The Archaeology of the North American Fur Trade

THE AMERICAN EXPERIENCE IN ARCHAEOLOGICAL PERSPECTIVE

UNIVERSITY PRESS OF FLORIDA

Florida A&M University, Tallahassee
Florida Atlantic University, Boca Raton
Florida Gulf Coast University, Ft. Myers
Florida International University, Miami
Florida State University, Tallahassee
New College of Florida, Sarasota
University of Central Florida, Orlando
University of Florida, Gainesville
University of North Florida, Jacksonville
University of South Florida, Tampa
University of West Florida, Pensacola

THE ARCHAEOLOGY OF THE
North American Fur Trade

Michael S. Nassaney

UNIVERSITY PRESS OF FLORIDA
Gainesville / Tallahassee / Tampa / Boca Raton
Pensacola / Orlando / Miami / Jacksonville / Ft. Myers / Sarasota

This book may be available in an electronic edition.

20 19 18 17 16 15   6 5 4 3 2 1

Library of Congress Cataloging-in-Publication Data
Nassaney, Michael S., author.
The archaeology of the North American fur trade / Michael S. Nassaney.
    pages cm — (The American experience in archaeological perspective)
Includes bibliographical references and index.
    ISBN 978-0-8130-6157-3
    1. Fur trade—North America—History. 2. Fur traders—North America—History.
3. Archaeology and history—North America. I. Title. II. Series: American experience in
archaeological perspective.
HD9944.N62N37 2015
338.3'729709709009—dc23   2015029218

The University Press of Florida is the scholarly publishing agency for the State University
System of Florida, comprising Florida A&M University, Florida Atlantic University,
Florida Gulf Coast University, Florida International University, Florida State University,
New College of Florida, University of Central Florida, University of Florida, University
of North Florida, University of South Florida, and University of West Florida.

UNIVERSITY PRESS OF FLORIDA
15 Northwest 15th Street
Gainesville, FL 32611-2079
http://www.upf.com

To my parents, Joseph and Josephine Nassaney

Contents

Illustrations

Figures

Tables

Textbox

Preface and Acknowledgments

My interest in the fur trade emerged from a fascination with the myriad outcomes of interactions between Europeans and the original inhabitants of North America. As the project director of the excavation of a seventeenth-century native cemetery in southeastern New England, I came to understand the complexity and severity of colonial encounters, their ramifications for our reconstructions of the past, and their role in shaping the present. When I began investigations of the eighteenth-century site of Fort St. Joseph, I was afforded the opportunity to view interactions from the European side, only to learn that the sides were not as neatly defined as I once thought. My training in critical archaeology at the University of Massachusetts compelled me to consider how interpretations support vested interests and how an alternative narrative could be constructed from the detritus of everyday life.

The influences that contributed to my understanding of the fur trade and the scores of mentors, associates, family members, and friends who made this work possible are too numerous to name here, though I would be remiss if I neglected to thank a number of individuals and institutions for support that led to the completion of this book. I stand on the shoulders of many able archaeologists who came before me. This project began with an excessively long chapter on the North American fur trade for the *Oxford Handbook of Historical Archaeology* (Nassaney 2014). When I heeded James Symonds's suggestions to cut it by half, I was left with the outline for a book that I was eager to write. Most of the research and writing was conducted while I was on sabbatical leave from my teaching duties at Western Michigan University

(WMU) during the 2013–2014 academic year. I obtained funding from the WMU Support for Faculty Scholars Award program for travel to study fur trade sites and collections in Minnesota and Wisconsin in 2013. The WMU College of Arts and Sciences Travel and Research Award helped defray costs associated with travel to Colony Ross in 2009. Doug Wilson of the National Park Service supported my visit to Fort Vancouver in 2011 to discuss my research and view collections.

My research focus on the western Great Lakes region is the result of my fortuitous participation in the Fort St. Joseph Archaeological Project. Had I not answered the phone when Hal Springer of Support the Fort called me to solicit my help in finding the old fort, I would not have written this book. I often relied on members of the Niles, Michigan, and WMU communities and my research collaborators for inspiration and encouragement. These include José António Brandão, Terrance Martin, the late William M. Cremin, the late Joseph L. Peyser, Carol Bainbridge, Juan Ganum, Larry Sehy, William Sauck, and scores of students over the past fifteen years. The staff at Waldo Library helped me obtain works that were not locally available through interlibrary loan. Several fur trade historians and archaeologists welcomed my queries and provided references and suggestions for sites to visit, particularly José António Brandão, Douglas A. Birk, Kent Lightfoot, and Jeff Richner.

Many generous colleagues assisted with translations, provided access to collections, showed me sites, shared unpublished data and references, sent images, and reviewed portions of the text for accuracy. These include Amelie Allard, Douglas A. Birk, James Bradley, Amanda Brooks, Catherine Cangany, Cathy Carlson, Cathrine Davis, Erica D'Elia, Vincent Desroches, Jackie Eng, Lynn Evans, John Franzen, Jay Johnson, Kent Lightfoot, LisaMarie Malischke, Rob Mann, Terrance Martin, Gail Moreau DesHarnais, Vergil Noble, Ken Sarkozy, Diane Sheppard, Suzanne Sommerville, Richard Veit, Steve Veit, Doug Wilson, and Mike Zimmerman. Mary Ann Levine made critical comments on an early draft of the first two chapters that provided timely encouragement. José António Brandão, Greg Waselkov, and Doug Wilson reviewed the entire manuscript, noted inaccuracies, and suggested revisions for a clearer and more accessible text. Kate Babbitt recommended many editorial improvements for which I am grateful. Finally, thanks to Meredith Morris-Babb at the University Press of Florida for soliciting the manuscript and working with me to see it into print.

Preparation of the manuscript required uninterrupted days and months of study as I aimed to synthesize a significant body of literature and link the fur trade to the American experience. My wife, Nadine, and my sons, Andrew and Alexander, recognized and respected the seriousness of my endeavor and granted me precious solitude and offered welcome distractions on occasion. I am lucky to have such a nurturing environment for pursuing my intellectual, personal, and professional dreams.

1

Furs, Materiality, and the American Experience

For millennia, Native North Americans obtained furs, pelts, skins, and robes from a variety of indigenous mammals predominantly for their own use, until overseas demand driven by declines in European supplies led them to intensify the capture and processing of fur-bearing animals to satisfy global markets (Wolf 1982, 158–194). Furs were exchanged for imported goods such as cloth, iron tools, glass beads, brass kettles, alcohol, and other commodities that natives deemed desirable. The spatially and temporally extensive phenomenon known colloquially as the North American fur trade varied in the types of animals collected, how they were processed and shipped, the relationships that developed among groups in the course of extraction, and the uses to which products derived from these animals were put. The fur trade was implicated in numerous encounters between Europeans and native peoples for centuries over vast stretches of the North American continent, from the Atlantic to the Pacific and from Hudson's Bay to the Gulf of Mexico. Unprecedented demand for furs in North America stimulated by European markets beginning in the sixteenth century arguably fueled exploration, colonialism, imperial conflicts, and manifest destiny and had a profound impact on the daily lives of natives and newcomers well into the nineteenth century. I refer to this period as the fur trade era.

It may be difficult to identify any North American site or historical event of the fur trade era that was not implicated in some way in the trading of furs. For instance, furs were intimately tied to Native American and African slavery in the American South. English and Irish immigrants acquired furs and native captives to create the wealth to purchase enslaved Africans (Wilder 2013, 90–91). The fur trade also stimulated industrial developments in New England, particularly the mass production of skinning knives that were used in the Southwest and upper Missouri country in the 1840s and 50s (Nassaney and Abel 2000, 245; Woodward 1927, 1970, 64–68). These connections underscore the extensive reach of the fur trade and challenge researchers to delineate the scope of its study. For Canadian historian Harold Innis (1962, 178–179), the fur trade had broad political significance. He attributed major confrontations such as the American Revolution and the Seven Years' War to the struggle between settlers and fur traders. England waged war on New France because the success of the French in the fur trade had limited westward expansion of the English colonies. Similarly, American patriots opposed the British fur trade, which also threatened manifest destiny. Other colonial wars (e.g., the Pequot War, King Philip's War, Pontiac's Rebellion) were also associated with the fur trade. But the goods exchanged for furs and the restructuring of the traditional rhythm of daily life were the most pervasive impacts of the trade. These affected everyone.

From local to global scales of analysis, the outcomes of fur trade interactions varied according to "geography, native culture type, and the specific nature of the European group—its size, composition, national and cultural origin, religious denomination, economic motivation, and general motivation" (Fitzhugh 1985, 6). The similarities of goods distributed to Native Americans who participated in the fur trade are "largely irrelevant to the individual histories of the groups involved" (Fitzhugh 1985, 6). That the fur trade experience was diverse and complex in nature (Rogers 1990, 21) is an understatement.

In a landmark exhibit catalog devoted to the Great Lakes region fur trade, Carolyn Gilman (1982, 1) proposed that while the fur trade has been perceived as a model of extractive industries that depleted resources, a mechanism of acculturation, and an example of intercultural economics, it was foremost about communication. Douglas A. Birk and Jeffrey Richner (2004, 1) expounded by noting that "beyond the mere swapping of furs and goods, the trade involved . . . [the] exchange of ideas, languages, worldviews, commodities, practices, technologies, diseases, and genes." In the course of obtaining beaver furs, deerskins, buffalo hides, and sea otter pelts in the fur trade era, Native Americans and Europeans learned much about each other and the natural world in a dynamic relationship that was by no means temporally or spatially monolithic. There were in reality many fur trades (Morantz 1980) that produced many fur trade societies (see Van Kirk 1980). This requires separate models to describe the trade in different geographical regions at particular historical moments (White 1982, 122). Often "economic activities were only one thread in an elaborate fabric of interaction involving the trade of tangible and intangible commodities" as well as services, "information, languages, loyalties, and people" (White 1982, 122).

Much has been written about the North American fur trade. The purpose of this book is to capture some of the salient issues that English-language scholars have addressed, particularly with regard to the materiality of the trade. Specifically, I aim to examine what an archaeological perspective can tell us about the fur trade and its legacy for the American experience. Though material goods harbor their own biases, the objects made, used, and discarded in the course of the fur trade can provide insight into the exchange relationships among the participants and their lifeways. And given the temporal duration and geographic extent of this expansive phenomenon, it seems reasonable that the way exchange was conducted, resisted, and transformed to meet various needs has left an indelible imprint upon the American psyche, particularly in the way the fur trade has been remembered and commemorated (Nassaney 2008a).

The North American Incubator

The North American fur trade was nurtured by a host of environmental, ecological, geographic, economic, social, political, and historical factors that are elaborated on throughout this book. As Mann (2003, 28) succinctly states, "The most salient features of the landscape for traders were fur bearing animals, Native labor, and rivers to transport furs to world markets." Here I briefly summarize the conditions that made the fur trade possible. Until large-scale urbanization, suburban sprawl, and accelerated population growth reduced wildlife habitat in many areas of North America in the twentieth century, fur-bearing animals (beaver, bison, deer, lynx, marten, mink, muskrat, and sea otter, to name the predominant species targeted for exploitation) were plentiful (figure 1.1). While Europeans had familiarity with some of these animals (e.g., deer), most wild species had been eradicated in proximity to living spaces in the Old World except in the countryside that was set aside for hunting by the nobility. Having relied on domesticated animals for food since the Neolithic, most Europeans had limited knowledge of game habitat and hunting techniques. In contrast, Native Americans had exploited a host of species for subsistence and raw materials (e.g., bone, antler) to produce essential goods for generations. Europeans readily depended upon native producers to capture animals and process furs to supply distant

Figure 1.1. Furs from select species are still collected, processed, and sold along the north shore of Lake Superior in Hovland, Minnesota, where animal populations have been sustained or have rebounded from earlier overexploitation. Photo by Michael S. Nassaney.

markets (e.g., Lapham 2005, 9–12). A notable exception is the Rocky Mountain system, by which "mountain men" trapped beavers for their own profit, "competing directly with the Indians who were seeking the same animals" (Wood et al. 2011, 99).

Natives had also effectively solved the problem of transportation throughout the interior of this immense continent by taking advantage of the elaborate network of lakes and rivers linked together by portages. The technology of birch bark canoes allowed furs to be moved by natives and voyageurs to entrepôts such as Albany and Montreal, from which they were shipped to overseas markets (figure 1.2; Kent 1997). These portable vessels then returned along the same routes filled with imported goods to supply native consumers. Native Americans also developed land transportation to supplement aquatic routes. They used toboggans on frozen ground during the winter in the north. They also captured feral horses from Spanish herds in the Southwest and traded them onto the Plains by the eighteenth century (Wood and Thiessen 1985, 63).

With these conditions in place, the driving forces needed to stimulate the fur trade were consumer demand for furs and production centers ca-

Figure 1.2. Birch bark canoes, like this replica at Grand Portage located along the north shore of Lake Superior in Minnesota, were integral to the movement of goods and people in the Great Lakes fur trade. Photo by Michael S. Nassaney.

pable of providing goods in exchange. Furs supplied felt, leather, and other products that Europeans of all social classes needed. European workshops produced all manner of finished goods that would find their way into native hands, even if only as raw materials to be altered into forms that were more suitable to native tastes. Although scholars have suggested that principles other than supply and demand operated in the fur trade and that the exchanges that took place were more than merely economic in nature, an economic motive clearly fueled the trade (see Innis 1962; Juen and Nassaney 2012, 6–7; White 2011, 94–141). Both producers and traders understood a fair bargain, even if rates changed in accordance with the social context of exchange or fluctuations in global prices. It is unlikely that the trade could have been sustained if either side felt cheated on a regular basis (Ray and Freeman 1978).

Sources for the Study of the Fur Trades

The study of the fur trade was initially the domain of historians, who recognized its economic, social, and political importance to the settlement of North America (e.g., Chittenden 1902; Innis 1962; Norton 1974; Phillips 1961; Turner 1891). Their work has produced an enormous historiography on the fur trades (see Cuthbertson and Ewers 1939; Donnelly 1947; Hanson 2005; Peterson and Anfinson 1984). Researchers have relied on a voluminous archive of primary sources such as journals, letters, company records, public documents, account books, bills of sale, vouchers, private papers of prominent fur traders, maps, drawings, voyageur contracts, newspapers, and unpublished manuscripts to produce a mountain of books, dissertations, and articles in scholarly journals.

Until recently, most document-based histories have generally ignored oral histories, archaeological data, and additional forms of materiality that provide insight into the fur trade (cf. Miller 2000). Yet investigations of fur trade sites were among the earliest developments in historical archaeology (Orser 2004, 31–33). As the heyday of the trade came to a close in the late nineteenth century, antiquarians sought material manifestations of sites that had been identified in the documents, thereby laying the groundwork for what would become historical archaeology (Beeson 1900). They were followed by archaeologists who sought to analyze the material traces of the fur trade through the lens of the research questions current at the time (e.g., Caywood

1967; Greenman 1951; Maxwell and Binford 1961; Quimby 1939; Woolworth and Wood 1960). The trend continues to the present; fur trade archaeology mirrors the development of the field in microcosm and reflects changes in research priorities that are influenced by factors both internal and external to the discipline (Klimko 2004; Nassaney 2012a).

Archaeologists have long recognized that written and material sources are created in different contexts and can exist in healthy tension for contemporary researchers. Gregory Waselkov (1998, 200) pointed out some of the discrepancies that exist between trade lists and archaeological evidence and why we need these complementary data sources. For example, cloth is well represented on trade lists, yet it seldom preserves in the ground. In contrast, brass thimbles are generally absent from trade lists, yet they frequently appear in archaeological sites. Each line of evidence has relative merits and biases as a tool for reconstructing the past. Historical archaeologists recognize the benefits of documents (Bradley 1987, 115). First, documents provide details that may be absent from archaeology, such as the names of site occupants. Second, written records contain independent chronological data that can be compared with archaeological data. Finally, written accounts suggest what people were thinking and their motivations for action.

Historical archaeologists actively consult historical documents when they are available to reconstruct the cultural contexts within which material objects were made, used, and discarded. They understand that documents carry the implicit biases of their authors and the cultural milieu in which they lived and wrote, so they must be used critically. Many of the foundational histories of the fur trade were produced in the late nineteenth and early twentieth centuries and reflect intellectual thought embedded in ethnocentric, racist, and evolutionary world views (Trigger 2007, 159, 167–170). Many popular notions about the fur trade derive from this early scholarship (Peers 1998). Furthermore, historical documents often neglect the lived experiences of significant segments of the population, including women, children, Native Americans, and commoners. In contrast, the wrought and the wrecked objects that ultimately became deposited in the archaeological record are arguably more democratic representations of the site residents, albeit not without their own biases. Unlike historical documents, which may suggest prescriptive behaviors, material remains often express actual use contexts. Finally, many historical contexts, as in the case of early fur trade sites in the Arctic (and elsewhere), simply lack documents, making archaeology particularly important for gaining a fuller understanding of what happened in the past and who was involved (see Arndt 1996, 26, 77).

There are nearly as many ways to interpret the material world as archaeologists who attempt it. Many agree that material objects serve as an active medium of communication among their makers, users, and viewers instead of being "a passive by-product of human behavior" (Nassaney and Johnson 2000, 5). When we consider that archaeological materials were often deposited in contexts after their users reinterpreted them in culturally appropriate ways, we are better positioned to understand how their actual functions may have deviated from those intended by their original makers.

Historical Context of Fur Trade Studies

The desire to memorialize the fur trade began even before historians turned their attention to its study. An early form of commemoration was the Beaver Club, an elite dining association founded in 1785 by wealthy Montreal merchants who had wintered in the North American interior (Podruchny 1998). Theirs was not a scholarly pursuit; they passed the evenings consuming large quantities of alcohol and elegantly prepared foods obtained from the hunt in a bonding ritual that reaffirmed their brotherhood in the trade. Major historiographical works began to appear on the subject just as the old-time fur trade was fading into obscurity. Some of these authors aimed to celebrate its role in manifest destiny (Biggar 1901; Chittenden 1902; Johnson 1919; Turner 1891). They presented history as a "moral success story" that emphasized the inevitability of Euro-American dominance in the trade and the defeat and dependence of native peoples in its wake (Wolf 1982, 5, quoted in Mann 2003, 80). These fur trade histories often disparaged Native Americans and marginalized them in the wilderness, stuck in the evolutionary stage of savagery (Saum 1965, 216–217). Such ideas were both a product of a larger social context and served to legitimize the social inequalities imposed on disenfranchised groups. In short, studies forged in the heat of racialized America distorted our understandings of the fur trade.

Prior to the 1960s, archaeologists were attracted to trading posts but were generally uninterested in native groups who participated in the trade because they saw such groups as tainted by the influences of civilization (Maxwell and Binford 1961). As such, many archaeologists believed, they offered little to the study of pristine culture (cf. Quimby 1939, 1966). Thereafter they began to study change and continuity in the context of the so-called contact period and wanted to understand how native societies adapted socially, economically, technologically, and politically in response to the European presence (Bradley 1987; Fitzhugh 1985; Krause 1972; Nassaney 1989). This shift was ultimately inspired by work conducted in the 1950s, namely salvage archaeology in the Missouri River Valley and ethnohistorical studies initiated by the Indian Claims Commission that sought archaeological evidence to corroborate written testimony in the process of restoring land to Indian tribes (Galloway 1993, 92, 99; Krech 1999, 347). Native activism and the changing political climate of the late twentieth century led scholars to reconceptualize the fur trade and the roles natives played in it (e.g., Rogers 1990; see also Nassaney 2012a). As issues of power became important in the discipline, archaeologists suggested that the focus should be on autonomy and control (as opposed to change and continuity) and noted that Native Americans persisted in pursuing indigenous strategies for survival until their sovereignty was compromised (Jordan 2008, 351). Consequently, the early years of the fur trade were likely to contrast with later periods, when Europeans and their descendants had managed to appropriate native lands, greatly diminishing the political and economic capacity of native peoples (Bamforth 2003, 169).

Previous research showed that the fur trade had profound social, material, economic, and ideological influences on American society. Thus, its study continues to attract both popular and scholarly interest across disciplinary and international boundaries even as perspectives on the trade have changed (e.g., Brown et al. 1994; Carlos and Lewis 2010; Dolin 2010; Juen and Nassaney 2012; Nassaney 2011; Sleeper-Smith 2009). Nine conferences were devoted exclusively to the topic from 1965 through 2006 (e.g., see Buckley 1984; Brown et al. 1994; Fiske et al. 1998; Gilman 1967). Eric Dolin (2010) recently authored a book on the "epic history of the fur trade" that is accessible to a general audience. The Museum of the Fur Trade in Chadron, Nebraska, welcomes visitors from all over the world, publishes *The Museum of the Fur Trade Quarterly*, and operates The Fur Press (see Hamilton 1987; Hanson 2005). The fur trade is also the focus of numerous heritage tourism destinations operated by municipal, county, state, national, and private organizations (e.g., Birk 1989; Deseve 2009; Lightfoot 2005; Morrison 2007, 131–137; Nassaney 2011; Veit 2011; Wilson and Langford 2011). As can be said of any subject matter, scholarship on the fur trade reflects the social and political concerns of the era in which it was produced (see Nassaney 2012a). Public interpretations seem to lag behind scholarly understandings.

The North American fur trade can be a daunting topic because of the enormity of the subject. Many studies have examined it by region and time period, which often results in a failure to appreciate the fur trade as an extensive and interlocking continent-wide enterprise that Europeans and native peoples participated in for centuries (St-Onge 2008, 17). Studies that relate to the fur trade are sometimes subsumed under alternate labels such as colonialism or culture contact that are equally broad topics (Cusick 1998; Ferris 2009; Jordan 2009; Silliman 2005). Be that as it may, the fur trade was a global phenomenon in geographic scope and had significant impacts on social relations, economic practices, demographic expansion, and environmental perceptions in the past; its legacy persists to the present. Moreover, the fur trade had widespread material consequences. This is why its study falls squarely within the domain of historical archaeology (Little 2007). Despite the significance of this enterprise in American history, its role in the settlement and exploitation of the continent, and its material implications at multiple scales, there is no synthetic treatment of the fur trade in the archaeological literature to date. This book attempts to fill that gap.

Mosaic or Melting Pot?

Most of the places and people examined in this book occupied territories that would eventually fall under the legal, political, and ideological domains of the United States of America, though the Canadian fur trade cannot be ignored. Yet national policies, practices, and beliefs associated with the fur trade created a distinctive legacy that persists to the present and is filtered through the experiences of those who consider themselves Americans. How the fur trade is remembered (and commemorated) varies in accordance with national values, different understandings of the past, and the significance of the trade to the present (Klimko 2004; Peers 1998).

Research conducted since the 1970s has been more sensitive to the role that Native Americans played in the fur trade (see Peterson and Anfinson 1984). No longer portrayed as passive victims of an inevitable process, native peoples have been granted a central place in the history of the fur trade. Consequently, contemporary research aims to characterize the role of native peoples in the trade and their receptivity to it. In the course of the cultural interactions required by the trade, native peoples often attempted to sustain previous lifeways, accommodated to changing material circumstances, and viewed alien institutions such as Christianity and mercantile exchange within their own world views. Europeans also adopted practices and beliefs that accorded with those of the Native Americans. This conjunction—often referred to as fur trade society—produced cultural practices that were neither fully native nor fully European in content or form (White 2011). Hybridization and creolization are normal processes in colonialism (Beaudoin 2013). Yet for much of the twentieth century this blurring was ignored in favor of a model that saw cultures colliding with and displacing each other (Wolf 1982). This leaves open the question of whether the fur trade legacy was one of a melting pot or a mosaic. Did fur trade interactions between traders and producers entail a blending of cultural practices that created entirely new cultural forms? Or did the process lead to a cultural mosaic in which distinctive practices were maintained but modified in the context of intimate interactions? It appears that under some conditions, new cultural practices emerged, as in the well-known case of the middle ground of the western Great Lakes, where exchange was reinterpreted to suit the needs of both natives and newcomers (White 2011). At other times and places, mercantile and reciprocal exchange systems operated simultaneously. And in others, systems of exchange were geared toward mutual benefit with each side driving a hard bargain in an attempt to maximize returns, as in the maritime trade of the Northwest Coast (Gibson 1992).

However one chooses to characterize the economics of the fur trade, information was constantly being exchanged and gift giving greased the wheels of economic and diplomatic relations (White 1984, 185). Gifts aided in establishing and affirming social relationships necessary for trade in the western Great Lakes region (White 1984, 186). For many native societies, such as the Ojibwes, the exchange of goods and services was a prerogative of kinship (White 1984, 186). A particularly salient gift was tobacco; its role in the calumet ceremony cannot be underestimated. The smoking of the calumet throughout much of the Mississippi River Valley and Great Lakes region was a means of ensuring amicable relations among complete strangers (Mann 2004). Thus, the exchange of goods (including clothing) and smoking the calumet could turn potential enemies into friends (White 1984, 188).

Intercultural marriage was perhaps the most intimate of exchanges (White 1984, 189) and was a hallmark of fur trade society wherever it developed, creating further opportunities for cultural blending. Often a trader's influence and success with native fur producers was dependent upon the strength and renown of his father-in-law. By "marrying a chief's daughter, the trader gained a powerful ally among his Indian customers" (White 1984, 195). Marriages across ethnic lines resulted in *métis* offspring who were truly children of the fur trade. Often they could operate in both white and native worlds. However, in the increasingly racialized climate of the late eighteenth and nineteenth centuries, some *métis* would be seen as neither white nor native and were forced to assimilate to one or the other or live a life of destitution in a dichotomous world in which blended identities were shunned (see Peterson and Brown 1985; Pollard 2011; Sleeper-Smith 2001). Furthermore, not all fur trade unions were welcome or accepted. Despite evidence of miscegenation along the Northwest Coast, mariners seldom established permanent settlements among native people there, and the offspring of mixed marriages were held in low esteem by both whites and the local population (Gibson 1992, 239; Pollard 2011). They would have been more numerous had it not been for mothers who practiced infanticide when white fathers refused to allow their mixed offspring to have their heads flattened. Unflattened heads would surely rank them as slaves, and thus their mothers preferred them dead. The variety of new and old practices that accompanied the fur trade is both enlightening and overwhelming. I can only hint at this diversity in the pages that follow and leave the empirical investigation of fur trade contexts that I have unintentionally ignored here to future scholars.

Navigating This Book

I cannot hope to capture the enormity of the fur trade in this overview, as it involved dozens of trading companies, scores of native groups, hundreds of settlements, thousands of traders, millions of trade goods over four centuries, and nearly 10 million square miles. My treatment of the archaeology of the North American fur trade is by no means exhaustive. Rather, I attempt to provide an introduction to the works that have influenced my understandings of the subject by exploring the contributions of historical archaeology to the study of the fur trade and how the fur trade contributes to a better understanding of the American experience. The focus of this volume is the fur trade era, when the demand for furs in North America, stimulated by European markets, was unprecedented and marked by profound transformations among natives and newcomers. I aim to examine the consequences and legacy of the fur trade from an archaeological perspective. Was it a force of cultural disruption and an early form of colonial relations between Europeans and Native Americans (Peers 1998, 115)? What is the legacy of the fur trade and how has it influenced the American psyche today?

I have selected examples that illustrate how archaeologists have approached the subject of the fur trade and what their investigations and analyses have revealed. Thus, this book is intended to be an expanded literature review based on my reading of and familiarity with the literature as a historical archaeologist who has worked on fur trade sites in New England and the western Great Lakes region. Though this synthesis is not complete, it aims to highlight some of the significant developments in the fur trade—particularly the events and activities that were instrumental in the American experience—and their treatment in archaeological studies. I aim to identify the historical conditions that contributed to the broad fur trade narrative that the dominant society constructed and to expose contrary material evidence that demands space for alternate voices and new understandings.

The next chapter surveys the interpretive frameworks that archaeologists have used to make sense of the dizzying array of sites, artifact patterns, and social processes that characterize the fur trade era of our collective history. A critical perspective for examining the political and academic forces that influenced the design and outcome of the archaeology of the fur trade enables me able to shed light on the blind spots that reflect ethnocentric Euro-Canadian and Euro-American biases and illuminate the role of native peoples (see Klimko 2004). The questions that count in fur trade archaeology are similar to those that are pursued in the broader field of historical archaeology. Moreover, they represent concerns that emanate from larger social contexts.

In chapter 3, I provide a broad summary of the history of the North American fur trade based on contemporary thinking. I give particular attention to the material and social outcomes of the interactions between fur producers and fur traders at places that have yielded archaeological remains in order to provide a better understanding of the similarities and differences in the fur trade era. This discussion provides the basis for a closer examination of the ways archaeologists have investigated fur trade sites and what they have learned from this material record. A number of prominent themes that have emerged from the literature serve as the framework for discussing archaeological contributions in chapter 4. I also explore how changes in the discipline have influenced the archaeology of the fur trade.

Chapter 5 provides more detail about the historical archaeology of several fur trade systems, emphasizing the materiality of the trade. I integrate historical documents and oral and material sources to demonstrate what historical archaeology has taught us about the fur trades at particular historical moments in select geographical areas where the archaeological record speaks to the issues that were raised in previous chapters. In chapter 6, I highlight the archaeology of Fort St. Joseph, an eighteenth-century fur-trading post in the western Great Lakes region that has been the focus of historical archaeological research for more than a decade. The project illustrates in detail some of the goals of fur trade archaeology and what investigations of this site contribute to our understandings of the fur trade in the St. Joseph River Valley under the French regime. In the concluding chapter, I suggest some directions for future research and offer my thoughts about the relevance of fur trade archaeology in the twenty-first century. I discuss how information about the fur trade as known through archaeology is disseminated to the public and the significance of this work (Peers 1998). Finally, I suggest why the fur trade was significant in the formative experience of contemporary America and how the lessons that emerged from the study of the fur trade can help us forge a more inclusive American identity in the future.

2

Interpretive Frameworks for the Study of the Fur Trade

Although what happened in the North American fur trade remains unchanged, our perceptions of it are constantly in flux because of shifts in the way we see the world based on sociopolitical conditions, theoretical frameworks, personal predilections, and a host of other factors (Nassaney 2012a). Contemporary understandings of the fur trade are filtered through interpretive frameworks that structure our assumptions about the people who inhabited the past, the motivations for their actions, the relationships between individuals and their cultural milieux, and a range of other variables that we constantly evaluate implicitly or explicitly to make sense of the past. These frameworks serve both to structure and give meaning to the documentary and material evidence of the past as we impose spatial and temporal order on what is demonstrably an expansive, pervasive, enduring, and multifaceted phenomenon. Many of the debates about what happened in the fur trade take place at the level of theory, though assumptions may remain implicit. At the risk of oversimplification, fur trade analysts often believe that all people are either essentially the same or they are all different (Cook 1998, 80) and that the trade was either beneficial or detrimental to native peoples (Wike 1958). Scholars have been particularly interested in explaining the social, material, economic, political, and ideological outcomes of the fur trades and the cultural changes they engendered.

Fur trade archaeology mirrors in microcosm the development of the broader field of historical archaeology (see Klimko 2004 for a review of fur trade archaeology in Canada). While contemporary theory informs recent approaches to the fur trade and colonial encounters, traditional concerns persist (e.g., Nassaney 2012a). Some of these concerns are driven by the public's desire for reconstruction, tourism, and commemoration, and thus fur trade archaeology has a long history of public appeal (Klimko 2004, 172; Nassaney 2011). Scholarly interest in chronology, architecture, spatial organization, subsistence, technological change, cultural interactions, and ethnogenesis allows for varying approaches to coexist and makes possible new syntheses grounded in practice and social relations. It is useful to discuss some of the broad theoretical frameworks that have informed the archaeology of the North American fur trade before examining what fur trade archaeology has contributed to our understanding of the American experience.

The fur trade, by its nature, brought people of different cultural traditions into contact with each other. These interactions ranged from antagonistic and conflicted to peaceful and harmonious. The consequences of fur trade interactions are critical to anthropologists who are interested in examining how contemporary American beliefs, values, and practices are rooted in the formative conditions and events of our national history.

Even before historical archaeologists became interested in the material residue of fur trade life, historical agents were judging the behaviors of individuals and groups they encountered in the fur trade (Saum 1965). Much of what was recorded in historical documents emanated from literate, white, male Europeans, and thus the record they left reflects a narrow world view. Most (if not all) participants in the fur trade were cognizant of and sought to understand cultural differences among the myriad groups they encountered in daily life. There were no shortages of opinions regarding the vices and virtues of fur producers and traders, many of which have been recorded and summarized (see Saum 1965). While it is difficult to generalize about what fur traders thought about Native Americans (and even more so about what Native Americans thought about fur traders), it is clear that impressions varied over time and space. Despite the disdain with which some traders treated natives, most traders understood that the trade could not thrive without them, since they were the primary producers on which the system relied. And many native groups saw the benefits of European allies. Generally speaking, the success of the trade was dependent on cooperation between Europeans and natives, as each group had something the other wanted (Saum 1965, 42–43). North West Company partners and other fur traders regarded native peoples as belonging to one of two classes: those with furs and those without (Saum

1965, 46). In contrast to that gross oversimplification, traders apparently acknowledged individual differences among Native Americans and saw within native societies individuals of every type, from those who were as grave as judges to merry jesters and from those who were generous to those who were miserly (Saum 1965, 59). In the course of their dealings with natives, fur traders created and perpetuated some remarkably enduring stereotypes, such as the notion that natives were indolent, had childish dispositions, were belligerent, and were frequently inebriated (see Saum 1965, 153–177).

The thoughts and views of fur-trade-era observers were influenced by the dominant ideologies of the time. Clearly, I cannot summarize in detail the social, political, and economic milieu of Western Europe from the age of discovery through the age of Enlightenment and the industrial revolution. Moreover, European ideas about the Other (i.e., non-Western peoples) changed considerably over this period and European nations had different perspectives about their ultimate goals in geopolitical relations and in the colonial project of which the fur trade was a part. For example, Dutch traders aimed to realize a handsome profit in the seventeenth century, whereas French Jesuits and civil servants sought to dominate the Iroquois religiously and politically (Cook 1998, 80, relying on Dennis 1993). These economic and political strategies had an impact on how native peoples were perceived, and this variation must be understood in any attempt to deconstruct colonial remarks.

With this background, anthropologists and archaeologists have employed a number of interpretive frameworks to examine the fur trade phenomenon. I present them in roughly chronological order, but they should not be seen as replacements for paradigms. Some approaches are complementary, while others are clearly contradictory and developed in response to the shortcomings of previous perspectives.

Early Anthropological Contributions

When anthropology was coming of age in the nineteenth century, the nascent discipline was evolutionary in orientation (Trigger 2007). Cultures were organized in stages that were judged predominantly by their technological accomplishments, a reflection of the importance of technology and the nineteenth-century belief in progress. Societies were held up to the standards of Western civilization—namely writing, centralized bureaucracies, standing armies, and technological advancements, particularly in the physical sciences (e.g., metallurgy, armaments, navigation). Groups found lacking these traits were prime targets for the colonial project. In North America, most of the societies that engaged in the fur trade were hunters and gatherers, though agriculturalists often provisioned the trade. The former groups generally made fewer capital investments in landscapes, thus appearing landless to covetous imperial eyes. Colonial regimes in which the fur trade was embedded appropriated native lands by conquest or justified their claim for sovereignty through the principle of *terra nullis*. Since Europeans viewed native practices of land use (e.g., the seasonal round) as impermanent, they considered territory ripe for the taking so they could create settlements and landscapes that suited European sensibilities and were regarded by other European powers as the means of establishing legitimate claims of ownership (Gosden 1997).

Economic, political, and social power was always part of colonial contestation, and the fur trade was one way that power could be exercised. As Europe established colonial settlements around the globe, more European goods were marketed to consumers and European systems of governance were forced on the populace. Arrogant rulers believed that their subordinates were becoming civilized when they embraced compulsory foreign practices (Wolf 1982). Anthropologists played two important roles in creating and perpetuating this colonialist history. First, they developed evolutionary and hierarchical models of human society that employed innate cultural and physical characteristics to legitimize colonial expansion. Second, they aimed to document disappearing cultures, thereby establishing a gulf between the West and the rest. Anthropologists were generally attracted to traditional cultural values and practices—those that had not been tainted by Western civilization. Societies that were least influenced by the penetration of capitalism, Christianity, and other markers of the West were often viewed as the most primitive and therefore worthy of anthropological study.

In order to understand these Western influences on indigenous peoples, anthropologists developed the theory of acculturation to examine the mutual borrowing of cultural traits between interacting cultures (Redfield et al. 1936). In reality, they emphasized the diffusion of cultural practices and material goods from more powerful, centralized capitalist societies in the West to less complex, Stone Age societies such as those that were providing furs for European markets.

For most of the twentieth century, acculturation was the dominant interpretive framework for understanding the cultural interactions between Europeans and native North Americans, including those who participated in the fur trade (Carlson 2006, 201–203; Orchard 2009, 3; Wagner 2011, 12–13). Stated simply, acculturation as conceived by these early anthropologists assumed that European culture was destined to replace native cultures because it was racially and technologically superior. According to this model, this process explained the drastic and continued decrease in native population and the proclivity of the survivors to adopt European goods. Researchers employed a relatively straightforward—though in hindsight theoretically unsophisticated—research methodology to compare quantities of traditional and imported objects as a way of assessing the extent to which natives had become civilized. The increase in western goods over time demonstrated the inevitable course of cultural decay. George Quimby's work (1939, 1966) is pertinent in this regard because he sought to examine changes in material culture and native lifestyles brought about by the fur trade in the western Great Lakes region from the seventeenth through nineteenth centuries. He observed that by 1760, native peoples of the western Great Lakes region had changed as a result of their involvement in the fur trade. Their adoption of imported goods had produced a cultural uniformity throughout the region. One observation that was inconsistent with acculturation theory was rather telling, yet Quimby failed to realize how its implications challenged his assumptions. He noted that despite significant material culture change, Chippewa (Ojibwe) economic activities of the 1760s "were still linked to [the] physical environment and the seasons, probably much as they had been in pre-European times. Thus there seems to be a continuity and conservatism of subsistence and settlement pattern that is lacking in most aspects of material culture" (Quimby 1966, 179).

It was easy for researchers to ignore such anomalies when they were working under the influence of a reigning paradigm that "equated Native American utilization of European-made goods with technological decay, social disintegration, and dependence" (Wagner 2011, 12; see also Witthoft 1966). And until native peoples began to reassert some degree of social and political power in the late twentieth century, acculturation remained relevant in American anthropology as an explanatory framework. For example, in the early 1980s the Anthropological Society of Washington sponsored a series of presentations that sought to examine from an archaeological perspective the earliest period of contact in eastern North America, namely the sixteenth and seventeenth centuries (Fitzhugh 1985, 5). The focus was "not on changing material culture and technology per se, but rather of the effects of European contact on the institutions that organized native societies" (Fitzhugh 1985, 5). Not surprisingly, some of these societies participated in the fur trade (e.g., Robinson et al. 1985; Thomas 1985). The goals of the presentations were to explore cases "in which a native American society was undergoing initial acculturation or adaptations to changes from pre-contact conditions" that were "instructive in terms of acculturation theory and studies of historical process" (Fitzhugh 1985, 5). A series of case studies was assembled to explore differences in acculturation stages between different regions. Studies conducted from an acculturation perspective generally assume the outcome of interactions that took place in the fur trade, namely that European societies were able to reproduce themselves in new environmental and social contexts and that native societies gradually but inevitably became more similar to European ones. Little attention was paid to the range of strategies Europeans used in their pursuit of the colonial enterprise or the active resistance, accommodations, and politically savvy tactics native peoples practiced in their efforts to maintain their autonomy.

Early historically oriented archaeological investigations of fur trade sites aimed to provide a more complete narrative of European settlement and colonialism from a humanistic (particularistic) rather than an anthropological (nomothetic) perspective (e.g., Caywood 1967; Greenman 1951; Maxwell and Binford 1961). Many of these studies were primarily descriptive and focused on material culture that complemented existing historical works or that clarified historical details, particularly at sites associated with the historic preservation movement. The earliest historical archaeologists also recognized a native presence at these sites, since many of them were trained in pre-Contact archaeology (Douglas Wilson, personal communication, 2014).

In the mid-twentieth century, anthropologists attempted to establish historical links between the societies Europeans observed at first contact (or shortly thereafter) and their pre-Contact ancestors. By using the so-called direct historical approach, archaeologists could use ethnohistorical records as an aid in archaeological interpretation (Galloway 1993, 93; Rogers 1990, 103). Practitioners often incompletely understood the extent to which native societies had been influenced by interaction with Europeans and Euro-Americans and their manufactured products. In his study of Algonquian land tenure in the Northeast, Frank Speck argued that eastern subarctic and northeastern

Algonquians adhered to a rather "uniform system of land tenure . . . called the family hunting territory system" (Martin 1975, 117). This system involved the absolute right of ownership by individual families of fur-bearing animals within defined territories. Moreover, he claimed a pre-Columbian origin for the system. Seeking to deconstruct this understanding, Calvin Martin (1975, 117) astutely noted that Speck's interpretation came at a time when American values of individualism and free enterprise were threatened by global developments and American capitalism was under fire. The idea that precapitalist societies could have a concept of land ownership called into question their communal basis.

Speck was immediately attacked and his argument was largely put to rest with the publication of Eleanor Leacock's doctoral dissertation (1954). Leacock was able to show that Montagnais hunting territories were a product of the international fur trade (Martin 1975, 118; Moore 1993, 12). She supported her argument by establishing that the traits commonly associated with the family hunting territory system, such as a dependence on imported foods, exhibited a clinal distribution, such that "native groups living in proximity to trading posts displayed more of these diagnostic elements than did more remote groups" (Martin 1975, 118). Leacock's work demonstrated the articulation of tribal economies with the larger global system and its dynamic qualities (Moore 1993, 12). Subsequent researchers across disciplines explored these issues further and recast them in the idiom of world economic systems.

Economic Approaches to the Fur Trade

Economic historians recognized the wealth generated by the fur trade and sought to understand the factors that contributed to its growth and expansion. In his comprehensive study of the Canadian fur trade first published in 1930, Innis (1962) explained the dynamic relationships between relatively complex European and simpler Native American cultures. Implicitly using evolutionary thinking, he (1962, 116) described how "European culture had reached [an industrial] stage" that involved specialized production and "a manufacturing system which demanded large quantities of raw material." He suggested that beaver fur, which was the type of commodity that was valuable, in demand, and available on a large scale, was well suited to the operation of seventeenth-century trade. In turn, the industries that supplied the European goods of metals and cloth were stimulated by external demand (figure 2.1). Innis had begun to outline how long-distance trade relationships operated in the Atlantic world. The relentless demand for raw materials was the driving force for the expansion of the trade from the St. Lawrence Valley to the Pacific and Arctic regions.

Economically oriented anthropologists such as Eric Wolf and others in the 1950s rediscovered Marxian approaches in anthropology and resuscitated a concern for political economy (e.g., Diamond 1974; Leacock 1954; Wolf 1959; see also Moore 1993). This approach focused on how labor is organized and how surplus is mobilized on a global scale (see Cobb 1993). John Moore (1993, 15) noted that political economists share the "opinion that most social and cultural events . . . find their roots and explanations in matters of production, trade, and consequent political conflict."

What emerged is world systems theory, which was first presented coherently by Immanuel Wallerstein (1974, 1979). World system theorists seek to

Figure 2.1. Brass kettles, like this eighteenth-century specimen from the vicinity of Fort St. Joseph, near the present-day city of Niles, Michigan, are among the iconic manufactured goods of the fur trade. Photo by Roger Rosentreter. Courtesy of the Fort St. Joseph Museum.

explain the factors that lead to global inequities by identifying the dialectical relationship between core areas of resource accumulation and peripheral areas of resource extraction (Kardulias 1990). They examine globalization as a system of social relations that links distant places such "that activities in each place are shaped by events occurring elsewhere" (Giddens 1990 quoted in Pierson 2011a, 69–70). Gold and silver mines in Spanish-claimed territories, English plantations that relied on the labor of enslaved Africans, and the French and Dutch fur trades are some of the labor formations Europeans organized that underdeveloped and economically marginalized their colonial subjects. In the case of the fur trade, primary producers were induced to capture and process fur-bearing animals that would be transformed into commodities in the core and semi-peripheral areas of the world. Cheap labor and raw materials from the periphery were used to produce cloth and other high-value goods for new markets created by fur traders—the vanguards of civilization—who were expanding the frontier.

The primary archaeological application of world systems theory has often been associated with the expansion of the modern mercantile capitalist economy in the age of exploration, beginning in the sixteenth century (see Orchard 2009, 5; Wolf 1982). P. Nick Kardulias (1990) employed a world systems framework to characterize the North American fur trade. He rightly noted that the world economy was marked by a division of labor and contained a multiplicity of cultures (Kardulias 1990, 25). European nation-states competed for control over access to resources in peripheral areas in order to increase profits (Kardulias 1990, 26). He argued that natives played a role in peripheral areas through their procurement activities that led to the intensification and specialization of fur production (Kardulias 1990, 52). As a consequence of incorporation into the world economic system, many local ecosystems were degraded and native societies experienced changes that included a dependence on western goods (e.g., provisions, cloth, metal implements). Changes in settlement patterns involved abandoning some areas and relocating to sites that were closer to European trading posts. Plains Indian men practiced polygyny in order to gain more wives, who were needed to process hides. Kardulias (1990, 52) concluded that natives acted in their own self-interest by adopting economically rational behaviors that allowed them to compete in order to expand their exploitative activities to meet the demands of a capitalist market economy.

In his political economic analysis of the buffalo hide trade on the Plains in the nineteenth century, Alan Klein (1993) argued that world systems approaches have privileged exchange over production. Native Americans and working whites were organized into a complex division of labor that rendered these racially and culturally dissimilar groups into a powerless, unstable class (Klein 1993, 137). Members of the dominant culture used racial and cultural differences to obscure economic similarity and hinder class solidarity.

One of the outcomes world systems theory predicts is that peripheral societies will become dependent on the products (goods and services) of the core. This is a result of their increased allocation of labor to the production of cheap raw materials (i.e., furs) that the core requires and an accompanying decrease in the production of subsistence and other goods needed for biological and social reproduction. There is ample documentary and archaeological evidence of instances when native peoples relinquished traditional technologies and adopted imported technologies in their place (e.g., Innis 1962, 18, 109–110; Nassaney and Volmar 2003). Firearms, hatchets, knives, scissors, needles, fire steels, and copper kettles had all become common, noted traveler Peter Kalm in the 1740s, at the end of the French regime (Innis 1962, 109–110). More than a century earlier, in the early seventeenth century, an Indian in the St. Lawrence Valley was reported to have remarked that "the beaver does everything to perfection. He makes for us kettles, axes, swords, knives, and gives us drink and food without the trouble of cultivating the ground" (Innis 1962, 28). Clearly, at least some natives were induced to acquire beaver as a means to an economic end.

In fur trade societies throughout North America, goods that were once luxuries soon became necessities. Oscar Lewis (1942, 36, cited in Klein 1993, 143) noted that the Blackfoot people of the northern Plains had forgotten how to make pottery a mere decade after adopting iron kettles from British traders. With the disruption brought about in the trade following Pontiac's War (1763–1764), "even those tribes who had remained peaceful desperately needed European goods" (Norton 1974, 212).

While world systems theory has exposed dependency for some analysts, others suggest that natives often struggled to maintain autonomy and only relinquished it when they had no other options. For instance, Charles Cleland (1993) examined the effect of the fur trade on the transition from traditional modes of livelihood to wage labor and a market economy among the Lake Superior Chippewas in the early nineteenth century. He argued that the fact that the Indians drove hard bargains and were economically astute does not mean that they wholly adopted mercantilism. Since traders were not re-lated by kinship, they operated in a different sphere of exchange. The Chip-pewas "were able to rectify the barter system of the fur trade with their own social, political, and economic interests" by circulating goods paid to native workers in a reciprocal exchange system (Cleland 1993, 119). This supports the idea of a coexistence of exchange systems rather than the replacement of traditional systems of exchange with mercantilism.

Richard White (2011) argued that the fur trade must not be seen in solely economic terms dictated by market principles and the laws of supply and de-mand. He also questioned the degree to which native peoples had become dependent on foreign goods in the early years of the trade in the western Great Lakes region based on the limited volume of trade goods that actually made their way into the region. Models of gift giving and reciprocal exchange more closely describe how each side met their needs (see also Murray 2000). It might be useful to think about the fur trades at different historical mo-ments as lying along a continuum from commodity exchange, a price-form-ing process that establishes a relation between the objects exchanged, to gift exchange, which establishes a relation among the exchanging subjects (Mur-ray 2000, 39, citing Strathern 1988). Though it may be difficult to generalize about these processes, there may be ethnic and temporal trends that can be discerned through careful study of the documentary and archaeological re-cords.

The extent to which groups were incorporated into the world system greatly influenced the degree of dependency, and this often changed over the course of generations. The Athabascan-speaking Chipewyans (or "Northern Indians" as the Hudson's Bay Company referred to them) and the related groups that stretched from Churchill Factory on Hudson's Bay west to the Rocky Mountains and north to the Arctic Ocean were relatively isolated geo-graphically (Allen 1983, 303). As a result, they were able to remain somewhat economically independent. Even though they had adopted some European goods, they "periodically reverted to their traditional hunting and fishing economy" and preferred to hunt and fish for food instead of hunting beaver for the trade (304). These discriminating traders generally refused liquor in exchange for furs, were reluctant to trade their meat provisions in the winter, and resisted the dictates of the newcomers (304).

Whereas world systems theory was a robust model for explaining the growth of mercantile capitalism, it often failed to account for the diversity of responses at the periphery and denied native producers the exercise of agency in their actions and avenues for self-expression, accommodation, and resistance. It often assumed that Native Americans abandoned traditional technologies and adopted European goods (Brain 1979; Lohse 1988) to use in ways intended by their European makers. The presence of imported goods at native sites was once interpreted as evidence that natives were passive participants in a burgeoning mercantilist system that immediately and inevitably created dependency. This supposedly made them increasingly reliant on imported goods and necessitated an increased commitment to the fur trade, thus diverting labor away from traditional pursuits (subsistence and otherwise) in a continuous spiral that led to poverty and cultural alienation. This model reaffirmed the inherent superiority of European ways and demonstrated the virtues of civilized life that culminated in government policies of assimilation that aimed to "kill the Indian to save the man." While this ideology was not fully developed until the late nineteenth century, early traces of it appeared in the writings of the whites who were the arbiters of the evolutionary and racial standing of all Americans (see Nassaney 2012a).

Beginning in the 1970s, anthropologists began to reimagine the inherent technological superiority of European goods and the consequences of the fur trade on native peoples. This revisionist thinking accompanied social changes that aimed to empower marginalized peoples and questioned the production of knowledge that reproduced relations of domination and subordination (see Peers and Coutts 2010; Nassaney 2012a). First under attack was a formalist economic logic that cast people of all cultural backgrounds as capitalist consumers who sought to maximize benefits. A substantivist perspective was offered that examined systems of exchange that were not predicated on cost-benefit principles (see Sahlins 1972). When Trigger (1985) summed up the debate between formalists and substantivists with regard to the evidence relating to the fur trade in the St. Lawrence Valley in the first half of the seventeenth century, he concluded that native trading practices were embedded in political and social institutions yet exhibited important elements of economic rationalism insofar as they sought to profit from exchange (see Cook 1998, 76). Thus, market exchange was not the only economic rationality that operated in the fur trade. Indeed, empirical studies demonstrate that "precapitalist relations of production play an active role in the transitions to some sort of capitalism"—the simpler forms do not merely crumble (Klein 1993, 136). Negative reciprocity, in which exchange takes place between socially distant partners, shares with market exchange the objective to maximize profits. Such practices were not alien to Northwest Coast groups who occupied incipient class-based societies in which meticulous and complex systems of exchange through competitive feasting predated Europeans.

Thus, empirical, theoretical, and political forces impinged on anthropologists, prompting them to consider the voices of native activists and simultaneously reexamine the contexts in which material goods were put to use. Similarly, historical analysis suggested that native peoples were active agents and creative consumers who were crafting their own cultures and making their own histories from among the choices they were given, so long as they had some autonomy to selectively adopt, reject, and/or meld new material forms and cultural practices (see Ray 1980; Kehoe 2000).

Reflexive and Indigenous Perspectives

European sentiments regarding relations of dependency emanated from a colonial world view that justified the supposed benefits of western goods and anchored the belief that native societies were doomed to be replaced by superior, more evolved, civilized societies. Yet anthropological voices began to challenge this canon as early as the mid-twentieth century. For example, Joyce Wike (1958) questioned the premise that the fur trade was "favorable and [economically] stimulating" for native communities, based on her research on the maritime trade on the Northwest Coast. She evaluated what she called the "enrichment thesis" that posited that the fur trade brought technological improvements, increased the value of native commodities, and incorporated native communities into a more "advanced" economic system. While it is true that natives had ready access to steel traps, axes, and guns through the fur trade, the expedited production of pelts that such tools encouraged often depleted the supply of fur-bearers. Wike also argued that the increased returns natives initially received were not sustainable; they could be maintained only if natives could retain some degree of economic and political autonomy. She also challenged the assumption that natives profited from the penetration of capital by noting the patterns of uneven development that occurred. Not all benefited from the trade, economic inequalities became exacerbated, and trade often intensified the incipient class structure of pre-Contact society.

Well before anthropologists challenged the dominant ideology, native peoples promoted a different view of the fur trade and their role in it (e.g., Bibeau 1984). Of course, their words often were not recorded, were generally ignored, or were misinterpreted because native peoples were politically marginalized and their views rubbed against the grain of received wisdom and challenged the status quo. They did not need to be reminded that they had not vanished. Some called upon researchers to consider the implications of the persistence of native groups for scholarship, despite centuries-long campaigns of genocide and efforts to force them to assimilate. Michael Wilcox (2009, 11) called for the "active dismantling of *terminal narratives*—accounts of Indian histories which explain the absence, cultural death, or disappearance of Indigenous peoples." Archaeologists in the late twentieth century began to listen to these once-muted voices and recognize that material remains are the explicit products of native actions that can be decoded from a native point of view (see Jordan 2008). The heightened sense of reflexivity that emerged in the context of postmodern and postprocessual thinking at the end of the last century had its roots in critical theory, another organizing framework that owes its genesis to Marx and his predecessors and one that has played a role in contact and fur trade studies (Klimko 2004; Lyons 2014; Nassaney 1989, 2012a).

Critical theorists posit that knowledge claims emanate from positions of power and serve to substantiate unequal relationships. Contemporary social and political conditions influence interpretations of an archaeological record that only exists in the present, even though it was created in the past. Because there is a relationship between the present and the past, interpretations of the past are ideologically charged and reflect the personal and political predilections of the interpreter and his or her cultural milieu. Critical theory calls us to recognize that the archaeological record is underdetermined and has ample room for bias to creep in that often reflects a dominant ideology.

More than three decades ago, Donald Bibeau (1984) alerted fur trade historians to the unconscious bias the literature harbors. He used a native perspective to question four key assumptions embedded in the received wisdom surrounding the fur trade. First is the rate of culture change among natives. Numerous examples have been assembled over the past few decades to demonstrate that change was not as rapid as many students of the trade have claimed (e.g., Bamforth 1993, 50). Second is the fiction of native dependency. Again, a close look at native choices during the fur trade suggests that natives were active consumers rather than passive victims of a system that left them dependent on European goods soon after they encountered them (e.g., Ray 1980). Third, Bibeau urges scholars to examine the presumed legitimacy of European claims over North America. Those in power failed to consider the legal rights of indigenous "ownership." Finally, he questions the artificial dichotomy between civilization and savagery that has been used to characterize Europeans and natives, respectively, because it views "civilization" as the preferred state and denigrates native practices as inferior by virtue of their association with those whom Europeans sought to conquer and dominate.

Earlier historiography emphasized the machinations of European powers and cast native people in the roles of minor players at best or passive victims at worst. Commemorations of sites such as Casa Grande, Cahokia, and Chaco Canyon suggest that ancient Native Americans were nobler than their descendants who participated in the fur trade. These views are no longer tenable. Revisionist histories over the past four decades have laid to rest perspectives that emphasized the history of the fur trade as a testimony to the triumph of the civilized over the savage or the Christian over the heathen (Nassaney 2008a) or viewed the fur trade as the precursor to inevitable settlement (C. Gilman 1982, 1). While the fur trade undoubtedly had severe consequences for native peoples throughout North America, their centrality in the institution of the trade must be granted (Peterson and Anfinson 1984) and celebrated. Ethnohistorical and archaeological studies are sensitive to the formerly muted voices of native peoples and acknowledge that the history of the fur trade is an important component of native history (Ray 1978; see also contributions to Nassaney and Johnson 2000 and Podruchny and Peers 2010). Furthermore, native history is integral to understanding national history.

While critically informed historical and anthropological inquiries have prompted revisionist perspectives, the politics of colonialism remain deeply embedded in public interpretation. This is particularly apparent when scholars examine the messages fur trade sites communicate to nonspecialists. In her study of several reconstructed fur trade sites, Laura Peers (1998, 104) noted that the fur trade is portrayed as a foundation of national history in ways that highlight "the deeds of European men and downplay the roles of Native people." Similarly, the repetitive array of trade goods represent tokens of civilization offered to the savages in the wilderness; they reinforce the idea "that Native people became dependent on European trade goods; . . . they thus affirm the underlying assumption that European cultures have always been superior to those of 'Others'" (Peers 1998, 105–106). Detailed portrayals of daily activities (e.g., processing hides, cooking) deflect attention away from social relations involved in the trade (Peers 1998, 106). Reconstructions emphasize European actions and depict native sites as small encampments occupied by a few people beyond the walls of the fort (figure 2.2). This disguises the importance of natives to the trade and denies the cross-cultural nature of the trade (Peers 1998, 107–108).

Fortunately, native interpreters are present at many of these sites to challenge "prejudice and stereotypes through their performances" and replace dominant narratives of cultural disappearance and salvage with stories of revival, remembrance, and struggle (Peers 1998, 112–113). Since the 1970s, natives have made efforts to gain control over public and scholarly representation of their cultures and pasts. As "part of a worldwide trend within the global context of decolonization, Native peoples across North America have

Figure 2.2. Reconstructed wigwams at the Forts Folle Avoine Historical Park near Danbury, Wisconsin, segregate native people from the palisaded North West Company settlement, assigning them a lesser role in the fur trade. Photo by Michael S. Nassaney.

critically explored and problematized the relationship between the dominant elements of nation-states and their academic and public representations of minority groups" (Peers 1998, 103).

New messages are being communicated to the public that can change negative assumptions that still permeate nationalist ideologies, sour native-white relations, and maintain inequalities in North American society (Peers 1998, 103). They can be stated briefly: 1) native peoples adapted creatively to the trade; 2) some natives and whites were able to bridge cultural differences; 3) natives were astute traders; and 4) natives had sophisticated cultures of their own. These messages emerge from native experience and inform both scholarly inquiry and public interpretation.

The politicization of knowledge threatens to cast the past as merely a construction. Yet the materiality of the past forces us to avoid extreme constructivism; material traces limit the range and significance of any particular historical narrative and constrain our interpretations of the past (Mann 2003, 93; Trigger 2007, 540). Archaeological data constitute an "alternate archive" that can be used to reverse the narrative that has plagued the study of the fur trade as nationalist history (Mann 2003, 96). It follows that formerly disempowered stakeholders in excluded positions can use archaeology to challenge the status quo and subvert a dominant ideology. In the post–Native American Graves Protection and Repatriation Act world, an indigenous archaeology has emerged that aims to reintegrate "Indigenous materials, remains, history, and research with contemporary Indigenous peoples" and their concerns (Wilcox 2009, xii). The approach can be extended to other marginalized groups such as voyageurs and women who may have been illiterate but were not powerless (see Scott 1991a). By making fur trade archaeology more inclusive, the "narratives that explain the disappearance and alienation" of native peoples can be reversed and attention can be focused on explaining the survivance of such peoples in contemporary society 500 years after Columbus. The archaeologies that result from this practice and our understandings of the fur trades will be fundamentally transformed by an indigenous archaeology.

The critical analysis of material culture can demonstrate how the interactions of indigenous economies with a global European market were mediated by local cultural schemes (Hamell 1983; Mann 2003, 2004; White 2011). George Hamell (1983) provided a now-classic example in his analysis of glass beads—an iconic category of fur trade goods. Raising the question of why trinkets such as glass beads would seem to be so desirable (read: valuable) in native societies of the Northeast, he examined the qualities they possess from a native point of view. He noted that glass beads shared several attributes with traditional goods that were esteemed in native societies, judging from their placement in mortuary contexts. Marine shell, copper, quartz crystals, and other siliceous stones are traditional material culture expressions of a "metaphysics of light" when they are consecrated for ritual use among the Iroquois and other Native American groups (Hamell 1983). Reflective objects such as glass beads were material embodiments of a "metaphorical conceptualization for semantic domains of highest cultural value synonymous with 'life,' 'mind,' 'knowledge,' and 'being'" (Nassaney 1992, 318). When we reduce glass beads to their exchange value, we fail to understand how natives perceived them and integrated them into their daily life. Copper and other raw materials likely played similar roles that elude a strictly economic explanation for their place in fur trade society (see Bradley 1987; Waselkov 1989, 122).

Creolization, Glocalization, and the Comparative Method

A comparative perspective that juxtaposes evidence (however defined) across sites, regions, or time periods to search for meaningful patterns of similarity or difference is often implied, if not explicit, in fur trade studies (and in much of historical archaeology and anthropology). The comparative method has been a hallmark of anthropology for decades. Comparative studies can take place at varying scales of analysis, from artifact to empire. The field of comparative colonial studies aims to examine how the fur trade and other empires laid the foundation for the globally connected world in which we live today. The materiality of the fur trade provides the opportunity to track comparatively the flow of ideologies, institutions, commodities, practices, and peoples over time and space. With so many fur trades (beaver, bison, deer, sea otter, raccoon, and muskrat) and varied native responses to strategies for mobilizing labor and resources, it would behoove us to look for similarities and differences in the way the trade was organized from French Montreal to English Charlestown and Russian California. This is just the type of work Katherine Arndt (1996) advocated in her study of Russian and British trading activity on the Middle Yukon, which compares native responses to the Russian-American Company and the Hudson's Bay Company. Comparative studies can reveal relational histories that are global in scope but were experienced locally.

The ways large-scale processes (i.e., fur extraction and the marketing of manufactured goods) are negotiated and experienced at the local level is an example of glocalization (Robertson 1995). Sociologists originally borrowed the term from Japanese businessmen to describe how a global product is transformed into another shape in order to meet the needs of local consumers. The fur trade is a prime example of glocalization and deserves to be viewed from the perspective of the global and the local simultaneously.

Kent Lightfoot, Thomas Wake, and Ann Schiff (2003, 2) advocate a similar approach in their study of Russian California and urge researchers to recognize that native peoples engaged in the fur trade were subjected to a wide range of colonial practices that elicited different kinds of responses from them. Inspired by postcolonial studies, they seek to be as inclusive as possible in their efforts to understand the social identities of all people entangled in the fur trade and the outcomes of those entanglements (Gosden 2002). Postcolonial theory foregrounds "the processes of colonialism from the perspective of the colonized, and recognizes that Indigenous peoples had the ability to resist domination and to continue with their traditional patterns of life" (Carlson 2006, 204). Proponents of this theory argue that the study of native strategies in colonial contexts should be undertaken on a case-by-case basis and should examine the nature of native societies prior to contact; the presence and effects of disease vectors; and colonial policies. By undertaking case studies within specific historical contexts, "we may better understand how different native societies responded to colonial policies of agrarian expansion, mercantilism, proselytization, and slavery. In this way, we may begin to compare how various kinds of native societies reacted to particular colonial practices" (Lightfoot et al. 2003, 2).

Scholars have long recognized the importance of variation in the operation and the outcomes of the fur trade. C. Gilman (1982, 2) urges us to "be aware that methods of trade changed over time, and that networks of political-commercial relationships in North America changed over space. The challenge is to untangle the confusion of variations and identify some of the broad patterns." Her prescription remains as useful today as it was over three decades ago. The material variation observed in colonial settings suggests that Europeans pursued different strategies in their efforts to put imperial designs into practice. It also demonstrates that native producers were active agents who had their own political and economic agendas that frequently came into conflict with the desires of white traders. Materiality also expresses the racial, ethnic, class, and gender diversity that populated the fur trade and can be revealed through comparative analysis (e.g., Ewen 1986; Scott 1991b, 2001b).

A postcolonial perspective forces us to consider that the outcomes of fur trade interactions are much more variable than was previously thought. Europeans, who were often far from their homelands, required creativity to survive and prosper in foreign lands. Their strategies often involved extensively borrowing cultural traits in a process of creolization—a form of ethnogenesis in which new cultural forms emerged. Richard White (2011) was among the first to elaborate on the cultural creativity that characterized fur trade society in the western Great Lakes region in the first edition (1991) of his perceptive study. He proposed the concept of a middle ground—a metaphorical space that the French and native peoples created that borrowed from both cultural contexts yet led to entirely new cultural practices. For much of the seventeenth and eighteenth centuries, the trade was never completely divorced from the relations in which it was embedded. Furthermore, domination by market principles never occurred, as is indicated by the prevalence of credit and gift giving. When trade worked properly, natives satisfied their needs and French Canadians gained a profit (Mann 2003, 154). The blurring, mixing, and blending that occurred in fur trade society challenges essentialized categories such as dominant/subordinate, colonized/colonizer, and even native/newcomer that were familiar dichotomies in colonial discourse. Postcolonial theory compels us to view identities as increasingly fluid and situational and no more fixed in matters of policy than they are in material practices.

Adjusting Our Interpretive Lenses to See a New Fur Trade

In sum, interpretive frameworks for examining the fur trade have emerged from general anthropological principles and modes of historical inquiry that were current at particular historical moments. As histories have become more inclusive for political and pragmatic reasons, the study of the fur trade has begun to reflect new theoretical and practical concerns that have moved beyond reproducing nationalist ideologies to efforts to empower groups whose ancestors were marginalized in the past (see Klimko 2004; Peers and

Coutts 2010). The archaeology of the fur trade, with its theoretical ebb and flow, gives us an opportunity to rewrite the past by interpreting material remains in new ways in the twenty-first century. As we continue to address old questions and raise new ones that count in fur trade archaeology, we simultaneously narrow the possibilities of what happened in the past, who did it, and why.

3

A Concise History of the Fur Trade

The sheer spatial breadth and temporal scope of the fur trade make it difficult to present a concise history. The extraction of furs from wild animals for commercial purposes was organized by no fewer than six colonial powers (the English, French, Dutch, Spanish, Russians, and Americans) in interactions with scores of native groups. The trade extended from the St. Lawrence River Valley in the sixteenth century to the Pacific Northwest in the nineteenth century. Each nation had different imperial interests that motivated their participation in the trade. Their motivations also varied over time, making it difficult to characterize, for example, French or English strategies.

This has not prevented scholars from making broad claims, some of which can be supported with documentary and archaeological evidence. For example, the literature is rife with examples that compare and contrast differing colonial policies related to the fur trade (see Dolin 2010; Laird 1995; White 2011). Some claim that the English, in particular, attempted to re-create their way of life in the New World (Washburn and Trigger 1996, 74). According to this argument, while all Europeans traded, fought, and sought to dominate native peoples to varying degrees, English-style settlement was paramount for the English and eclipsed efforts to exploit, plunder, intermarry, or trade with natives. Thus, English ownership and use of land conditioned their interpretations of natives, their role in the fur trade (Washburn and Trigger 1996, 74), and America's Anglo legacy.

The trade was so pervasive that practically every North American site and historical event in the fur trade era was influenced by the trading of furs. The fur trade also affected the vast majority of Native North Americans. Native women developed a trade economy that paralleled the one run largely (but not exclusively) by their male relatives that included marketing food (e.g., rice, pemmican), pottery, baskets, and even rope (Gregory Waselkov, personal communication, 2014). These extractive activities benefited native women, but they also underwrote colonialism. Although native groups were not initially part of Europeans' imperial designs, Europeans soon were attempting to manipulate them to ensure their own competitive advantage in territorial expansion. While the history of encounters and appropriation varies in its details, the fur trade era in North America precipitated a recurrent series of social, political, economic, and ideological contests that pitted native against newcomer in a struggle for power and hegemony.

In the discussion that follows, I track the development of the fur trades at different historical moments and in various places on the landscape. The goal is to illuminate the impact of the fur trade on the material and social lives of its participants. Regions that have yielded archaeological remains provide a better understanding of the materiality of this global phenomenon.

The First Fur Traders

Much of what has been written about the fur trade comes from historical documents. While the written record is by no means the only line of evidence, primary sources were the basis of historical understandings of the trade for decades, and they continue to be mined for the valuable observations and insights of their authors. When read critically, documents can also be used to reconstruct some native activities associated with the hunting and processing of fur-bearing animals in pre-Columbian times. The archaeological and ethnohistorical records suggest that native peoples were enmeshed in intricate and extensive interaction networks that moved resources, including animal products, over long distances (Nassaney and Sassaman 1995). Desirable goods such as minerals, exotic stones, marine shells, feathers, and furs circulated through exchange systems that linked various regions across the continent (Swagerty 1988, 351–352). In the early years of the trade, native people dominated the system and the trade should be viewed as an aspect of native history (Birk 1982, 116). In other words, "the white man did not 'invent' commerce in North America" but rather "tapped, rearranged, and expanded existing trade networks" (116). Thus, trade was by no means a novel practice for Native Americans, though their motivations for participating in and their perceptions of exchange relations differed markedly from those of the Europeans (White 2011, 94–141). Natives were well acquainted with various ways of hunting, trapping, and processing animals for subsistence and other products, including their furs, long before Europeans induced them to harvest fur-bearers for a global market.

Native North America was culturally diverse. It included more than 300 ethnic groups whose members spoke nearly 300 languages that can be organized into some 60 discrete linguistic families. Europeans lacked the conceptual framework to account for these human groups when they first encountered them in the sixteenth century, and this led to many different ideas about their history and origins. The tendency to stereotype natives is perpetuated today in the gross generalities used to characterize similarities in native practices that ignore significant differences. Thus, scholars risk oversimplification in any attempt to describe the indigenous people of the entire continent.

Prior to European exploration, mobile hunter-gatherers, semi-sedentary horticultural societies, and more centralized agricultural groups occupied most of North America north of the Rio Grande. Farmers who depended on maize, beans, and squash were concentrated in the eastern woodlands and in arable areas of the Southwest. Other groups relied on the natural bounty of environments that yielded plant and animal food resources that varied by season and locale. Some groups modified the landscape to increase resource productivity by constructing raised fields, irrigation ditches, fish weirs, and wing traps to capture animals (e.g., Arkush 2000). Many also managed resources through controlled burning that encouraged edge areas and promoted other ecological benefits. Native peoples everywhere scheduled their activities and movements in accordance with the spatial and temporal distribution of resources and devised social networks that provided a buffer against resource fluctuations.

Native groups engaged in reciprocity as the means by which they distributed and consumed goods. Exchange was embedded in native social and political relations, and when they encountered Europeans they assumed that the newcomers had the same values: "Natives expected whites to distribute goods as gifts when traders had much and Natives had little" (Saum

1965, 144). Concepts of resource accumulation, particularly of foodstuffs, were rare in all but the stratified societies of the Northwest Coast. This stands in marked contrast to European capitalist relations of production in which goods were bought and sold to realize a profit, wealth was accrued, and workers became alienated from the means of production through a system of wage labor (Wolf 1982). These differences have led to divergent assumptions that had profound implications for relations between natives and Europeans. It is important to understand the consequences of the entanglement of these two fundamentally different political economies.

Unlike European societies in which status and class structured social relations, kinship was the dominant metaphor in native societies. Through kinship, roles were assigned to individuals according to age, gender, and skill. Women were generally seen as life givers and were in charge of reproduction, gathering plants, cultivation, and rearing children. Men played a more public role; they spent much of their "time away from their villages and families, hunting, trapping, fighting, and conducting diplomacy" (Kicza and Horn 2013, 22).

Political positions were achieved or hereditary, depending on the ethnic group. Power was seldom monopolized because leaders were expected to lead through example and consensus was usually sought. While men held many of the political offices in native societies, women were known to fill important political roles and could exert influence both directly through the leaders they selected for office and indirectly through gossip and other informal means. In general, male and female roles were seen as complementary in native societies. Neither had dominion over the other, in contrast to European patriarchy (Nassaney 2004).

Native cosmology recognized various inanimate forces at work in the universe that included This World, the Upper World, and the Under World (Hudson 1976, 122). Phenomena and objects as diverse as trees, the wind, illness, stone tools, animals, and celestial bodies were seen to have inherent qualities that were to be respected as part of an interdependent web of connections that were important to sustaining human life. Ritual acts were often oriented toward maintaining those interconnections in balance in order to achieve and renew the physical, social, and ideological well-being of individuals and, more importantly, the community. This is the world view that guided many native peoples as they sought to "achieve peaceful relations with the intruders" and fit them into their social order (Cook 1998, 80).

European Instigation of the North American Fur Trade

The mercantile economy in Europe expanded in the fifteenth century. European societies had the capital and infrastructure to seek out raw materials and luxury goods in distant lands (Wolf 1982). Explorations across the north Atlantic were motivated by efforts to exploit rich sources of codfish for profit and seek a more direct route to the Far East. In the search for a westward passage, Europeans explored the waterways along the North American coast and determined the geographic extent of the North American landmass. At first, encounters with native peoples were unintentional and incidental.

José António Brandão (2008, 1) suggests that "the fur trade in northeastern North America was [arguably] . . . a consequence of Christopher Columbus's failed search for a water route west to Asia." He argues that the possibility of such a route or riches that would match Spanish booty in Central and South America was intoxicating to the French and their competitors for decades. In the course of exploring the northern reaches of the continent in their search for precious metals, spices, and a northwest passage, Europeans settled for what began as less lucrative resources, such as fish, timber, and furs. Europeans relied on native peoples to harvest and process the furs, as the latter were familiar with animal habitats and local landscapes. The desire of Europeans for furs of various sorts was matched by their eagerness to create new markets for a range of manufactured goods, including cloth, metal implements, weapons, and drugs (Eccles 1988; Innis 1962). Exchange was one of the most significant mechanisms of interaction between Native Americans and Europeans; it served social, political, and economic functions.

For many native groups, the capture and delivery of furs was integrated into their seasonal round and was minimally disruptive until they lost autonomy and control over critical resources (Bamforth 2003, 169; Jordan 2008, 351). The fur trade was compatible with traditional native lifestyles and was economically viable so long as parity of power existed and natives had access to land (Gilman 1974, 18). Regardless of time and place, it may be useful to conceive of the fur trade in three phases (C. Gilman 1982, 2–3). In the first phase, European participation was tenuous and uncertain; natives organized the trade and Europeans depended on them to bring in furs. In the second phase, Europeans moved into the interior and began to control the transportation of goods, though they still relied on Native Americans to collect and process pelts and supply food and information. During this phase, intermarriage accelerated as a means of establishing kinship relations. The third phase was characterized by highly organized fur-trading companies that were associated with expanding industrialized nations. These companies engendered disease, depopulation, land displacement, proletarianization of a multiethnic labor force, and heightened conflict.

The desire of Europeans for furs predated interactions with native North Americans. When local European sources of fur began to diminish in the eleventh and twelfth centuries, merchants turned to Norse and Slavic sources in the north and east. As anthropologist and ethnohistorian Lydia Black (2004, 5) has noted, trade was critical in the economic life of Russia, and "no other trade item was as important as fur." Furs were used in marriage settlements and as compensation in various disputes. Squirrel, marten, sable, lynx, fox, and wolf were available, although sable eventually emerged as the most desirable fur (Black 2004, 5). Moscow gained control over this market in the fifteenth century and expanded east, exacting tribute (*iasak*) from conquered peoples. Delivery of *iasak,* in the form of furs, symbolized submission to a higher authority (Black 2004, 6). Cooperation between the state and private entrepreneurs in this fur trade had propelled Russians across Siberia and the Bering Strait and into the Pacific Northwest by the eighteenth century.

French, Dutch, and English Pursuits and North American Prey

Basque, French, and other western European fishermen encountered native peoples who offered furs in exchange for iron and brass trifles in the early sixteenth century, when they first landed on the North American coast near the waters of the Grand Banks to dry their fish (table 1; Eccles 1988, 324). Although at first it was a mere trickle, the flow of furs and hides fueled the trade that became pervasive throughout North America for the next four centuries.

The French were especially active in the fur trade partly because beaver and other fur-bearing animals (e.g., mink, otter) were present in the areas that they settled (figure 3.1). Jacques Cartier sailed up the St. Lawrence River in 1534, hoping to find that the wide Gulf of St. Lawrence would provide a water route to Asia. He encountered Micmac Indians on the Gaspé Peninsula who were willing to trade furs for European goods, which suggests that the practice was already well established. In his study of the early fur trade in New France, Henry Biggar (1901) reasoned that trade goods found their way

Table 1. Predominant nationalities of North American fur traders, select native trading partners, and preferred prey species through time by region

	Northeast	Western Great Lakes and Upper Mississippi Valley	Subarctic and Arctic	Southeast	Missouri River Valley and Northern Plains	Greater Southwest	Pacific Northwest
Nineteenth century		English, Americans, Ojibwes, Kickapoos, **muskrat, buffalo, raccoon, deer, beaver**	English, Russians, Iñupiat Eskimos **beaver, fox, wolverine, lynx, land otter**	Americans, Cherokees, Creeks, Choctaws, Chickasaws **deer**	Americans, Mandans, Arikaras, Hidatsas, Cheyennes, Blackfeet **bison, beaver**	Americans, Spanish **beaver**	Russians, Americans, English, Tlingits, Haidas, Secwepemcs **sea otter, beaver**
Eighteenth century	French, English, Americans, Senecas, Onondagas **deer, *menu pelteries***	French, English, Spanish Potawatomis, Ojibwes, Miamis, Piankashaws, Weas **beaver, deer, elk, *menu pelteries***	English, French, Crees, Chipewyans **beaver**	English, French, Cherokees, Creeks, Choctaws, Chickasaws **deer**	English, French, Mandans, Arikaras, Hidatsas **beaver, deer, *bison, menu pelteries***	Spanish, French, Navahos, Apaches, Comanches, Kiowas, Pawnees **buffalo**	French, English, Americans, Russians, Tlingits, Haidas, Aleuts, Nootkas, Kashaya Pomos, Chinooks **sea otter, bear**
Sixteenth– seventeenth centuries	French, Basque, Dutch, English, Micmacs, Narragansetts, Pequots, Wampanoags, Hurons, Pocumtucks, Squakheags **beaver, *menu pelteries***	French, Odawas, Ojibwes **beaver, *menu pelteries***	English, French, Crees, Montagnais **beaver, marten**	English, Spanish, Cherokees, Creeks, Choctaws, Chickasaws **deer**		Spanish, **buffalo, deer, rabbits, antelope**	

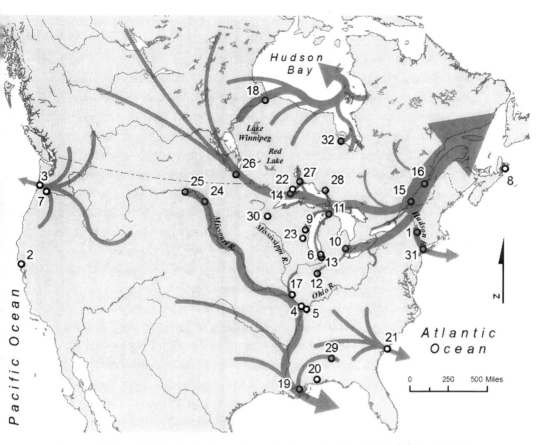

Figure 3.1. Select colonial sites, trading posts, and trade routes of the Dutch (D), the English (E), the French (F), the Russians (R), the Hudson's Bay Company (HBC), the North West Company (NWC), and the American Fur Company (AFC) with dates of establishment. 1. Albany, D-E, 1614; 2. Fort Ross, R, 1812; 3. Fort Astoria, AFC, 1811; 4. Fort de Chartres, F-E, 1721; 5. Fort Massac, F-E, 1756; 6. Fort Miami, F, 1679; 7. Fort Vancouver, HBC, 1825; 8. Fortress of Louisbourg, F, 1714; 9. La Baye, F, 1634; 10. Detroit, F-E-AFC, 1701; 11. Fort Michilimackinac, F-E, 1671; 12. Fort Ouiatenon, F-E, 1717; 13. Fort St. Joseph, F-E, 1691; 14. Grand Portage–Fort Charlotte, F-NWC, 1765; 15. Montreal, F-E, 1642; 16. Quebec, F-E, 1608; 17. St. Louis, F, 1765; 18. York Factory, HBC, 1682; 19. New Orleans, F, 1718; 20. Mobile, F, 1718; 21. Charlestown, E, 1663; 22. Fort William, F-NWC-HBC, 1679; 23. Fond du Lac–Fort St. Louis, F-NWC-AFC, 1793; 24. Fort Clark, AFC, 1830; 25. Fort Union, AFC, 1828; 26. Fort Garry, HBC, 1822; 27. Nipigon, F-HBC, 1683; 28. Michipicoten, F-NWC-HBC, 1725; 29. Fort Toulouse, F, 1717; 30. Sayer's Fort, NWC, 1804; 31. New Amsterdam, D-E, 1624; 32. Fort Albany, HBC, 1769. Drawn by Jason Glatz, Western Michigan University Libraries Mapping Service.

into Iroquoia from coastal sources in the sixteenth century. Archaeological evidence suggests that by the second quarter of that century, native peoples had severed their connections to the north and were acquiring imported goods and marine shell from the south (Bradley 1987, 100–103).

In 1608, the English explored Hudson's Bay; six years later, the Dutch explored the Hudson River. Both bodies of water provided access to the resources of the continent's interior. The English, Dutch, and French quickly realized that furs were plentiful and potentially profitable. Beaver was the preferred (but by no means the only) fur-bearing animal in much of North America. The French initially referred to the pelts of other animals (e.g., mink, lynx, fox, otter, muskrat) as *menu pelteries* because they were generally of less value to the trade than beaver. The desirability of beaver was dependent on native methods of treating the fur and the felting process (Innis 1962, 14). As luck would have it, the furs Europeans desired the most were those that natives had processed into clothing and worn for a considerable amount of time. Native techniques varied somewhat over time and space, but some basic steps were regularly followed. Pelts were scraped on the inner side and rubbed with the marrow of certain animals (Innis 1962, 14). Each pelt was then trimmed, and several were sewn together to form a robe. These were worn with the outer side of the fur against the body. The longer guard hairs would eventually rub off, leaving the short undercoat in prime condition to be sheared and matted into felt for hats in Western Europe. The value of a fur, skin, or robe was influenced by location; the time of the year it was taken; its size, color, and thickness; and the way it was processed, among other factors (Innis 1962, 64–65; Lapham 2005, 9–12).

Other animals were deemed desirable for various purposes; trade eventually developed in buffalo, sea otter, muskrat, raccoon, and deer fur (typically buffalo and deer hides or skins; sea otter, muskrat, and raccoon furs), among others. The American Fur Company acquired the furs of well over a dozen species of animals in the nineteenth century (Clayton 1964, 94–112). Whatever the specific resource, European traders generally relied on native peoples to capture and process the furs, for which they obtained manufactured, imported goods that cemented the relationships that were more than merely economic in nature (figure 3.2).

Before 1700, natives brought furs to trade with the French in the St. Lawrence River Valley. Montreal became the center of exchange (Innis 1962). In the 1650s and 1660s, trade fairs in Montreal were a flurry of activity each

Figure 3.2. Baling needles and thimbles, like these specimens from Fort St. Joseph, were probably used to sew heavy cloth around fur bundles to protect them during shipment. Photo by John Lacko. Courtesy of the Fort St. Joseph Archaeological Project.

summer. Hundreds of natives who were ready to trade for European goods and renew alliances with the French would travel to Montreal in birch bark canoes loaded with furs. The Hurons and later the Odawas made the trip regularly, often acting as middlemen for western Indians. Native peoples had considerable autonomy in the fur trade in this period and exchanged goods within the framework of a pre-Contact trade they controlled (C. Gilman 1982, 2; Kay 1977, 90).

Gradually, westward exploration brought the French and the sites of exchange closer to the source of the furs. Jeanne Kay (1977) claims that as explorers and traders traveled inland (e.g., to Green Bay) and traded directly with natives, native control began to decline. In 1660, when Radisson and Groseillers entered Lake Nipigon from Lake Superior, they discovered a bounty of prime beaver (Morrison 2007, 11). In 1681, in order to regulate the number of men who left the colony in search of furs and restrict the supply, French officials created a licensing system. They issued a limited number of *congés* (permits) to trade. However, independent fur traders, known as *coureurs de bois* (literally "runners of the woods"), managed to circumvent this legality. When trade extended into the interior, merchants incurred higher costs for transportation and other expenses. As a result, a small number of large merchants came to monopolize the trade (Innis 1962, 58).

Fluctuating, if not diminishing, sources of furs along the Eastern Seaboard and a desire to bypass middlemen drove exploration into the interior of the continent. In an effort to find new sources of furs and markets for imported goods, the French began establishing trading posts along a network of waterways connected by a series of portages. In 1727, the French Crown authorized Pierre de la Vérendrye to establish a series of forts that extended westward from Lake Superior. This expansion presented a challenge to the Hudson's Bay Company traders who aimed to enter the interior (Wood et al. 2011, 25). By 1731, the French had begun using the Grand Portage–Pigeon River route from the western end of Lake Superior and had established seven posts in the region that extended from Rainey Lake to the Saskatchewan River (Morrison 2007, 15). From these strategic locations, they drew the trade of western natives away from Hudson's Bay and made inroads into what would become a very lucrative trade in the Middle Missouri River Valley (from present-day Nebraska to Montana) among the Mandans, the Hidatsas, and the Arikaras (Morrison 2007, 15; Rogers 1990). In 1738, La Vérendrye established Fort la Reine on the Assiniboine River and continued south and west, where his expedition reached the Mandan villages at the mouth of the Heart River. He was lured there by native accounts of a river that flowed to the west, which some French explorers hoped might be a route to the Pacific Ocean (Wood et al. 2011, 26). Thus, the fur trade came to include the heartland, the home of the bison that would replace beaver as the mainstay of the trade in the next century. By the 1750s, the French had gone as far west as the Rocky Mountains (Ray 1978, 28). French exploration and expansion of the trade was made possible by support from the Crown, knowledge of the interior gained from natives, and a desire to claim new lands before other Europeans did (Brandão 2008, xxiv–xxv).

The French were never able to attract settler populations as large as those of the English or Spanish, and amicable relations with natives were essential for their survival in North America. The fur trade was the glue that bound the French and their native allies together against their enemies, the English and the Iroquois. This partnership demonstrates that alliances were not always built along cultural lines. French claims to native lands were in name only. Unlike English colonists, the French built their outposts with native permission on native-controlled land. These settlements, which seldom supported more than a few dozen residents, depended on native allies not only for trade in furs but also for the food, technology, and knowledge needed to survive the challenging conditions of the frontier.

Interactions between the French and their native allies facilitated cultural exchange (Juen and Nassaney 2012, 22). Languages and cultural practices were shared. For example, the French readily adopted aspects of native culture and technology that were well suited for living in a northern climate (Gilman 1974). This contributed to a mixing of material culture assemblages. Snowshoes and toboggans made it possible to move over frozen surfaces, and the lightweight birch bark canoe was an appropriate technology that used products of the northern forest—birch bark for the canoe skin, cedar wood for the frame, *wattap* (spruce root) to bind the bark skin to the frame, and spruce gum to waterproof the seams (figure 1.2). The French also practiced native hunting techniques and consumed wild rice, maple sugar, and pemmican (a high-protein mix of buffalo fat and berries). Residents of New France wore moccasins (*souliers sauvage*) (Cangany 2012). In addition to their receptivity to native technologies, clothing, and cuisine, the French often married native women (Peterson and Brown 1985; Sleeper-Smith 2001; Van Kirk 1980).

Although it was mutually beneficial for fur traders of all ethnic backgrounds to marry across cultural lines, the French engaged in this practice more often than most other groups for political and demographic reasons. Intermarriage ensured native women access to European trade goods, and it gave fur traders access to the choice furs of their wives' brothers, fathers, and other kin. The offspring of these marriages, known as *métis*, were uniquely positioned to participate in the fur trade. Since they shared ties to both cultures, some became diplomats who could operate in both native and French environments (Juen and Nassaney 2012, 23). In 1765, George Croghan, a British deputy Indian agent under Sir William Johnson, recognized the underlying French superiority in the fur trade:

They have been bred up together like Children in that Country & the French have always adopted the Indians Customs and manners, Treated them civily & supplied their wants generously, by which means they gained the Hearts of the Indians & commanded their Services, & injoyed the Benefit of a very large Furr Trade. (Quoted in Laird 1995, 237)

French relations with Native Americans were generally better than those of the English (Eccles 1988, 328; White 2011). The French lived among native peoples, mastered their languages, were willing to court them, and held values much closer to those of the natives than "the English traders[,] who thought only of buying cheap and selling dear" (Eccles 1988, 328).

In order to secure the interior, establish alliances with natives, and thwart the efforts of the British and the Iroquois to expand westward from the Atlantic Coast, the French established a string of posts in the western Great Lakes region beginning in the late seventeenth century (figure 3.1). Known to the French as the *pays d'en haut* (upper country), the western Great Lakes region was particularly strategic for the French. It had a large native population and extensive riverine systems that provided both suitable beaver habitats and a network for transporting goods, and the French established several settlements there in the late seventeenth century that persisted until the Seven Years' War. These included posts at Michilimackinac, St. Joseph, Ouiatenon, Green Bay, and Detroit. However, by the late seventeenth century, the storehouses of Montreal were filled with an oversupply of beaver pelts, and the Crown was forced to close many of these posts. The French government reopened several Illinois and Michigan posts in 1701, including Fort Michilimackinac, Fort St. Joseph, St. Louis de Illinois, and Frontenac (Laird 1995, 13), because of its concern that the English would expand into the Great Lakes region. The political and military significance of these posts were such that the Crown was willing to receive devalued furs in exchange for imported goods, effectively underwriting the fur trade at an economic loss. Collectively, the Michigan posts shipped nearly 2,000 packs of furs and hides (approximately ninety-seven tons) at the height of the French fur trade in 1755. This amounted to more than a quarter of all the furs obtained from New France, including Canada, Louisiana, and Hudson's Bay (Brandão 2008, xxvii).

While the French controlled much of the trade in the St. Lawrence–Great Lakes riverine system, the English established settlements along the eastern seaboard, beginning in Virginia and Massachusetts. From Jamestown (1607), they hoped to raid Spanish vessels returning to Europe laden with precious metals. Though the region would soon support a considerable population that profited from tobacco production (some of which made its way into the fur trade), as early as 1612 colonial traders were receiving deerskins in return for "copper, beades, and such like" (Lapham 2005, 7). By the end of the century, trade for deerskins and other pelts was common.

The English settlement at Plymouth (1620) was founded for religious free-dom in an area where native groups had been decimated by disease trans-mitted through casual contact with European explorers and fishermen. The remnant population there welcomed the English as potential political and military allies against the Narragansetts, who had been less affected by the epidemics (Kicza and Horn 2013, 153–154). English settlements grew rapidly at Boston (1630), Providence (1636), Springfield (1636), and Hartford (1638) and soon were placing pressure on native lands in the region. In the 1650s, in an early effort to confine native groups to small tracts of land in eastern Massachusetts, John Eliot established a series of "praying towns" that were ostensibly designed to convert native peoples to Christianity and assimilate them to English society. The success of this scheme was marginal. Had these New England natives been supplying the Massachusetts Bay colonists with furs, they might have been encouraged to roam more freely.

Dutch involvement in the fur trade followed Henry Hudson's voyage in 1609 to the river that bears his name. In the vicinity of what is now Al-bany, New York, "the people of the Countrie came flocking aboord. . . . And many brought us Bevers skinnes, and Otters skinnes, which wee bought for Beades, Knives, and Hatchets" (Norton 1974, 3). A year later, Dutch mer-chants sent a vessel to trade with natives and explore the region, and in 1614, the Dutch built an outpost known as Fort Nassau a few miles south of where the Mohawk River enters the Hudson (Bradley 1987, 112). By 1624, the Dutch West India Company had established Fort Orange near present-day Albany and New Amsterdam on the island of Manhattan. The company operated a profitable trade until 1644, when it discontinued its operation at Fort Orange. Competition ensued over control of the fur trade among the people of northern New Netherland, while the colonists to the south at New Amsterdam were killing, subjugating, or displacing the local natives (Norton 1974, 5). Because the natives and Dutch to the north depended on each other, they developed means for settling their differences. From the English conquest of the colony in 1664 until the mid-eighteenth century, Albany was ideally situated for acquiring pelts and negotiating with the Iro-quois (Norton 1974, 6–7). Moreover, Albany was an alternate market for native furs in northeastern North America until the late eighteenth cen-tury.

Natives of the western Great Lakes region (e.g., Odawas, Potawatomis, Ojibwes) brought some of their furs to the Senecas, who traded them at

Albany (Bradley 1987). Material evidence of this interaction includes the presence of red pipestone from western sources at Seneca sites, indicating their involvement as middlemen in the fur trade (Bradley 1987, 304–309). This role gave the Senecas another means of involvement in the trade, supplementing a new emphasis on deer hunting and deerskin production as beaver declined in importance. This suggests that the fur trade in Iroquoia was vital well into the eighteenth century, contrary to assertions that it had receded rapidly and was eclipsed by the exchange of lumber, land, and crops by that time (Richter 1992, 270–71, quoted in Jordan 2008, 331–32).

The French secured much-needed wampum, which was not available in Canada, from Dutch traders in Albany, despite prohibitions on this illegal trade between the French and other foreign traders at Albany (Norton 1974, 126). This was probably how wampum made its way into French colonial sites in the *pays d'en haut*. Wampum became a medium of exchange in the fur trade (Woodward 1970). The beads, which initially were produced by native peoples in coastal New England and Long Island from marine shell, had various functions in native societies and have been recovered archaeologically throughout the Northeast and even west of the Mississippi River. In the context of the colonial trade, wampum "served as a record of transactions in diplomatic exchanges between tribes as well as with Europeans" (White 1984, 189). It also became an official currency in the mid-seventeenth century when specie was in short supply (figure 3.3).

Since both the English and the Dutch sought to profit from the fur trade, they frequently coveted native lands in areas that yielded few furs and in areas where wampum was "minted" (Ceci 1990). Coastal New England and Long Island offered a poorer habitat for beaver and other fur-bearing animals than interior regions, but marine shell was plentiful there. Thus, even though Roger Williams established a trading post among the Narragansetts at Cocumscussoc in the 1630s and it continued under the proprietorship of Richard Smith and his son into the later decades of the seventeenth century (Rubertone 2001, 134–135), there is little mention of furs being procured from the area, perhaps because they were either inferior (by interior standards) or because fur-bearing animals were depleted early on. English settlers obtained grazing rights for their sheep on Conanicut Island in Narragansett Bay in 1638, and soon after that (1657), they sought "clear and absolute title to the land" conveyed in exchange for wampum (Robinson 2000, 399).

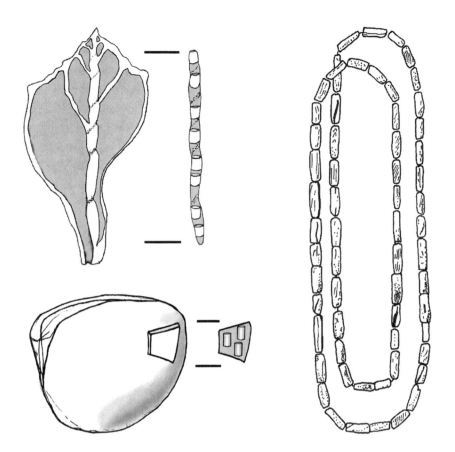

Figure 3.3. Wampum made from northern Atlantic whelks and hard-shelled clams became one of the currencies of the fur trade. Adapted from Nassaney 2004, figure 3. Drawing by Charlotte Taylor.

Nevertheless, the Narragansetts and neighboring coastal groups in southern New England played important roles in the colonial political economy throughout the seventeenth century because they participated in the fur trade by producing wampum. Dutch, French, and English settlers became aware of the importance of wampum early in the seventeenth century (Ceci 1990). The French learned that wampum was "'esteemed more highly' than trade goods by northern fur suppliers, who would buy them 'very dear'" (55). While the origins of the wampum-for-furs exchange system are obscure, Lynn Ceci (58) has described a trade triangle that was in place by the early seventeenth century. First, European investors sent trade goods (cloth and other imports) to coastal areas, where they were exchanged for wampum. Second, Europeans shipped the wampum and some imports inland and exchanged them for furs. Third, the furs were transported back to investors, who sold them at a considerable profit. Through networks such as this, native peoples acquired European goods long before they saw the traders themselves. Records testify to the profitability of this commodity chain. In 1633, Dutch cargo from New Amsterdam increased in value by nearly 500 percent. The commoditization of wampum led to competition and conflict, including the Pequot War and other intertribal animosities (Hauptman 1990).

The English also sought to acquire furs from interior regions before they were depleted by overhunting and habitat destruction (Cronon 1983). In 1636, William Pynchon and several other men and their families settled Springfield, Massachusetts, in the middle Connecticut River Valley. Pynchon "found a ready market for the wampum, cloth, and other items he had transported from the coast" (Thomas 1985, 142). In exchange for these goods, he and other traders acquired maize and beaver pelts. The interdependence of the English and the native residents of the valley encouraged peaceful coexistence. The Pocumtucks and other native groups provisioned the English with surplus agricultural products that were grown locally. The furs the English acquired came from local hunters, middlemen who traveled to the north and west, or directly from distant suppliers (142–143). As was the case with native groups elsewhere, for the Pocumtucks, exchange marked social relationships within families, villages, and between political allies. Imported goods were grafted onto this extant system.

Fur trade records show that natives had access to a wide range of goods that included glass, iron, and copper alloy items, but cloth exceeded all categories in monetary value (146). In addition, the export of beaver pelts declined steadily from 1652 to 1670, particularly in years marked by regional conflict. Finally, colonists opted to seize native land as collateral for credit extended to Native Americans and as a valuable substitute for furs (145). By the 1670s, native peoples had been dispossessed of most of the prime agricultural bottomland in the valley, which effectively terminated the fur trade. Within a generation of its establishment, the exchange system that united English and native interests in the Connecticut Valley collapsed. The European population quickly forgot the importance of their native alliances of a generation earlier.

Deer and the Southern Hide Trade

While the northern reaches of North America provided beaver and other small fur-bearing animals, beginning in the late seventeenth century, a robust trade in deer hides developed that extended from New York to southern Georgia and west to the Mississippi River Valley and the American Southwest (Weber 1971). Hunting deer to obtain hides for commercial trade evolved into a substantial economic activity for many Native American groups throughout this vast region (Lapham 2005; Pavao-Zuckerman 2007). Deer were the dominant source of skins in the American Southeast south of the Ohio River Valley. Much of the history of the Old South is dominated by slavery, the Civil War, and the plantation economy, but furs were the basis of that economy until they were replaced by rice in 1720. The "Indian trade [predominantly in furs] was South Carolina's principal economic activity. . . . It produced more wealth in the colony than indigo, cattle, hogs, lumber, and naval stores combined" (Hanson 2005, 49). As elsewhere, colonial traders supplied Native Americans with a variety of imported goods in return for finely processed hides that were sent to England to be manufactured into "book covers, fine leather gloves, and other apparel and accessories" (Lapham 2005, 11). Lower-quality hides were sold to local leather manufacturers or northern American colonies.

Eighteenth-century government documents provide information about the regional intensity of hide production. From 1699 to 1710, more than 800,000 hides were exported to Great Britain from Virginia and the Carolina colonies—an annual average in excess of 68,000 deerskins (Lapham 2005, 6–7). Further evidence of the intensification of deer exploitation can be found in changing hunting practices and skin-processing activities that have been documented archaeologically (J. Johnson 1997, 2003; Lapham 2005; see also chapter 5).

The Hudson's Bay Company and French Competition

The English also sought to access furs from the interior through a more northerly route. They chartered the Hudson's Bay Company (HBC) in 1670 and established several posts along the shore of the bay to keep down costs (Klimko 2004, 160–161). From these northern posts they were able to divert some of the best beaver furs away from the French (Innis 1962, 48). They soon faced increased competition from the French, who established posts along the north shore of Lake Superior at Nipigon (1678) and Kaministiquia (1680–1681) (Innis 1962, 49). As the French and English penetrated the interior in search of pelts, their economic rivalry developed into a political struggle over the continent; each sought the allegiance of various native tribes (Norton 1974, 6).

The attempts of the English to exploit furs from the St. Lawrence River Valley and its tributaries were generally unsuccessful until their victory in the Seven Years' War. Then they were able to acquire furs from the interior and trade them in Albany, which was the center of trade and diplomacy for the northern English colonies from the 1680s until the fall of New France (Laird 1995, 62). The Dutch traders who remained in Albany well into the eighteenth century willingly did business with the Canadians both in peacetime and during wars (70). Beginning in 1680, English traders also attempted to compete directly with the French by channeling furs to the north through their posts along Hudson's Bay. The 1713 Treaty of Utrecht suppressed French competition in the north and left the Hudson's Bay Company in control of all of the posts on the bay (Ray 1978, 28). Despite the shifting balance of trade, data on the quantities of beaver exports from Canada indicate that neither the English nor the French had a clear advantage in the competition for furs (Cox 1993). As William Eccles (1979) has noted, natives may have preferred to trade with the French but did not hesitate to trade with the English to maintain a viable trading alternative. This underscores the agency natives exercised throughout their involvement with the fur trade, as long as they had economic autonomy. Even after that was lost they still maintained social and political sovereignty (Klein 1993, 137).

Aboriginal groups north and west of the Great Lakes were compelled to travel to the HBC posts to trade since the company seemed content with "sleeping at the edge of a frozen sea" (Allen 1983, 285). The company's charter granted it a monopoly in the fur trade over an enormous region and the right to go into the interior by water and land, "provided the trade went through Hudson Bay" (285). Like the French, they hoped to discover an accessible route across the continent (the elusive northwest passage) to the Pacific and the markets of China and the Far East. Since the company ignored the potential of the untapped interior and confined itself to trading establishments on the coast for almost 100 years, natives developed an intricate system of intertribal trade in which the distant tribes traded through middlemen who brought the furs to the factories at the bay. This spared the company the costs associated with inland transportation (285). However, as with the French situation, the presence of independent traders who traveled into the interior in the late eighteenth century eventually forced the HBC to construct inland posts, beginning with Cumberland House in 1774 along the Saskatchewan River and continuing south of the 49th parallel. The company also expanded west (Klimko 2004, 161), stretching all the way to what would become British Columbia and the U.S. Pacific Northwest to contest its rival, the North West Company, which had already established successful posts there. In this arena the HBC would soon be forced to compete with the American Fur Company and the Russian-American Fur Company.

The earliest HBC explorations that took place in the interior were aimed at pacifying natives so they would hunt and trade more beaver. The HBC was initially at a decided disadvantage because of transportation problems related to the unavailability of birch and cedar for canoes, the discontentment of Orkney laborers in such isolated conditions, and a smallpox epidemic (1780–1781) (Allen 1983, 291). The Plains Indians were reluctant to undertake the long journey to trade at the bay because they had not yet acquired horses and were unfamiliar with canoes. Furthermore, native middlemen, particularly the Crees, jealously guarded their profitable position in the trading system and prevented more distant tribes from passing through their territory to the HBC factories (286). In 1810, a scheme was proposed to reorganize and improve the management of the HBC. The objectives were to undermine the North West Company (NWC), which began as a consortium of independent traders that formed after the fall of New France, and establish an agricultural colony in the Winnipeg district of the HBC's territory to enhance their self-sufficiency. This would place the HBC colony in the path of NWC routes to the northwest and in the midst of the Métis, who provisioned the NWC with pemmican (311, 314).

The French Canadians, who "talk[ed] several Indian languages to perfection," had made inroads in the region and were beginning to collect and transport furs to Montreal (288). The HBC responded by establishing posts in the interior in the manner of the French. The Peace of Paris in 1763 may have ended the imperial influence of France in North America, but it did not ensure a peaceful and unopposed monopoly for the HBC in Rupert's Land, the name given to the watershed of the rivers and streams that flowed into Hudson's Bay and covered approximately 1.5 million square miles. In Montreal, British and American colonial traders and knowledgeable French Canadian voyageurs of the old regime who realigned themselves with independent traders of various nationalities called "pedlars" flagrantly ignored trade restrictions and aggressively pushed their trade into the northwest (286–287).

The "pedlars" continued the French practices of establishing interior posts and wintering among natives with great success. Furs were acquired during the winter and spring and transported to Grand Portage at the western end of Lake Superior and then on to Fort Michilimackinac (287). Competition among independent traders led to their consolidation as the loosely formed North West Company in the 1770s. One of the partners, Alexander Mackenzie, traveled as far as the Arctic and Pacific oceans, in 1789 and 1793, respectively (Morrison 2007, 23). By the 1790s, the NWC was extracting furs from a vast region that stretched from eastern Canada to the Rocky Mountains. The company was directed by Simon MacTavish, who was of Scottish descent (Birk 1989, 8). In less than three decades, it established some 120 outposts that stretched from Lake Superior in the south to the Arctic Ocean in the north. It consolidated with the HBC in 1821.

Transportation, Provisions, Logistics, and Labor Organization

The modes of transportation in the fur trade and the means of provisioning laborers were based on native cultural developments (Innis 1962, 389). Benjamin and Joseph Frobisher discussed the importance of transportation in this intensive inland navigation system in a report on the fur trade in 1784 (Innis 1962, 213–214). Birch bark canoes were essential for plying the inland waterways and moving furs and goods to markets and consumers. Their portability made them practical since they had to be carried over as many as 90 portages between Montreal and the Lake of the Woods. Half the men in the business transported goods from Montreal to the Grand Portage in large canoes (*canot du maître*) that were capable of carrying four tons and could be navigated by eight to ten men. The other half delivered such goods into the interior in smaller canoes (*canot du Nord*) designed for this purpose (figure 1.2). The latter generally spent the winter in the interior, obtained furs directly from natives, and returned with their quarry to Grand Portage in early summer, only to repeat the process beginning in the later fall.

Extensive travel in the fur trade "required a highly developed organization for the supply of provisions" (231). Native agriculture, maize, and native methods of capturing buffalo and making pemmican were critical to the development of a network that could reach into the interior of the continent. Supply depots were established to overcome "the difficulty of carrying large supplies of provisions" by canoe (232). The need to provision workers in the fur trade had broad implications for labor allocation throughout fur trade society. In some instances, large segments of the native population devoted considerable time to creating food surpluses that would support trade workers, including wild rice, maize, fish, and pemmican. These practices underscore the trade's ancillary effects and represent another native contribution in most regions of the continent that were involved in the fur trade.

For the sake of efficiency, the NWC organized its territory into departments and districts that varied by size, productivity, and logistical problems (Birk 1989, 8; Ray 1988, 341–342). A strict hierarchy of specialists managed daily affairs. The shareholders who were known as the wintering partners, or *bourgeois*, traveled into the interior to conduct the actual bartering and supervise their employees (Wheeler 1985, 18). Merchants acted as agents who purchased and packed trade goods and hired guides, interpreters, and voyageurs, a group of specialists that was collectively known as *engagés*. Clerks kept journals and settled accounts, which were important tasks in a system based almost entirely on credit. The social and economic positions of these partners afforded them different diets, clothing, shelter, and other material amenities. While these positions were class based, they also had an ethnic dimension; the labor force was organized according to essentialized characteristics that served as convenient markers for recruitment into the fur trade (Mann 2003, 115–120). Thus, the *bourgeois* tended to be of Scottish or English descent, whereas voyageurs were often French Canadian or *métis*. By the early nineteenth century, British and Americans had instituted a racial and ethnic hierarchy that subsumed all members of fur trader society in an inferior class marked by material distinctions such as vertical timber housing in the western Great Lakes region and the two-wheeled carts that symbolized Red River communities (figure 3.4; Mann 2003, 127). Colonials did not hide their efforts to dominate native peoples economically and politically. An anonymous author of a letter dated 1822 at the HBC's Fort Garry opined that "[natives] must be ruled with a rod of Iron to bring and keep them in a proper state of subordination, and the most certain way to effect this is by letting them feel their dependence upon us" (quoted in Innis 1962, 287). The author urged withholding credit from northern natives unless they were inclined to be industrious. However, some groups, such as those

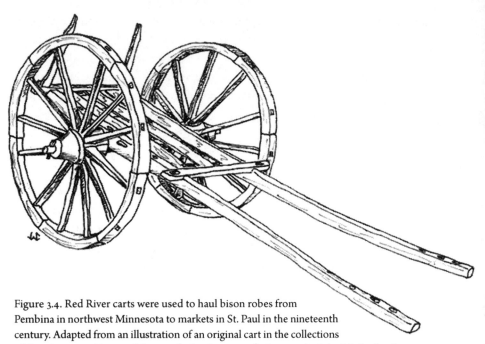

Figure 3.4. Red River carts were used to haul bison robes from Pembina in northwest Minnesota to markets in St. Paul in the nineteenth century. Adapted from an illustration of an original cart in the collections of the Minnesota Historical Society (Wheeler 1975, 36). Drawing by John W. Cardinal.

that occupied the Plains, maintained a degree of independence; in the early years of the trade they could revert to their bows and arrows and abstain from alcohol and tobacco if Europeans could not provide ammunition and other staple articles (288).

The Canadian fur trade in North America reached its apex in the early nineteenth century (Gilman 1974, 11). Business was funneled through three major centers—Detroit, Mackinac, and Grand Portage—that lay in American territory after Jay's Treaty in 1796. In 1798, another fur-trading company, the XY Company (XYC) was formed (Birk 1989, 10). It often built its posts adjacent to the NWC in order to monitor the affairs of its rival. Each firm was intent on ruining the reputation and finances of the other. The NWC attempted to overwhelm the upstart XYC by expanding relentlessly in the hope of bankrupting its undercapitalized adversary (Birk 2008, 144). For natives, competition meant options for bartering; they could obtain the maximum return for their furs by playing one trader off another. Traders were known to entice natives with alcohol, a gift that seems to have crystallized the idiom of kinship more than any other (White 1984, 191). Rum came to represent mother's milk and signified the concern of a parent for a child and the loyalty of a child to his mother (192). While this consumable was often de rigueur in the trade, some natives recognized its deleterious effects and resisted its use (e.g., Allen 1983, 304).

In order to acquire furs directly from natives at their settlements and encourage hunters to be productive, traders often sent their men *en dérouine* (for short visits or stays as itinerant peddlers) among natives (Birk 1989, 10). Successful trade was dependent upon industrious natives who would provide traders with a steady supply of furs and essential food provisions.

American and Russian Escapades

Following the Treaty of Paris (1783) the United States claimed the Northwest Territory, which included northern Michigan, Wisconsin, and much of Minnesota, even though the new nation could exert little political control over the region. Many of the British and French Canadian inhabitants remained loyal to Britain (Kay 1977, 209). While the HBC and the NWC competed for the wealth of the vast inland area north and west of the Great Lakes, American interests led to the incorporation of the American Fur Company (AFC) under John Jacob Astor in 1808. The history of the fur trade for much of the nineteenth century is complicated by the involvement of numerous companies and their subsidiaries and "shifting business alliances that led to dissolutions, mergers, and reorganizations of these firms" (Wood 1990, 9). By the end of the War of 1812, Astor and the AFC controlled the fur trade south and west of the Great Lakes (Dolin 2010, 192–197; Gilman 1974, 13). They effectively ended Canadian influence in the middle Missouri region and shifted the focal point of American trade from Montreal to St. Louis. Astor's domination extended to the far west by the 1820s (Clayton 1964).

A poor but ambitious German immigrant, Astor was introduced to the fur trade in the 1780s through his work with a New York fur dealer. He took trips into the backwoods in the mid-Atlantic region to acquire furs for sale and export. Astor became one of the few American fur traders operating east of the Mississippi River and soon expanded his enterprise to participate in the Pacific maritime fur trade. To stake his claim on the furs that could be harvested from the lands newly acquired in the Louisiana Purchase, he proposed to build a series of trading posts along the trail of Lewis and Clark up the Missouri River, over the Continental Divide, and along the Columbia River to the ocean (Dolin 2010, 194). Among the notable posts established during this period were Fort Union (1829) and Fort Clark (1831). Astor supported his plan by claiming that his aim "was to improve relations with the Indians and pave the way for peaceful settlement of the West," effectively hiding his economic motives (Dolin 2010, 195). He also mounted a patriotic argument for his exploits by accusing Canadians of taking American furs from the west and selling them in Montreal, thereby raising costs for American consumers. With government support, Astor created a second company, the Pacific Fur Company (PFC), in 1810 in an effort to control the U.S. fur market from the Great Lakes to the Pacific as well as markets in Asia, particularly the lucrative China trade that Boston merchants were finding profitable (Clayton 1964, 132).

Arriving by sea, the employees of Astor's PFC established a fur-trading post in 1811 in what is today Astoria, Oregon, making it the first permanent American settlement west of the Rocky Mountains (Wilson et al. 2012). This fort, commonly called Fort Astor or Fort Astoria in honor of its founder, quickly became the hub of a regional fur trade centered on the lower Columbia River. The fort was operated by PFC employees who were French Canadian, Scottish, American, and Native Hawaiian and members of various eastern Native American ethnicities. A diverse group of tribes also converged there. The NWC also explored the upper reaches of the Columbia River and began trapping there. To avoid direct competition, Astor invited the NWC to purchase a share of the PFC's profits and join in his endeavor, but the NWC refused. Astor countered by hiring numerous Canadians, whom he admired as the best in the business (Dolin 2010, 196–197; St-Onge 2008).

During the War of 1812, Fort Astoria became the focal point of international tensions in the region. PFC employees transferred ownership of the fort to representatives of the now-British-owned NWC in 1813. The fort continued to operate as before, under the new name of Fort George. In 1818, the fort was ceremoniously returned to the United States, under the terms of the Treaty of Ghent, but it continued to operate as Fort George under the direction of the NWC. The HBC assumed management of the fort in 1821 and used it as its principal depot in the region until Fort Vancouver was built in 1825. Fort George was gradually eclipsed in its regional significance by Fort Vancouver, but it continued to operate as an HBC fort until 1848, when the Oregon Treaty designated Astoria as indisputably American territory. Despite its gradual decline, the fort was a major trading center for tribes of the Pacific Coast and the lower Columbia region, and it was a cornerstone of Anglo-American settlement in the region. These fur-trading enterprises had a profound effect on the outcome of the colonial conquest of the Pacific Northwest, and the goods they introduced had a significant impact on the native peoples of the region (Doug Wilson, personal communication, 2014).

After the American Fur Company withdrew from the Northwest, it concentrated on developing a vibrant business in the Great Lakes region (Clayton 1964, 20). The fluctuations in the supply of and demand for furs prompted James L. Clayton (1967, 66) to divide the American fur trade "into three major eras characterized by the dominant fur of the time": 1790–1820s (beaver); 1820s–1860s (raccoon); and 1870s–1890s (fur seal). He also suggests that the period before the 1830s (the period when beaver declined) should be called the "fiber trade" because fine furs played only a minor role in comparison to the beaver's undercoat (67). As beaver, bear, and buffalo declined in the 1830s, the smaller fur-bearers such raccoon, mink, and muskrat became popular and remained abundant even as settlement increased (Clayton 1964, ix–x). Records of the AFC indicate that the fur trade was growing rapidly in the 1820s and was not generally in decline. By the 1830s, muskrat accounted for 95 percent of the furs the company shipped from the Upper Mississippi Valley; deerskins were second in prominence (Gilman 1974, 18). Some of these deerskins may have supplied the moccasin industry that was active during this period (Cangany 2012). Muskrat, buffalo, and raccoon were the most important species by value that the AFC obtained in the Great Lakes trade in the 1830s (Clayton 1964, 50). Muskrat alone averaged over 400,000 pelts annually from 1835 to 1842, and these were supposedly very poor muskrat years (49). The Detroit Department of the AFC was especially productive.

During the early 1820s, Ramsay Crooks assumed the leadership of the company under Astor's lax supervision (143). Over the next decade he committed himself to increasing the company's profits for its stockholders and was a vocal opponent of the government trading houses first established in 1796 to sell goods to the Indians at cost (141). Crooks supported a prohibition movement that led to the effective curtailment of alcohol use in the trade, since he believed that "sober Indians were better hunters" (244). The AFC was the most important fur company in the United States. It handled more furs than any other organization, though independent traders continued to operate throughout its existence.

The AFC and the HBC were staunch rivals; their territories overlapped only near the 49th parallel before this became the U.S.-Canadian border in 1846. After the NWC merged with the HBC in 1821, the Hudson's Bay Company reduced the size of its labor force and retired or terminated some *métis*. Many of these former employees took up residence in Red River Colony (present-day Manitoba), where they were allowed to "trade with Indians in the southern areas of Rupert's Land so long as they obtained their goods from, and sold their furs to, the Hudson's Bay Company" (Ray 1988, 344). The Red River traders began buying goods and selling furs south of the U.S. border, likely to AFC agents, in a clandestine trade that violated HBC policies (344).

Farther west, the HBC established the headquarters of its Columbia Department at Fort Vancouver in 1825 in an effort to anchor Britain's claims to the Oregon Country (Wilson 2011, 7). Over the next two decades the fort became the fur trade capital of the Pacific Northwest. It had warehouses, access to locally produced goods, and enough agricultural surplus to supply fur brigades, Native Americans, settlers, and up to two dozen other company posts in the department "from Russian Alaska to Mexican California and from the Rocky Mountains to the Pacific Ocean, a territory of approximately 700,000 square miles" (Wilson 2011, 7).

The expansion of French, English, and American trade into the Pacific Northwest occurred after the Russians discovered the economic value of sea otter pelts to the Chinese. Warm winter garments made of fur were needed in China, where the scarcity and cost of fuel restricted its use to cooking and ceramic production (Gibson 1992, 54). The fur of the sea otter is exceptionally dense, and its "thick, dark, lustrous pelt became the most valuable fur on the world market" (Gibson 1992, 6). The Russians began to acquire pelts and market them to Chinese merchants in the seventeenth century. Fur seal and beaver skins were likewise in demand, and the Russians crossed the Bering Strait in 1742 to exploit sea mammals for their fur (Lightfoot 2005). From 1743 to 1800, Russian fur traders obtained more than 8 million silver rubles' worth of skins (Gibson 1988, 376). In 1799, Tsar Paul granted the Russian-American Company (RAC) a charter, giving it a monopoly over all Russian economic activities in North America. The RAC, which employed Hawaiians, Aleuts, native Californians, and creoles (the offspring of Russian and native unions), instituted a system of forced labor in which coastal Alaskan natives hunted furs in Pacific waters as far south as northern California. Sea otters were taken in the ocean and on shore. Nets, clubs, and harpoons were employed, sometimes from native kayaks called *baidarkas* (Black 2004, 71; see also Gibson 1988, 377).

Russian exploration along the California coast led to the establishment in 1812 of Colony Ross at the mouth of the Russian River just north of San Francisco Bay. The purpose of this settlement was to grow wheat and other crops to sustain Russian traders in Alaska, hunt marine mammals, and trade with Spanish California (Lightfoot 2005). The colony had been a successfully functioning multicultural settlement for nearly thirty years when the RAC decided to abandon it, due in part to the depletion of the California sea otter population. Mexican and American settlers also posed a challenge to Russian claims in the region, a demonstration of the fact that sovereignty in North America rested on the ability to seize, occupy, and hold territory, often by force.

Most of the maritime trade was not dependent on permanent European settlements. It was not necessary to take native lands in order to earn a profit from the trade along the coast from northern California to the Aleutian archipelago. On his third voyage, British commander Capt. James Cook sailed to the north Pacific in yet another attempt to find a northwest passage (Dolin 2010, 134). When he arrived along the coast of Vancouver Island in 1778, he was greeted by canoes filled with natives eager to trade the furs of sea otters, bears, and other animals for knives, buttons, nails, and other goods (135). He and his men obtained a good many pelts that brought a considerable return in China. News of this lucrative trade enticed Boston investors to enter the market the following decade. After the American Revolution, the former colonies had lost their trading relationships with the British Empire and were seeking direct access to Chinese goods (Vaughan 1982a, 3). News of Cook's good fortune precipitated two decades of active trade that linked New England, the Northwest coast, and Canton and generated profits on each leg of the journey (Gibson 1992, 58). Investors gave their factors considerable latitude "to improvise and respond flexibly to whatever situation arose" in their dealings with both the Indians and the merchants in Canton (Dolin 2010, 155). Since they were less constrained by regulations and strict oversight, the "Boston Men" (as they were known) could use their bargaining skills to gain a competitive advantage over their British, Portuguese, French, Spanish, Dutch, Danish, and Swedish rivals and brought some American capitalists as much as a 2,200 percent return on an initial investment in the voyage (155–156; see also Vaughan 1982b, 263).

Americans soon surpassed the Russians in this maritime trade. The Russians were permitted to trade with China only from a border crossing at Kyakhta. This required them to transport furs "from the Northwest Coast across the North Pacific and through Eastern Siberia to the Mongolian frontier" (Gibson 1992, 60). In contrast, Americans could trade at the port of Canton. From 1790 through 1818 American shipmasters transported approximately 10,000 skins annually to Canton (181). By 1818, the Russians were competing with both the Americans and the HBC on different geographic fronts. The declining stock in sea otter had forced the RAC to diversify its fur intake and seek untapped sources in Alaska (Arndt 1996, 20). Company employees penetrated the Yukon River Valley in the 1820s to obtain beaver, fox, and land otter skins in exchange for knives, kettles, tobacco, and pipes (23).

Meanwhile, the HBC was well established in the Mackenzie River region. In 1829 its directors began to consider the southwestern tributaries of the Mackenzie as possible routes to the Pacific trade. They also contemplated intercepting terrestrial furs destined for Russian hands (74). The HBC experienced supply problems in this remote area; Chilkat Tlingit traders, their competitors, used western goods they acquired from the coast, including guns, to barter for the furs of the region (75–76). Katherine Arndt (76–77) has called attention to the scarcity of information about the antiquity, extent, and routes of the fur trade in the upper Yukon drainage area; early accounts do not exist and well-dated archaeological evidence is rare. There are also questions about how native peoples gained access to critical goods such as firearms. What is clear is that native fortunes changed when sea otter populations declined in the 1820s, Russians came to rely on the pelts of land mammals, and "the Chilkat and other mainland Tlingit who controlled access to the interior became powerful middlemen in the coast-interior fur trade" (80). Interestingly, natives in these northern regions considered their own skin clothing superior to European cloth. They could not be induced to accept textiles in trade (Arndt 1996, 84), in contrast to many other regions of the continent, where the cloth trade was paramount.

Although the Russians were front-runners in the Pacific maritime fur trade, Americans began to collect furs aggressively in the late 1780s, using ships that sailed from Boston harbor and around Cape Horn, stopping in the Hawaiian Islands. Sir Francis Drake had visited the Northwest Coast in the sixteenth century, but neither the English nor the Americans established any permanent settlements there. The Boston–Northwest Coast–Canton triangular trade produced "a perfect golden round of profits," as F. W. Howay

(1923, 42–43, quoted in Gibson 1992, 58) described it. First, profit was made on the original cargo of trading goods that was exchanged for furs; second, profit was made when the furs were traded for Chinese goods; and, third, profit was made on Chinese goods when they were sold in America.

This lucrative maritime trade persisted for more than half a century. Over 127 American voyages between the United States and China via the Northwest Coast (Gibson 1992, 56) were made from 1788 through 1826. This fur trade stimulated economic development and industrial production in the United States. It enriched Boston merchants and ship owners and contributed to the accumulation "of the capital that enabled New England to evolve from an agrarian to an industrial society" (Gibson 1992, 296). By the first decades of the nineteenth century, American fur traders had begun to supplement foreign goods with domestic products to exchange for furs in the western Great Lakes region (the present-day states of Michigan, Minnesota, and Wisconsin), the Missouri River Valley, the Southwest, and the Pacific Northwest (see Woodward 1927).

The history of the fur trade demonstrates how global processes affected local production. For example, when the Russians lowered their fur tariff in 1837, Russian Jews and Poles imported more raccoon skins from the United States to meet the demand for coonskin caps like those associated with Davy Crockett. When the Russian czar banned the use of raccoon skins in 1846, the German demand for the pelts to trim hats and coats increased (Clayton 1967, 68). Likewise, this history illuminates the varied imperial, corporate, and individual motivations for involvement. For example, Royal Way (1919, 222) has argued that Great Britain and Spain used the trade in the nineteenth century as part of an attempt to check the expansion of the United States. He suggests that the English and Spanish befriended native peoples and attempted to influence them to oppose American advance. In this scenario, the United States countered by trying to win Native Americans over through trade, despite the practices of unscrupulous traders.

Beginning in 1775, the policy, if not the practice, of the United States was to secure alliances with natives to ensure westward expansion and remove the dangers of continual native conflicts (Way 1919, 223). A system of government-owned trading posts known as factories (in reference to the merchants, or "factors," who carried out the trade) was established in 1795 in an effort to create harmony with tribes, convert them to Christianity, and make them more dependent upon government-supplied goods and thereby more subject to government control (Prucha 1962, 84–93; Wallace 1999). The factory system began as an attempt to eliminate the worst excesses of the fur trade by prohibiting the sale of alcohol, gifts, and credit and by providing goods to natives at wholesale prices (Way 1919). Over a dozen factories were located in the South and in the Old Northwest Territory (see table 2). In exchange for quality goods at a fair price (e.g., clothing, tobacco, utensils, and sometimes weapons and ammunition), the government trader, or factor, obtained animal skins and furs. The factor at each trading house was supposed to keep rather extensive financial records for the time, including daybooks, ledgers, journals, letter books, cashbooks, and invoice books. The AFC aggressively opposed the system as the company sought to monopolize the fur trade; Astor claimed it placed commercial traders at a disadvantage because the factories sold goods below cost. Be that as it may, the factory system was abolished in 1822 because it was costly, inefficient, and unpopular and could not compete with free enterprise, particularly the mammoth AFC (Hanson 2005, 99–103).

Credit was common in the fur trade; cash, or specie, was seldom used (Pendergast 1972). In much of the commercial (i.e., nongovernmental) trade, goods were credited to natives in the fall and offset by furs the following spring (37). "It is the established custom of the fur traders to supply the Indians with goods on credit, extracting from them a promise to deliver, in return, a stipulated number of beaver skins, or an equivalent in other furs" (Douglas 1816, 44, quoted in Pendergast 1972, 39). Such a system worked to maintain relationships and encouraged dependency, as some natives went further into debt. Traders were eager to collect on bad debts when tribes were forced to sell land to the U.S. government. Traders also profited from annuity payments the government promised natives, which were sometimes paid directly to traders to offset debts or new purchases (Gilman 1974, 18).

Retrospect

Participants in the fur trade shared the experience of novel goods, information exchange, technological transfer, and the creation of new forms of cultural practice (Rogers 2005, 352–353). Historians have documented the diversity of ways the fur trade worked. The motivations for participating in the trade, the goods exchanged, and the way labor was organized to collect and process furs differed over time and space. For example, in the early

Table 2. Years of operation of U.S. government factories
in order of their establishment

Colerain (Georgia), 1795–97 (Creek)

Tellico (Tennessee), 1795–1807 (Cherokee)

Fort Wilkinson (Georgia), 1797–1806 (Creek)

Chickasaw Bluffs Factory (Tennessee), 1802–18

Detroit Factory (Michigan), 1802–5

Fort St. Stephens (Alabama), 1802–15 (Choctaw)

Fort Wayne (Indiana), 1802–12

Arkansas Factory (Arkansas), 1805–10

Belle Fontaine Factory (Missouri), 1805–9

Chicago Factory (Illinois), 1805–22

Natchitoches–Sulphur Fork Factory (Arkansas), 1805–23

Ocmulgee Old Fields (Georgia), 1806–9 (Creek)

Sandusky Factory (Ohio), 1806–12

Hiwassee (Tennessee), 1807–10 (Cherokee)

Fort Madison Factory (Iowa), 1808–15

Mackinac (Michilimackinac) Factory (Michigan), 1808–12

Osage Factory (Missouri), 1808–22 (Fort Clark)

Fort Hawkins (Georgia), 1809–16 (Creek)

Green Bay Factory (Wisconsin), 1815–23

Prairie de Chien Factory (Wisconsin), 1815–22

Fort Confederation (Alabama), 1816–22 (Choctaw)

Fort Mitchell (Alabama), 1816–20 (Creek)

Fort Edwards Factory (Illinois), 1818–23

Sulphur Fork (Arkansas), 1818–22

Spadra Bluffs (Arkansas), 1818–22

Spadre Bluffs (Illinois Bayou) Factory, 1818–24

Fort Armstrong (Illinois), 1821–22

Marais des Cygnes (Kansas), 1821–1822

Source: RG75.3, Records of the Office of Indian Trade, 1795–1830,
National Archives and Records Administration, Washington, D.C.

nineteenth century, the Shawnee prophet Tenskwatawa urged his followers to disengage from the fur trade and return to "traditional" forms of subsistence and material culture to recapture sacred power and defeat the Americans (Wagner 2011, 227). In contrast, the native peoples of the Northwest Coast maritime fur trade were shrewd traders who were just as eager to trade as the Euro-Americans. They aimed to maximize profits and obtain more than equivalent values for their furs (Gibson 1992, 114–117). Native peoples in the western Great Lakes region and elsewhere were always willing to play the French against the British to ensure exchanges that symbolized a favorable alliance.

As Native Americans became dispossessed from their land, they were unable to procure animals and process them for the trade. By the end of the nineteenth century, it was no longer commercially profitable to obtain furs in the wild, particularly the furs of dwindling animal species such as the beaver, sea otter, and buffalo. Although hunting fur-bearing animals persists to date in marginal environments such as the far north, the number of animals harvested today pales in comparison to the number taken during the fur trade era.

This concise history of the fur trade demonstrates the interdependent relations that emerged between natives and newcomers beginning in the sixteenth century and persisting as long as natives remained the primary producers of the raw materials Europeans desired. The trade was not without negative consequences for native societies, particularly after they were dispossessed of the land base they needed to maintain some degree of autonomy in the face of European efforts at domination. The tensions, negotiations, and resolutions that resulted are manifest in the choices participants in fur trade society made. Moreover, many of these choices had material consequences that are amenable to archaeological analysis.

Numerous firsthand accounts detailed prescriptive behaviors. Little of what actually transpired in exchanges between traders and natives was recorded, making it difficult to reconcile contradictory viewpoints and draw any definitive conclusions about the everyday conduct of the trade (Laird 1995, 50). Archaeology can provide a different line of evidence to examine how these large-scale processes were experienced at the local level, since archaeological materials were deposited in contexts that reflect daily life. An archaeological perspective can also shed light on variation that may not be revealed through documentary sources alone, particularly with regard to native participation in the system (e.g., Carlson 2000; Kehoe 2000; Rogers 1990). The following chapter examines some of the significant research questions and methods that archaeologists have employed in their study of the materiality of the fur trade.

4

Themes in the Materiality of the Fur Trade

Historical archaeologists have addressed a range of research questions at sites from various time periods in their investigation of the North American fur trade. Studies conducted over the past 150 years under the broad rubric of fur trade archaeology mirror the development of the field of archaeology and reflect changes in its research priorities (Trigger 2007). The fur trade and fur trade–related archaeological sites that have been located and examined are too numerous to detail in a single book. In this chapter I select examples from throughout North America to illustrate prominent themes that have emerged in the literature and the methods archaeologists have employed in their investigations. The goal is to determine what the materiality of the fur trades can contribute to our understanding of the American experience.

The Genesis of Fur Trade Archaeology: Site Identification, Chronology, and Classification

Early investigations in North American archaeology were focused on pre-Columbian sites to determine the identity of the ancient mound builders and the origins of Native Americans (Trigger 2007, 160). There was limited interest in native sites of the post-Contact period because native peoples were perceived as in decline and as people who were soiled by the trappings of Western culture (Rubertone 1996). Working under the influence of the reigning paradigms of the day, practitioners saw evidence of Native American use of European-made goods as a sign of social decay and economic dependence (Wagner 2011, 12).

Historical archaeologists initially sought to identify European sites associated with "famous people or with events important in American or Canadian history" (Orser 2004, 30; see also Doroszenko 2009), although there were exceptions. For example, John W. Dawson conducted excavations in the 1860s on a St. Lawrence Iroquoian fortified village that Jacques Cartier visited in 1535 (Doroszenko 2009, 507; Waselkov 1997, 12). In the 1930s, Emerson Greenman (1951, cited in Orser 2004, 31–32) examined the graves of Native Americans in Ontario's Georgian Bay region to recover goods obtained from French traders in Montreal. In these studies, an interest in the fur trade was tangential to concerns with commemorating resourceful settlers who tried to subdue the wilderness and cultivate their values of civility in the face of the native presence. In the west, Louis Caywood (1967), a National Park Service archaeologist and founding member of the Society for Historical Archaeology, investigated fur trade sites starting in 1947, including extensive excavations at Fort Vancouver to collect data to aid in architectural reconstruction. In these studies of early contact and frontier life, we see the beginning of efforts to understand the economic, social, and political relationships between Europeans and native groups who were coincidentally entangled in the fur trade.

Efforts to investigate the routes of exploration and the locations of early fur trade sites in the American Midwest have parallels in other parts of North America (Nassaney 2009). Because Europeans and their descendants in the Midwest were confined to a few locations before the first quarter of the eighteenth century, archaeological sites dating to this period are rare and are limited to predominantly French fortified outposts. However, contemporaneous Native American sites are more common, particularly burials, and some have been examined from the perspective of the fur trade (e.g., Cleland 1971; Good 1972; Mason 1986; Quimby 1966; Trubowitz 1992a). Relatively small sites of limited duration or those for which later developments impacted earlier cultural components have left few intact archaeological traces, making them difficult to find. Nevertheless, there has been considerable interest in examining material evidence from early fur trade sites in the region, most of which can be tied to famous explorers or important places associated with historical documents. Nineteenth-century antiquarians frequently collected artifacts from fur trade sites such as Fort St. Joseph in Niles, Michigan (see chapter 6). Other sites were publically commemorated even in the absence of material traces, such as La Salle's Fort Miami at the mouth of the St. Joseph River (figure 4.1; Nassaney 2008a).

Figure 4.1. Commemorative marker for French explorer and fur trader René-Robert Cavelier, Sieur de La Salle, erected in 1902 near the site of Fort Miami in present-day St. Joseph, Michigan. Photo by Michael S. Nassaney.

Systematic excavations generally did not begin at places such as Fort Michilimackinac until the latter half of the twentieth century, although beginning in the 1930s George I. Quimby (1939, 1966) used museum collections associated with sites that could be dated through historical documents to establish a chronological framework for artifacts associated with the historic period in the western Great Lakes region. Most of the diagnostic artifacts he used to define the Early, Middle and Late Historic periods were trade goods such as silver ornaments and glass beads. Establishing an accurate chronology is an important theme in fur trade studies. Michael Shott (2012) recently revisited the utility of pipestem-bore values for dating seventeenth- and eighteenth-century sites, including fur trade settlements, demonstrating that archaeologists continue to refine their analytical tools to establish chronology.

Excavation at many sites was also motivated by the need for information to assist in reconstruction and site interpretation, as at Fort Michilimackinac, where archaeological work began in 1959 (Maxwell and Binford 1961). As was too often the case in both the United States and Canada, reconstruction and commemoration have been used to buttress national myths at the expense of a fuller narrative that engages multiple populations (Klimko 2004; Waselkov 1997, 13). Nevertheless, many of these sites and their collections still have value for addressing fur trade issues in the modern era. Since the 1970s in the United States and the 1980s in Canada, compliance with legislation has shifted investigations of fur trade sites "to more problem-oriented research with efforts to study subsistence, diet, status, ethnicity, social composition, acculturation, land use and symbolism of both European and aboriginal peoples involved in the fur trade" (Klimko 2004, 166). These interests remain current and focus attention on the role of different cultural and ethnic groups within a broader context of comparative colonialism and the fur trade.

In conjunction with written documents, archaeologists have used material remains to classify sites according to age and function so they can gain a better understanding of synchronic and diachronic variation. In addition to fortifications, there were also trading centers, farmsteads, villages, churches, cemeteries, and production sites. Some archaeologists see these settlements as hierarchically organized at different levels, from ports of entry and governmental centers down to regional and local distribution centers, reflecting the flow of goods from Europe into the hands of consumers. Judith Tordoff (1983) identified five site types with distinctive archaeological expectations based on the activities they supported and used the model to test predictions against archaeological data from Fort Ouiatenon, a fur-trading post along the Wabash River. Others have found it useful to distinguish sites that were engaged in the extraction and processing of natural resources such as furs or lumber from those associated with the production of agricultural goods that supplemented the fur trade (Keene 1991). Jacqueline Peterson (1985) identified three types of fur trade communities in the Great Lakes region: commercial and military centers, village or post settlements, and corporate trading towns. All of these sites supported different activities that have implications for the frequency and distribution of artifacts in archaeological contexts. In a society in which most people were illiterate and left no written records, archaeology can contribute to our understanding of the daily activities at these sites and the identities of their occupants.

At a larger geographical scale, we can propose "catchments" that mirrored the flow of goods and services between natives and Europeans. C. Gilman (1982, 3) identified four trading spheres that impinged on the Great Lakes region based on transportation networks and tribal alliances. These include: 1) the Algonquian system in the St. Lawrence River valley and the Great Lakes region; 2) the area north of the Great Lakes reaching toward Hudson's Bay; 3) the Iroquois network in New York State; and 4) a system operated by native-born French actors that originated near present-day St. Louis. The latter system reached all the way up the Missouri River during the late eighteenth and early nineteenth centuries.

Of course, there were other networks that linked to these and extended beyond the mid-continent to the Southwest, the Pacific Northwest, and New England and Long Island Sound. For instance, horses obtained from the Spanish in the Southwest expedited the hunting of bison on the Plains (Hanson 2005, 163; Lewis 1942; Weber 1971). Pacific marine shell ornaments were traded inland to the Plains Indians (Ewers 1954). Shell was also integral to the seventeenth-century economy of the coastal northeast (Esarey 2013). Although that region was depleted of fur-bearing animals by the mid-seventeenth century, the Narragansetts, Pequots, and other coastal groups produced wampum—"the magnet which drew the beaver out of the interior forests"—for use in an elaborate triangular trade (Ceci 1990, 58; Dolin 2010, 28). Europeans realized the utility of shell beads and ornaments and took over their production in the eighteenth century (Peña 2001). The spatial distribution of shell and imported goods is testimony to the scale of exchange networks and the means for their delivery.

Navigating the Fur Trade Landscape

Fur trade archaeologists employ the familiar dimensions of space, time, and form to order the materiality of the trade before they engage in comparative analysis. Even though they benefit from historical documents, they aim to use the detritus of daily life to create a fuller picture of fur trade history and culture. For example, archaeology has played a significant role in identifying sites that are poorly documented in written records. Archaeology can illuminate the location and appearance of many early trading posts that were formerly lost to time (Kenyon 1986, 10; Nassaney 1999; Oerichbauer 1982).

Given the ephemeral nature of some fur trade sites, surveying to locate archaeological evidence remains a priority. The Minnesota Historical Society has long been interested in identifying and preserving fur trade sites associated with the Grand Portage, which is now designated as a national landmark. In the early 1960s, the society initiated a long-term underwater search along historic canoe routes on the U.S.-Canada border that led to the recovery of a wealth of data from submerged contexts, including artifacts that were lost in canoe accidents centuries ago (R. Gilman 1982, vii; see also Birk and Richner 2004; Wheeler et al. 1975).

Once fur trade sites are located, preservationists are often motivated to investigate them to obtain information that will help with reconstruction and site interpretation (Birk 1989; Heldman 1991; Klimko 2004; Maxwell and Binford 1961; Peers 1998). Evidence has been obtained for the placement, size, and orientation of buildings, palisades, and other architectural features. This, combined with maps and other historical documents, has contributed to the re-creation of facsimiles of original sites. This was a popular strategy at places such as Fort Michilimackinac, the Fortress of Louisbourg, and numerous state and national parks throughout the United States and Canada (figure 4.2). To obtain accurate architectural information, archaeologists often excavated large horizontal areas in order to discern patterns of postholes, wall trenches, foundations, cellars, and other features. Excavations at Fort St. Joseph, a British military fortification and trading post constructed in 1796 in Ontario as a replacement for Fort Michilimackinac, located buildings that did not appear on period maps (Lee 1984, 146).

While building techniques varied widely from Maine to Manitoba in the fur trade era, most of the buildings were constructed of wood and few have survived. Nevertheless, archaeologists have benefited from studying extant structures, which provide insight into some of the styles represented in the archaeological record. Buildings, as might be expected, vary in construction techniques, size, function, and contents in ways that can reveal information about their makers and users (Mann 2008; Mullaley 2011).

Figure 4.2. Aerial view of Fort Michilimackinac facing south, showing the newly reconstructed Southwest Rowhouse. Courtesy of Mackinac State Historic Parks Collection.

Building styles in the St. Lawrence River Valley derived from northwest France with some modification. Most buildings were simple *poteau en terre,* or post-in-the-ground, structures that were built by setting upright posts in a trench and filling the interstices with *bousillage* (a mixture of clay and straw) or *pierrotage* (a mixture of stone and mortar) that was then covered with whitewash (a slurry of lime and water applied to walls to protect them from the elements). Sometimes the wall posts would be set on a sill placed on a stone foundation (known as *poteau sur sole*). Horizontal timbers (*pièce sur pièce*) were used only rarely, although that is the method used for the church at Fort Michilimackinac and many secular HBC, NWC, and AFC structures. Building size was dependent upon function; most residences were about 5 × 6 meters, or roughly 16 × 20 feet. Some French buildings at Forts Massac (southern Illinois) and Michilimackinac (northern Michigan) consisted of barracks or row houses that had shared walls (Heldman 1991; Walthall 1991), a style the HBC and the NWC also adopted (Birk 1989, 34). Stone fireplaces and hearths with stick chimneys chinked with *bousillage* were often placed at the ends or corners of habitation rooms; spaces lacking a source of heat might have been used for storage.

Habitation, storage, and other special-purpose buildings have been identified in the archaeological record, though a building's function or the identity of its occupants is sometimes difficult to discern in the absence of historical sources. For example, at Michilimackinac the powder magazine yielded a significant quantity of trade goods, suggesting that it was used not only to hold armaments but also served as a storeroom for traders. Donald Heldman (1991) has noted that both commoners and the privileged lived in *poteau en terre* structures, though those of material means lived in somewhat larger buildings, placed in locations that protected them from prevailing northwesterly winds, that yielded high-status goods. Rob Mann (2008) has argued that French Canadian fur traders persisted in using distinctive building styles in the late eighteenth and early nineteenth centuries in the Wabash Valley to differentiate themselves from the English and Americans.

Many of the forts were constructed according to the principles of fortification developed by the seventeenth-century military strategist Sébastien Le Prestre de Vauban. His design used bastions or projections at the four corners of a roughly square palisade to increase flank coverage during an attack. Such a spatial configuration is evident in the shape of the palisade at Forts de Chartres, Massac, and Michilimackinac, and was even adopted at HBC and NWC wintering posts such as the Snake River Post (figure 4.3; Birk 1989). The use of stone at Fort de Chartres and the placement of a moat at Fort Massac demonstrate further elaborations in the design of French forts, indicating that these were more military installations than loci of trade. Archaeological evidence has also demonstrated that the palisade was enlarged repeatedly at Michilimackinac to accommodate the growing fur trade.

Spatial patterns can be examined at different scales in investigations of fur trade activities. Habitation structures of the NWC typically had fireplaces with chambers made of rock bound together with mortar or daub. The chimneys or flues consisted of wood framing heavily lined and coated with daub. Some fireplaces had a subfloor vault beneath the hearth for storage of wild rice or high wine (Birk 2008, 145).

Archaeologists used microrelief to define fur trade post compounds at Brandon House and Rocky Mountain Fort, two HBC sites in the far north (Hamilton et al. 2005, 11). They focused on determining the location of

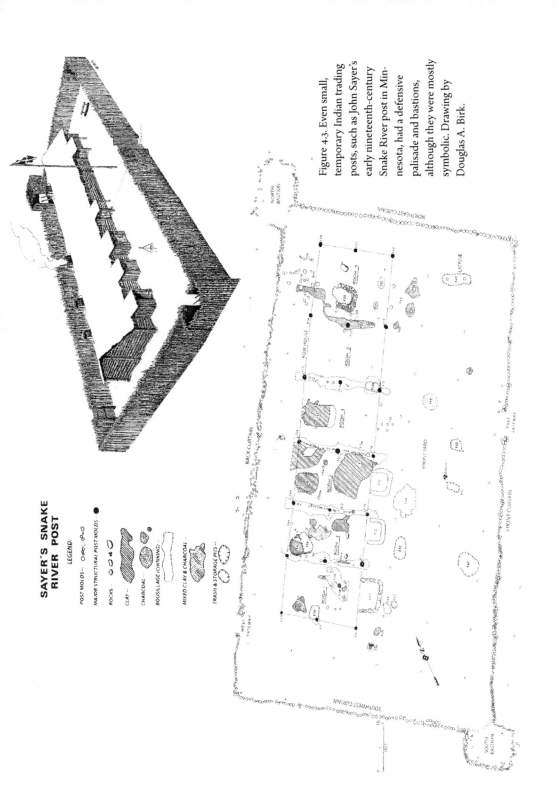

SAYER'S SNAKE RIVER POST

LEGEND:

POST MOLDS··
MAJOR STRUCTURAL POST MOLDS··
ROCKS··
CLAY··
CHARCOAL··
BOUSILLAGE (CHINKING)··
MIXED CLAY & CHARCOAL··
TRASH & STORAGE PITS··

NORTH BASTION

NORTHEAST CURTAIN

ROOM 2

ROOM HOUSE

ROOM 3

ROOM 4

ROOM 5

ROOM 6

ROOM 7

BACK CURTAIN

FRONT YARD

EAST GATEWAY

WEST GATEWAY

FRONT CURTAIN

SOUTHWEST CURTAIN

SOUTH BASTION

LATRINE

Figure 4.3. Even small, temporary Indian trading posts, such as John Sayer's early nineteenth-century Snake River post in Minnesota, had a defensive palisade and bastions, although they were mostly symbolic. Drawing by Douglas A. Birk.

buildings for accurate reconstructions and on recovering artifacts to use in future exhibits (48). They found that buildings were oriented around the inner margins of the palisade walls, a familiar pattern in British North American posts of the fur trade era (see Hamilton et al. 2005, fig. 24).

Buildings and fortified settlements were often designed to be imposing landscape features (Culpin and Borjes 1984). Architectural embellishments were also nonverbal forms of communication (Monks 1992). For example, although paint was clearly a luxury item during the fur trade era, quantities of paint in vivid colors were imported annually at Fort Vancouver. Painted fragments of wood and brick testify to the presence of painted buildings at the fort, although this was the case only for buildings persons of high rank occupied and used (Langford 2011, 41; see also Veit 2011, 28). Painted rooms would signal the wealth and refinement of the inhabitants to visitors to the fort, whereas brilliant surroundings would remind the officers and clerks of the power of their employer, the HBC (Langford 2011, 41).

Site locations also provide insight into settlement criteria. For example, site 21CW29 was placed on the northern end of Whitefish Lake for defensive and environmental reasons (see Birk 2008, 168). Pine Fort, a NWC trading post on the Assiniboine River, was similarly established in an ecologically rich area in proximity to a spring; essential resources for repairing canoes such as birch bark, spruce gum, and spruce rootlets (*wattap*); abundant wood for building; and fur-bearing animals (Tottle 1981).

The production and exchange of furs for imported goods also had an impact on regional settlement patterns. Europeans frequently located settlements to facilitate the movement of goods and the extraction of surplus. The French generally placed their trading posts along watercourses to minimize transportation costs. The British were often more concerned with defense than with ease of movement, as is indicated by a relocation of their settlement from the sandy shores of the Lower Peninsula at Michilimackinac (figure 4.2) to the rocky precipice of nearby Mackinac Island.

Native sites were also affected by the fur trade. In coastal New York in the seventeenth century, native settlements moved to locations with arable soil (Ceci 1977), perhaps in order to produce a maize surplus to provision the trade. Natives relocated to be in proximity to distribution centers such as Fort St. Joseph, Fort Ouiatenon, Thompson's River Post, and numerous other trading posts (Carlson 2000; Kohley 2013; Trubowitz 1992a). In 1762, some 200 Potawatomi warriors (perhaps representing some 600–800 people) lived across the river from Fort St. Joseph (Nassaney et al. 2012, 61). Leacock (1954) demonstrated "that a dependence on white foodstuffs, along with explicit encouragement by fur company agents, white neighbors, and relatives, prompted the Montagnais of the Labrador Peninsula to discard communal hunting for individual hunting of privately-owned tracts" (quoted in Martin 1975, 118) suggesting that the fur trade had an impact on land tenure, an aspect of settlement patterns.

Calvin Martin (1975) posited that metal kettles acquired by the Micmacs in central Maine influenced settlements as early as the seventeenth century. The mobility that cooking with copper kettles provided freed the Micmacs from a reliance on cooking in large stationary troughs or cauldrons hewn from tree stumps. The fur trade, Martin argued, triggered an urge to range widely in search of precious hides and pelts, which the Micmacs were capable of doing since they were no longer tethered to their obsolete wooden cauldrons. The copper kettle thus was a tool that facilitated movement over the landscape.

Mobility during the Fur Trade Era

Much of the North American landscape was a watery world, especially in the Great Lakes region and the drainage areas of the Mississippi and Missouri Rivers. Canoes were the main mode of transportation in the heart of the continent for much of the fur trade era (figure 1.2), though other methods of conveyance were used, particularly in areas where birch bark was unavailable. Because canoes were made entirely of organic components, they seldom survived as archaeological evidence. However, ethnographic specimens survive to the present and can provide insight into the technology of canoe manufacture and canoe performance characteristics. Under unusual conditions, remains of canoe parts and paddles have been recovered from the icy waters of the Pigeon and French Rivers and other northern waterways (Wheeler et al. 1975). These elements include paddle fragments made of white cedar and red oak, canoe thwarts, gunwale caps, spruce root lashings, and wooden sail toggles (figure 4.4; Veit 2011, 29; Woolworth and Birk 1975, 85–87).

Furs, trade goods, and personnel were moved between markets and consumers by various means, including Aleutian *baidarkas*; La Salle's sailing ship, the *Griffon*; HBC York boats; once-feral Spanish horses; steamboats such as the AMC's *Yellowstone*; in addition to the snowshoes, toboggans,

Figure 4.4. Organic remains from the fur trade are occasionally preserved and recovered archaeologically, like this canoe paddle from the Pigeon River in northern Minnesota. Photo by Douglas A. Birk. Courtesy of the National Park Service, Grand Portage National Monument, GRPO 16122.

and dogsleds that natives devised and Euro-Americans adopted to transport their precious cargo. A somewhat unusual and storied overland conveyance known as the Red River cart was adopted in areas marked by smooth ground such as the Red River Valley of Minnesota and North Dakota and the Canadian prairies (figure 3.4; Wheeler 1985, 36). These wooden carts were frequently used from the early 1840s to the late 1860s as a commercial vehicle for moving buffalo robes, pemmican, and furs from the Pembina region in northwest Minnesota to St. Paul. Red River carts probably originated in Europe, where similar forms occur. They made their appearance with the French *régime* in the old Northwest, and the NWC reintroduced them in about 1801. It was a "clumsy looking, but light, box cart with wheels six or seven feet in diameter, and not a bit of iron about the whole concern" (Innis 1962, 296). When a part broke, a thong of shaganappi united the pieces. Shaganappi in this part of the world did all that leather, cloth, rope, nails, glue, straps, cord, tape, and a number of other articles were used for elsewhere; it was the nineteenth-century version of duct tape. These high-wheeled carts cross the miry creeks when ordinary wagons would sink to the hubs (296). Capable of hauling almost half a ton over thirty miles in a single day, Red River carts could be heard for miles when they were in motion. The axles were greased with a mixture of lye and buffalo fat, but this quickly wore away, leaving the friction that produced the "lazy, creaking whine" that would "torture human ears" (Wheeler 1985, 36).

Because both the forms of transportation used in the trade and the trade goods themselves varied over time, they are good barometers of cultural change. Archaeologists have been examining material remains for the chronological and cultural information they contain for decades.

Calibrating Time in the Fur Trade Era

Chronology and classification were early concerns in the history of archaeology, though less so in historical archaeology, which benefits from historical records (Orser 2004, 94). However, most Native American sites associated with the fur trade lack documentation that would provide dates of occupancy. Thus, archaeologists have developed a suite of relative and calendrical dating techniques for calibrating time in the fur trade era. Most often they are able to take advantage of the known production dates of imported objects to establish when they were most likely used and deposited in the archaeological record. In a seminal study, Quimby (1939, 1966) used artifact assemblages from sites of known age, such as objects collected from Fort St. Joseph, to establish a tripartite chronological framework for the western Great Lakes region. He identified temporally diagnostic artifacts to distinguish and define Early (1610–1670), Middle (1670–1760), and Late (1760–1820) Historic periods. These, in turn, could be used to date native sites. This periodization of the fur trade era is still generally applicable today. Arthur Woodward (1970) was another pioneer in establishing the age of archaeological sites; he determined when Native Americans obtained temporally diagnostic objects.

Production techniques and styles of beads have also been used as chronological markers (e.g., Blair et al. 2009; Kidd 1979; Smith 1983). Beads have proven to be useful because they are ubiquitous, are often found at native sites, and changed throughout the fur trade era as new production and decorative techniques were introduced. While some types such as white, drawn seed beads were produced from the seventeenth through the nineteenth centuries, other colors, styles, and production techniques have a more limited duration that can be established within decades. For example, a three-part chronology for beadwork styles on the Plains includes the pony bead period (1800–1840) followed by the first seed bead period (1840–1865) and the second seed bead period (1870–present), representing the dominant bead styles in use at a particular time (McLaughlin 1987, 55; see also DeVore 1992; Lyford 1940). These changes were the result of native preferences and the Europeans' introduction of steel needles, cotton thread, and increasingly smaller beads.

Other artifacts besides beads have been classified chronologically, but because they are recovered from archaeological sites only sporadically, they are less useful as temporally diagnostic markers. For example, Kevin Gladysz

(2011, 121–140) recently organized French civilian flintlocks, many of which have been recovered on fur trade sites, into four chronological stages for the 1699 to 1760 period based on changing stylistic and formal elements of the furniture, barrel, and lock.

Gross chronological divisions have also been developed to organize imperial strategies or stages in the interactions between Native Americans and Europeans. For instance, Douglas A. Birk (1982, 118; Birk 1991) used a tripartite division to examine colonial strategies and the intensity of French involvement in the trade for Minnesota. He identified an initial or French contact phase (mid-1600s to 1702) that marked the tentative beginnings of cross-cultural exchanges between French and local Indian groups. From 1702 to 1713 the French withdrew from the interior and traded from Hudson's Bay, and local natives had to transport their furs to more distant posts such as York Factory (HBC), Michilimackinac, or Detroit. This was a disruptive period in the local fur trade and marked a transition between seventeenth- and eighteenth-century French activities in Minnesota (1991, 240). When the French lost their position on Hudson's Bay after the Treaty of Utrecht, they resumed interior trade in the French expansion phase (1713–1763). While Birk (1982) makes no mention of subsequent activity, the fur trade did not end in this region and its character changed as English, Scottish, and later Americans became active.

J. Daniel Rogers (1990, 79–88) organized the history of interactions between the Arikaras and Euro-Americans into "six periods, including one period before contact and five periods after" direct contact. Rogers put Arikara sites with access to European goods in chronological order as a way to determine the factors that led the Arikaras to adopt these goods. Changes in the types and frequencies of goods from initial indirect access in the late eighteenth century to the 1860s demonstrates that there was no steady increase of imported goods in native contexts, contrary to what an acculturation model would predict (220).

As noted previously, C. Gilman (1982, 2–3) has suggested that we conceive of the fur trade in three phases. In the first phase, European participation was tenuous and uncertain. Indians organized the trade and Europeans depended on them to bring in furs at locations such as Montreal, Fort Orange (later Albany, New York), and York Factory. Indians wielded power since they gathered and transported the furs. They transported European goods far inland where these novel objects were distributed through hand-to-hand exchange; Europeans gained little profit from this exchange network. In the second phase, Europeans moved into the interior and began to control the transportation of goods, though they still relied on Indians to collect and process pelts and supply food and information. While trade may have lost much of its ceremonial overtones, intermarriage accelerated as a means of establishing kinship relations (see also Sleeper-Smith 2001). The third phase of development saw the fur trade become an instrument of expanding industrial nations that laid the groundwork for Euro-American settlement. Natives were plagued by disease, depopulation, and appropriation of their land. These conditions, in concert with white trappers' replacement of native producers, heightened conflict between Indians and Europeans.

Gilman argued that these phases were independent of the political and ethnic affiliations of the participants. Furthermore, she posits that they had little to do with the depletion of game animals. However, it seems that the spatial expansion of these processes is partly related to exploitation patterns that significantly reduced animal populations in the face of increasing demands, pushing traders into ever more remote areas where they could exploit new animal communities and dispose of their goods.

The Materiality of the Trade

For archaeologists, the most tangible elements of the fur trade are the durable manufactured objects that were destined for native hands. Many of the goods Europeans used to barter with natives found their way into archaeological contexts through loss, abandonment, discard, or intentional deposition. Some substances such as cloth, tobacco, alcohol, and various foodstuffs were important elements of the trade but are difficult to trace archaeologically. Commercial fur production is also detectable, even though the furs themselves either did not survive or were exported to Europe to produce new commodities such as hats and gloves. As products were distributed from European workshops to native consumers, they acquired a rich biography that can be decoded through the context and frequency of their recovery. Among the most formidable challenges for fur trade archaeologists is the task of deciphering the meanings of these goods for their makers, users, and viewers. As natives became entangled in the fur trade, they also engaged in new practices or intensified old ones to meet the demands of a global market.

Typologies have been common since the inception of the discipline, and fur trade archaeologists have developed classificatory schemes to systematize their observations and to facilitate comparison. Quimby (1966, 9–11) organized artifacts into several groups to ascertain the extent of cultural changes. First, he recognized entirely new types such as guns and iron implements that were unknown to the natives. Second were new types that were copied from introduced models such as stone molds for casting metal. A third type were hybrid forms, as exemplified by beaded moccasins. Finally, he distinguished old artifact forms made from imported materials such as tinkling cones and hair pipes. In an influential study based on a sizeable collection from over a decade of large-scale excavations at Fort Michilimackinac, Lyle Stone (1974a) provided a detailed typology of various classes of material culture and sought to establish their temporal parameters and ethnic origins (French or English) based on associations of various artifact types and varieties.

Objects recovered from fur trade sites often directly reflect the exchanges that occurred among groups. Of course, so-called trade goods are not always easy to identify, as they may represent goods intended for European use, gifts given in order to maintain relationships with native allies, or commodities that were intended to be sold for a profit. The archaeological record is replete with objects that were intended for exchange, though it is sometimes difficult to distinguish these from goods European traders used themselves. When goods intended for the traders' use occur on trade lists, they often appear in smaller quantities than goods intended for distribution to natives (Anderson 1994). The glass beads, thimbles, finger rings, guns, kettles, knives, hoes, axes, and other metal artifacts found at archaeological sites confirm that such objects, which appear on trade lists, were destined for and desired by native consumers (e.g., Mason 1986). The lists also enumerate organic and otherwise perishable goods that are underrepresented archaeologically and were affected by preservation biases. For instance, cloth, alcohol, vermilion, and tobacco were important in the trade, but they often left only indirect archaeological traces.

Archaeologists subscribe to the dictum that form follows function. Thus, it is often easy to discern how consumers used most goods, although exceptions are noteworthy. Classification schemes are somewhat arbitrary, but they allow us to relate objects to activities in different realms of daily life. Archaeologists understand that goods can serve more than one purpose and that their meanings can differ, particularly as they are exchanged and adopted in new cultural contexts. They aim to explore what objects native peoples obtained in the fur trade and how they were used. While archaeologists used to distinguish between native and European artifacts and native and European sites, the intercultural nature of the fur trade makes it increasingly difficult to essentialize these categories. For example, the fact that many fur traders married native wives led to an amalgamation of different artifact patterns and usages. In the remainder of this discussion I draw examples from a range of fur trade sites to illustrate how archaeologists have analyzed their contents and their legacy for the American experience.

Fur or Food?

The exploitation and processing of furs for commercial use resulted in the deposition of animal remains that are frequently recovered archaeologically. Some of those same animals were a source of protein for natives and Europeans alike, raising the question of whether they were obtained for furs or food. Understandably, one need not exclude the other. Sheri Hannes (1994) examined faunal remains from a nineteenth-century fur-trading post on Leech Lake in northern Minnesota and compared them with a list of species the AFC collected for the fur trade. Her analysis demonstrated that although the faunal assemblage did include a wide variety of fur trade animals, fewer species were represented than expected based on historical accounts (50). Two discrepancies were noteworthy. First, her sample included no beaver bones, though beaver was among the furs the AFC collected (see Hannes 1994, table 7). Second, rabbits were well represented in the faunal assemblage, though they were relatively unimportant in the historical records. This suggested that they were important as a subsistence item. She concluded that the local economy was focused on both subsistence and fur trade activities. The faunal assemblage is more similar to food consumption remains from Ojibwe sites than remains from fur processing (82, 84).

Because fur processing was oriented to ensure choice pelts, animal selection and bone modification left archaeological signatures indicative of commercial exploitation and skinning (e.g., Lapham 2005). At Fort Albany, a seventeenth-century HBC settlement on James Bay, "disproportionately large numbers of skulls from small fur-bearing animals, mainly marten" were recovered among the mammal bones (Kenyon 1986, 16). The butchering practice evident at this site suggests how the animals were skinned. The mortality profile of a population can also be used to determine if particular sized animals were being hunted. Cut marks consistent with hide removal appear on certain skeletal elements in high frequencies. When cranial bones, teeth, and foot bones are recovered, the pattern is consistent with selective transportation in which pelts or skins were brought to the site but not meat (Jordan 2008, 282). Kurt Jordan (283, 289–290) reasoned that the high percentage of deer remains at the Townley-Read site, a Seneca village, indicates that deer had become the primary focus of native hunters by the eighteenth century, when the fur trade in the lower Great Lakes region became diversified and shifted away from its seventeenth-century emphasis on beaver pelts.

Europeans subsisted on predominantly domesticated plants and animals in their homelands. They made efforts to transplant this dietary regime into the New World with variable success. As a result, Europeans frequently relied on wild and locally produced plants and animals that native hunters, gatherers, and farmers obtained. Because many fur-bearers were also traditionally hunted for subsistence (e.g., deer, beaver, bison), there was often overlap between animals taken for food and animals taken for their fur.

Native subsistence changed very little over the course of the fur trade; that is, until native producers were dispossessed from their land or became unable to maintain the seasonal round that marked earlier food-collecting strategies. They were seldom induced to pursue new subsistence strategies despite the array of new tools (e.g., plows) and resources (e.g., domesticated plants and animals) at their disposal. William Cronon (1983) examined the disparate land use practices of natives and the English in New England, noting how domesticated animals such as hogs competed for resources that natives foraged and disturbed wild species' habitats (e.g., clam beds). In general, domesticated animals were inconsistent with native value systems and were adopted only as a last resort (see Pavao-Zuckerman 2007). The Shawnee prophet Tenskwatawa urged the Potawatomis who traded with the AFC in the upper reaches of the Kankakee River Valley in the early nineteenth century to give up domesticated animals and return to older hunting practices as an element of the native revitalization movements that swept the region (Wagner 2003, 110–112).

Food choices played an important role in a cultural discourse that served to define identity and belonging in the fur trade. Food was a symbolic means of creating and reproducing class, gender, and racial boundaries that helped define civilized British manhood (Vibert 2010, 137; see also Hamilton 2000). During the early nineteenth century in the Interior Plateau, a distinct racial hierarchy emerged based on subsistence in which fish was considered inferior to red meat (Vibert 2010). Despite this food preference, most commoners in fur trade society probably did not subscribe to elite notions of food consumption. Archaeology reveals the choices that often were unrecorded by providing copious and well-preserved assemblages of faunal remains that can disclose the types of animals regularly consumed at fur trade sites. For example, archaeological evidence and ethnohistorical accounts suggest that Native Americans dried, preserved, and shipped various types of fish, including salmon and sturgeon, along the Columbia River in the early nineteenth century and sold some to fur traders (Butler and Martin 2013). Between February and April 1813, traders purchased at least 300 large fish to provision Fort Astoria (Butler and Martin 2013, 86, relying on McDougall 1999).

Animal bone refuse and species composition from Nottingham House, an HBC wintering post on Lake Athabasca, reveal considerable variation in intrasite consumption and deposition patterns that expressed and reinforced social inequalities (Hamilton 2000, 260). In comparison to the subfloor storage pits under the officers' quarters, those beneath the laborers' quarters contain as much bone density as in the exterior refuse middens. This suggests that areas associated with the officers were kept conspicuously clean. Furthermore, the low frequencies of bone found in the officers' quarters displayed high proportions of mammalian (57 percent) and avian (34 percent) species and not much fish (9 percent). In contrast, fish accounted for nearly three-quarters (72 percent) of the bones associated with the laborers; birds and mammals made up the remainder in about even amounts (Hamilton 2000, 260). Thus, although red meat may have been preferred, the majority of the population frequently consumed fish.

Also at issue is the role of domesticated and wild animal species in the diets of fur trade communities. Charles Cleland (1970; see also Scott 1991a; Scott 2001a, 65) compared the faunal remains associated with the French and British occupants of Fort Michilimackinac. The French diet relied on local animal food resources, particularly the plentiful lake trout and whitefish from the Straits of Mackinac. In contrast, the British generally based their subsistence on domesticated animals such as chicken, pork, horse, and beef, although they did consume some wild animals, particularly birds such as ducks and geese. The British soldiers who occupied House D of the southeast row house at Fort Michilimackinac were considerably less dependent upon domestic species than other British-period households at the fort, suggesting that they had more time to hunt and fish or paid others to do so (Scott 2001a, 64). Various factors influenced food choices in the fur trade era besides environmental setting.

In his studies of the French colonial diet at a range of sites throughout the Midwest, Terrance Martin (1991a, 2008) proposed that subsistence was influenced by site location, site function, *and* the intensity of interaction with native groups. Martin, who compared sites that had different levels of involvement with the fur trade and native peoples, found that administrative centers in the Illinois Country housed larger numbers of soldiers, had limited involvement in the fur trade, and were more dependent on domesticated animals. For instance, the Laurens site, which is thought to be the first Fort de Chartres in the Mississippi Valley, was established just after 1718 and supported about sixty soldiers and a sizeable civilian population by the next decade. The faunal remains reflect a high proportion of domesticated animals, including cattle, pigs, and chicken, and lesser amounts of deer. Fish species were exploited from the main channel of the Mississippi River. The presence of black bear bones supports documentary evidence that the French viewed bear oil as a delicacy that they used for shortening and as a seasoning (Martin 2008).

In contrast, smaller posts such as Fort St. Joseph have yielded predominantly wild animal remains, including deer, beaver, porcupine, raccoon, turkey, and avian fauna. Such assemblages are a direct reflection of the intensity of interaction and exchange with native groups in fur trade society (Martin 2008). This was clearly a case where the French were adopting native cuisine. This is also reflected in the use of maize at Fort St. Joseph and the absence (thus far) of Old World domesticated plants such as wheat, oats, and barley. Formation processes may play a role in their absence, since these grains are typically processed before being consumed. However, they have seldom been recovered archaeologically, even at sites in the St. Lawrence River Valley or the Illinois Country, which was producing a surplus for shipment to New Orleans and French colonies in the Caribbean.

The animal assemblage from Fort Ouiatenon, a local distribution center established in 1717 along the Wabash River that housed a small detachment of about a dozen marines and fewer than twenty French families, is also dominated by wild species, most notably deer. Although domesticated animals are present, they were used to supplement the predominantly wild animal diet. Martin (1991b) noted that several modified animal remains might reflect trade with local native groups, the presence of local natives, or perhaps French accommodations to local native customs. A similar pattern occurs at Fort St. Joseph, where excavations have yielded bone tools, bone gaming pieces, and high frequencies of wild animal remains (Nassaney 2008b; see chapter 6).

Archaeologists have also addressed the issues of social stress and over-hunting through faunal analysis. Peter Thomas (1985, 154) reported evidence of the butchering of entire deer and bear carcasses at Fort Hill, a seventeenth-century native village in the Connecticut River Valley. This pattern suggests more localized resource exploitation, indicating that people hunted closer to the village than they had in earlier times due to increased hostilities. The evidence of overexploitation is equivocal and varied by species within regions and even locales. Gregory Waselkov (1998, 203–205) challenged the notion that deer were extirpated by the end of the eighteenth century by native overhunting in the Southeast on the basis of archaeological and documentary evidence. He noted substantial quantities of deer bone in the food refuse associated with several Cherokee and Creek villages occupied during the colonial and federal periods (203). Export figures for the ports of Augusta, Mobile, and Pensacola show increasing quantities of deerskins leaving those ports throughout the late 1760s, and the Pensacola-based Panton, Leslie, & Company was shipping over 100,000 deerskins a year to England in the 1780s (204). As late as 1801 it exported 203,000 pounds of deerskins, mostly obtained from the Creek trade (205). In other regions there were marked shifts in the types of species that were exploited. In the western Great Lakes region, the archaeological and documentary records clearly indicate that muskrat had replaced beaver in popularity by the nineteenth century (Clayton 1964; Franzen 2004; Gilman 1974).

In the early phase of the fur trade, natives often provisioned fur traders with local food resources that included maize, wild rice, pemmican, maple sugar, fish, fresh meat, and potatoes (Gibson 1992, 210). When natives began diverting more of their labor to commercial pursuits, they often came to rely on imported processed foods such as flour, refined sugar, and molasses that they obtained from traders. These dietary changes are reflected in high levels of dental disease among the Narragansetts in the seventeenth century (Robinson et al. 1985, 119). Since shipping food was a major expense, traders depended on local resources and tried to become self-sufficient. Maize has been found at sites where there was interaction with local natives, such as Fort St. Joseph, though it is not known if the French actually practiced maize agriculture or merely acquired it in trade from their indigenous neighbors (Cremin and Nassaney 2003). Old World domesticates have seldom been found at Midwestern sites, with the exception of rare occurrences of watermelon, peach, and wheat in the Mississippi Valley. This may suggest a reliance on local plant food resources in much the same way that wild animal species were exploited (Nassaney 2009, 51). Chief Factor McLoughlin encouraged agricultural activities at Fort Vancouver to produce food to supply employees and to sell to Russians in Alaska, Hawaiians in Hawaii, and American missionaries and other immigrants who began coming to the Pacific Northwest in the 1830s (Wilson 2011, 8). "At its height in 1845, Fort Vancouver was the nexus of a corporate farm that contained over 1,200 acres under cultivation, nearly 2,000 head of cattle, 1,500 hogs, 700 horses," and an orchard (8). Similarly, Fort Ross was established to provide agricultural products for the RAC. Thus, an ancillary component of the fur trade was intensified food production, often by women, that supported the specialized fur producers and traders who were removed from subsistence pursuits. Further archaeological study will likely document considerable temporal and spatial variability in the active subsistence choices and accommodations various participants in fur trade society made.

Technology, Crafts, and Daily Activities

Historical documents describe various technological objects that were used in crafting culture in fur trade society. Much of what has been recovered in the archaeological record pertains directly to technology, crafts, and daily activities, and this allows researchers to cross-check these data sources for redundancies and potential contradictions.

Iron and other metal implements were among the most desirable trade goods in much of North America. Their prevalence in the ground is partly a reflection of their durability, though iron is subject to corrosion. Metal objects frequently took the form of iron spears, chisels, knives, flintlock hardware, copper alloy kettles, kettle parts, and awls (Martin 1975; Quimby 1966, 63–80; Turnbaugh 1984). Archaeologists working from an acculturation perspective viewed such goods as superior to their native counterparts and considered them to be evidence that native groups abandoned their own less efficient technologies (e.g., Toom 1979; cf. Odell 2001). Thus, iron knives and axes were thought to be logical replacements for chipped-stone knives and ground-stone axes. Of course, the supply and demand for goods varied considerably over time and space, making it difficult to generalize about what was available and what natives wanted throughout the continent.

At the risk of oversimplification, it appears that natives often wanted goods that fit into their world view. As they acquired European goods, natives often abandoned traditional technologies such as stone tools and low-fired earthenware. Studies have repeatedly demonstrated that native peoples were active and discerning consumers who pitted French against English traders, walked miles to strike a fair bargain, and selectively adopted goods into their material repertoire (see Bradley 1987; Kehoe 2000; Ray 1974, 1980; White 2011). Natives often reinterpreted objects according to their own symbolic systems. Hamell (1983) was among the first to note that northeastern natives found glass beads so desirable, as noted above, because they fit native conceptual domains that equated beads with traditional light, shiny, and reflective objects (e.g., marine shell, native copper, mica, quartz crystals) that natives associated with well-being and clairvoyance. Symbolic meanings are further complicated by the roles that goods played in mixed cultural contexts associated with the offspring of French and native unions.

Iron tools in seventeenth-century French trading kits represent a class of objects that were handy for natives, particularly for scraping skins. James Bradley (1987, 145–146) examined how the Onondagas dismembered and modified axes from their original form to fabricate more "useful" implements. They bent knives into curved shapes to form crooked knives that were used for wood carving (149). Far from being seduced by these "toil-alleviating tools" (Ritchie 1954, 1), native people seem to have been more interested in adapting these implements into useful forms (Bradley 1987, 152). In essence, the Onondagas sought out European raw materials, not European objects.

It is also clear that natives did not always relinquish their own technology, much of which was very suitable for the tasks they performed in the fur trade. Jay Johnson (2003) noted the increase in thumbnail scrapers on eighteenth-century Chickasaw sites in Mississippi. Mark Cassell (2003) documented the recovery of fourteen chert end-scrapers that the Iñupiats in northern Alaska used to scrape hides for skin clothing. The working edges of these tools "are a studied balance of not-too-sharp yet not-too-dull," making them perfect for "[scraping] fat and tissue from the hides [of foxes] without cutting into and damaging [them]" (158). Ethnologist Diamond Jenness noted that Eskimos retained the use of the scrapers into the twentieth century; they "are more adapted to the purposes to which they applied than any implement which we can supply" (1918, 93, quoted in Cassell 2003, 162).

Archaeological evidence indicates that copper alloy (brass) kettles were among the first objects natives obtained in the trade (figure 2.1). Copper was a sanctified material among natives of eastern North America (Waselkov 1989, 122). It had a long history of use dating back to the Late Archaic period, and thus the appeal of kettles extended beyond their role in cooking and fetching water. Despite the ability of copper and brass kettles to withstand thermal and mechanical shock better than low-fired earthenware, they were initially used as a source of raw material in many societies (C. Gilman 1982, 94). Scraps of copper often made their way into the hands of distant groups long before they had direct contact with Europeans (Ehrhardt 2005). Brass forms "were routinely cut up and fashioned into body ornaments or utilitarian objects; initially, it would seem coastal Algonkian tribes had little inclination to use them as cooking vessels" (Witthoft 1966, 204–207, quoted in Martin 1975, 122). Bradley (1987, fig. 13) illustrated how the Onondagas recycled copper kettles to produce awls, projectile points, knives, beads, pendants, and tinkling cones (figure 4.5). Numerous sites throughout North America exhibit evidence of this type of reuse. By the beginning of the seventeenth century, some natives were also using kettles for cooking.

The timing and rate of the replacement of indigenous ceramic technologies with European metal, ceramic, and glass containers varied across the continent. The Onondaga ceramic tradition vanished in the early seventeenth century. It was replaced with lighter, less fragile, and functional copper or brass kettles (Bradley 1987, 121). In contrast, metal containers did not replace ceramic vessels in the Middle Missouri River Valley region of North Dakota and South Dakota until well into the nineteenth century (Krause 1972, 90; Toom 1979, 170–174). In the early 1830s, artists George Catlin and Karl Bodmer depicted Mandan ceramic vessels in traditional domestic earth lodge settings (Miller 2000, figs. 11.5, 11.6). Although these could have been anachronisms that were used to portray the Mandans as they once were, one writer remarked about the Arikaras during the same period that "[they] show considerable ingenuity in manufacturing tolerably good and well shaped vessels

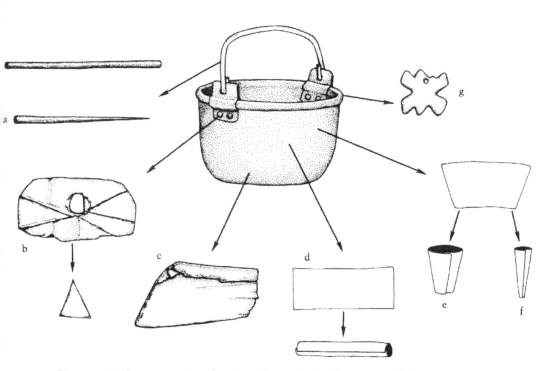

Figure 4.5. In the seventeenth and eighteenth centuries kettles were recycled into a range of useful products that included (a) awls, (b) projectile points, (c) knives, (d) beads, (e,f) tinkling cones, and (g) pendants. Adapted from Bradley 1987, figure 13. Drawing by Michael S. Nassaney.

for cooking out of clay. . . . These utensils though clumsy appear to be preferred by them to metallic ones" (Denig quoted in Toom 1979, 171). A Hidatsa woman said that metal pots made food taste strange and that her family did not begin cooking in them until about 1857 (Toom 1979, 172). Replacements were adopted after a period of trial and adjustment or when they were seen as more effective than their native equivalents (Smith 1972, 178).

Clearly, not all imports were equally embraced. The eighteenth-century traveler Peter Kalm remarked that Indians in the Northwest Territory "do not want our iron boilers because they cannot be easily carried on their continual journies, and would not bear such falls and knocks as their [copper] kettles" (1772, 391, quoted in Innis 1962, 110).

Unlike cumbersome iron kettles, natives welcomed guns because they were clearly at a competitive disadvantage with their neighbors if they did not. Guns were generally used for their intended purpose, though barrels and butt plates were known to have been recycled to make hide scrapers. Flint-lock muskets and, later, percussion cap rifles were initially unfamiliar objects that were challenging for some natives to obtain and maintain. Peter Kalm remarked: "The Indians have hitherto never tried to make muskets or similar firearms; and their great indolence does not even allow them to mend those muskets which they have. They leave this entirely to the Europeans" (1772, 391, quoted in Innis 1962, 11). While it is true that many French-allied tribes requested the services of a trained gunsmith, other groups learned the craft of metallurgy and became quite adept at fixing guns. Evidence for the disas-sembly of locks and apparent careful preservation of flintlock hardware re-covered from the Bell site (ca. 1680–1730) in Wisconsin suggest the Meskwa-kis may have been performing some basic gunsmithing on their own (Bodoh 2004; see also Hamilton 1987, 116–124). A native gunsmith would have been able to repair flintlocks by using parts from several nonfunctioning weapons to repair others. Such repairs would have been essential, particularly during open hostilities between the French and Meskwakis (Behm 2008, 55, 59). Na-tive groups at Plymouth in southern New England would have had to acquire guns from alternate sources (e.g., the French) and repair them on their own, since the English "forbade the repair of guns belonging to natives, and pro-hibited Indians from buying gunpowder" (see Wilder 2013, 38). This explains the presence of a blacksmith's tool kit associated with an adult male at site RI-1000 in southeastern New England (Robinson et al. 1985, 122, fig. 4).

Ammunition and gunflints were imported because native sources of suit-able raw materials were limited and were underexploited until the late eigh-teenth century (Lebeau et al. 2008). The English shipped at least two sizes of musket balls and buckshot, beavershot, and birdshot in at least five size grades to Fort Vancouver (Cromwell 2011, 63; Ross 1976). Ammunition was made locally in New France at sites such as Fort St. Joseph and Fort Michili-mackinac, as the presence of lead spatter, sows, and sprue indicates (Morand 1994, 40–44, fig. 18; Nassaney et at. 2007, 12).

Guns were mainly used in warfare and were not the principal means of hunting for some furs, despite the numbers of animal killed for the trade. Lead shot would ruin hides intended for breeches, coats, and other large gar-ments, though holes from lead shot in a beaver pelt would not diminish the value of its undercoat. The beaver trap became an iconic tool. It was essen-tial for the extraction of pelts for European and Asian markets, but not un-til the nineteenth century (C. Gilman 1982, 22–23; Juen and Nassaney 2012,

18; Wagner 2011, fig. 9.5c). Natives designed snares to capture and kill their prey. They also assaulted beaver in their winter lodges with chisels, axes, and spears (C. Gilman 1982, fig. 57). Traps and iron impaling tools commonly occur in trade lists, though less often in archaeological contexts because hand-wrought iron often decayed beyond recognition (Quimby 1966, 66; Wagner 2011, 132, tables 6.4–6.8, fig. 9.5d).

After fur-bearing animals were captured and killed, distinctive tools and facilities were involved in their processing. In addition to bone beamers, bone fleshers, and stone and metal scrapers, natives employed smudge pits in the final stages of handling a deer hide. Smudge pits are small earth ovens used to burn materials such as corncobs, pinecones, or other organic remains to produce a smoky fire suitable for smudging or smoking hides (see Binford 1967). Based on an analysis of their performance characteristics, technical attributes, and ethnographic evidence, James Skibo and associates (2004, 171–174) suggested that the pits they encountered on Grand Island are similar to those the Ojibwes used to smoke deer hides in order "to attain a golden color and to prevent them from getting stiff when wet." Smudge pits were the most ubiquitous feature (n = 79) at the Rhoads site, an early nineteenth-century Kickapoo village in central Illinois where furs were processed for the AFC (Wagner 2011, 98–100). Unlike the pits on Grand Island, which contained only charred pinecones, maize was present in 81 percent of the pits identified at Rhoads.

Artifacts related to hide processing occur most frequently at native village sites, though some have also been found at trading posts, where a limited amount of processing may have occurred. Patterns of faunal exploitation, together with the presence of processing tools (e.g., beamers, fleshers, thumbnail scrapers) and facilities (e.g., smudge pits) are clear archaeological signatures of native roles in the fur trade.

After traders acquired processed furs, they typically packaged them for transport to merchants in Montreal, Quebec, New York, Charlestown, or New Orleans. Then they were shipped across the Atlantic. Fur presses were used to compress the furs into bundles weighing about 100 pounds. Bundles were wrapped in canvas cloth to keep the pelts and hides clean and reasonably dry and inhibit deterioration and insect infestation (Wood et al. 2011, 86–87). Bundles of this size and weight were probably designed initially to fit into a canoe, and two or more could typically be portaged by a man using a tumpline. No presses survive from the fur trade era, but replicas can be found at reconstructed forts such as Fort William, Fort Vancouver, and Fort Union. Large iron needles, often triangular or diamond-shaped in cross-section, were used to sew the canvas wrapping (figure 3.2). These baling needles have been recovered in the kitchen area of the NWC depot at Grand Portage and at Fort St. Joseph in Niles, Michigan (C. Gilman 1982, 32; Juen and Nassaney 2012, fig. 60).

Imported tools were often used to create new forms of material culture or make native crafts more elaborate. Metal tools such as files, drills, knives, and chisels allowed for greater and more intricate work with shell, wood, bone, and stone. For example, wampum production increased and forms became more standardized after iron nails and drills replaced the stone tools that were used to perforate shell blanks (Brasser 1978, 87; Nassaney 2004). Knives, adzes, and chisels were used to carve wood into more expressive patterns. These are perhaps best known from the Northwest Coast, where formline styles appeared on objects as diverse as chests, canoes, mortuary masks, and totem poles (Brotherton 2000). Similarly, bone was fashioned into ornamental forms, as in the hair roach spreader recovered from the Rhoads site (Wagner 2011, 153–154). This was a decorative head crest made of animal hair and bone worn by warriors of the eastern woodlands and Plains who shaved their heads bald except for a single scalp lock. The bone component of the spreader was likely cut and drilled using metal tools. The Onondagas also carved bone and antler into intricate effigy forms that exhibited technical mastery made possible by the use of metal tools (Bradley 1987, 126, fig. 12).

Among southeastern New England groups, a lapidary industry emerged in the seventeenth century that produced ornate smoking pipes and other ritual objects (Turnbaugh 1977; Willoughby 1935; see chapter 5). Some of these goods were created to counter the ill effects of the fur trade and colonialism; others, such as Haida argillite pipes, were produced for Euro-American markets beginning around 1820 (Holm 1982, 134–143; Gibson 1992, 246–247; Mullins and Paynter 2000; Nassaney and Volmar 2003).

Natives sometimes used imported objects in ways that led to new cultural practices that became quintessentially American. Copper kettles and metal spigots facilitated the production of maple syrup; we do not know if this was a pre-Contact activity (see Mason and Holman 2000). Iron needles were used to embroider motifs, create intricate patterns in quillwork, and attach glass beads to garments. Silk ribbons were used to fashion complex ribbonwork designs that used imported raw materials to reflect native values of well-being (Neill 2000). As Cory Wilmott and Kevin Brownlee (2010, 49) observed, dress was an important means of cultural mediation in fur trade society; it was a means of achieving cultural mobility in the middle ground of European-native relations. While not all of these objects are directly recoverable in the archaeological record, they point to new forms of materiality and stylistic expression that many participants in fur trade society used to reinforce new social identities.

One indigenous American practice—tobacco smoking—provides insights into the new meanings of material culture in fur trade society. Tobacco was introduced in Europe during the sixteenth century and was soon considered a medicinal herb (Pierson 2011b, 84). The popularity of smoking explains why stone and clay pipes are so ubiquitous on fur trade sites in North America (see Fox 2015; Rafferty and Mann 2004). Heidi Pierson (2011b, 84) noted its prevalence at HBC establishments, where concentrations of pipe-stem fragments indicate places where customers congregated before entering a building to conduct their trade. As we might expect, pipe fragments are absent near the powder magazine, where a single spark would have been disastrous. Both men and women indulged in the practice, though its context of use varied by social class and ethnicity. Some researchers have argued that stone smoking pipes mark the presence of native peoples at fur trade sites (e.g., Pyszczyk 1989, 232–233), although production and use of stone pipes was not confined to natives (Mann 2003, 171).

Mann (2003, 2004) has examined the role of smoking pipes in the context of fur trade rituals designed to foster exchange relations at the early nineteenth-century Cicott trading post on the Wabash River. Smoking was a key precapitalist practice that provided Native American societies with an indigenous system for dealing with European "strangers." The practice helped maintain smooth trading relations because it integrated Europeans into native social structures as trading partners and kin (Mann 2003, 157, 162). Both stone and clay smoking pipes have been recovered from the Cicott trading post, although the latter are much more common; they represent 87 percent of the smoking pipe assemblage (168). Stone and clay pipes appear to have been used in different social contexts. The greater frequency of white clay pipes is indicative of their disposability, availability, and use in informal contexts. In contrast, the rarity of stone pipes suggests that they were highly valued, curated, and less subject to breakage, despite the presence of fragments that represent miscues during the manufacturing process. Local production and decoration of stone pipes suggest that they were more personal objects that were preferred over clay pipes during rituals of "cross-cultural exchange—when social relations were created or renewed" through the act of smoking (176). The power of tobacco in stone pipes eased tensions along ethnic lines between commodity-oriented and gift-oriented cultures "and enabled Cicott and his native customers to conceptualize the outcomes of exchange within their own cultural framework" (176; see also Nassaney 2004).

While stone smoking pipes clearly had profound symbolic meanings in the context of the fur trade, the white clay form was a ubiquitous commodity that seems to have been divorced from any ritual associations among native groups. They were produced in England, Holland, and France from the sixteenth through nineteenth centuries and appear in various contexts throughout North America (Fox 2015). Clay pipes and tobacco frequently appear on trade lists, so it comes as no surprise that pipes have been found in native villages, at *posés* (rest stops along portage routes), and at trading posts. It is also worth considering that tobacco obtained in exchange for furs (*Nicotiana tabacum*) "belonged symbolically in the secular, European realm" (Pego et al. 1999, 252) and may not have had the same cultural meaning as the tobacco (*Nicotiana rustica*) that was locally grown and smoked in the Micmac-style and calumet-style stone pipes that co-occur with pipes made from imported white clay (Mann 2004; Nassaney 2004, 129–130; Waselkov 2009, 623).

Hundreds of pipes have been recovered from Fort Union on the Missouri River (Sudbury 2009). Most of them were imported from Germany, including examples of "political pipes made in the likeness of U.S. Presidents that are frequently reported from 19th century American sites" (Sudbury 2009, 1). These pipes were probably not intended for trade to natives, since they seldom occur in native contexts, yet they mimic the anthropomorphic pipes that were common among seventeenth- and eighteenth-century Iroquoian groups. Perhaps they were a substantially cheaper version of the presidential medals that were distributed to native leaders in the nineteenth century to symbolize their alliance with the U.S. government.

Habitual practices associated with smoking, subsistence activities, and other activities involving repetitive motions often left telltale signs on skeletal tissue that can be detected using forensic approaches on archaeological remains (Kennedy 1989). Ping Lai and Nancy Lovell (1992), who analyzed features on three individuals in the Canadian fur trade, identified wear consistent with occupational stress. These remains were located at the Seafort

Burial site (FcPr100), which is located in proximity to a series of successively occupied nineteenth-century HBC fur trade posts along a stretch of the North Saskatchewan River near Rocky Mountain House. Lai and Lovell (1992, 222) identified three of the fourteen burials selected for analysis as males between the ages of 30 and 40 who were purportedly of mixed European and Native American ancestry, despite the difficulties in assigning ethnicity on the basis of skeletal remains. They base their inference on skeletal shape and size and contextual data: the males wore European clothing, they were buried in wooden coffins, and one was buried with a crucifix. Regardless of their ethnic or racial identity, these individuals displayed a variety of stress markers that indicated their involvement in the fur trade. Lesions, severe joint changes, bony growth, and compression of various vertebrae point to loading stresses that are consistent with the use of a tumpline for carrying heavy loads. These patterns are supported by the extreme skeletal robusticity and arthritis these males displayed. The features observed in this sample are consistent with the physical stress expected among voyageurs in the fur trade. For example, vertebral characteristics and "marked muscle attachments on the lower limb bones may reflect the stresses of jogging along the portage trail, often up and down steep inclines, while carrying a canoe or packs of goods" (229). Modifications to the jaw in two of the individuals may be "the result of facial tension due to tumpline force" (229). Finally, facets on the toes are consistent with habitual kneeling that was common in canoeing in order to maintain a low center of gravity to ensure "balance in turbulent water" (230). Lai and Lowell (230) concluded that the skeletal modifications seen in the three males "are consistent with the habitual lifting, carrying, and paddling or rowing performed by *voyageurs*" and provide insight into "the health and living conditions of the men of the fur trade."

Dressing for the Fur Trade

Material remains and historical documents testify to the importance of cloth in the fur trade (Anderson 1994; Davis 2014; Wagner 2011, tables 6.1, 6.4–6.11; Waselkov 1998, 200). In his analysis of the goods Montreal merchants shipped to several fur trade posts in the western Great Lakes region in the eighteenth century, Dean Anderson (1994) found that perishable fabrics and clothing were invariably the most common category of trade goods natives obtained in that region. They also appeared consistently in invento ries of goods the Wabash and Illinois River Outfits of the AFC traded with the Kickapoos (Wagner 2011, 64, 73). In contrast, less than 20 percent of an 1804 XYC invoice listed cloth, clothing, and blankets, whereas alcohol and tobacco accounted for 30 percent of the goods that were transacted (White 2004, 11). This small sample merely indicates that demand for cloth varied somewhat, but it was generally desired for some very practical reasons. In his narrative of his explorations in western America in the early nineteenth century, David Thompson (1916, 421–422) observed that woolen clothing had advantages over leather clothing for both Euro-American traders and natives: wool remains comfortable and warm even when wet, it dries quickly, and it keeps its shape (cited in Innis 1962, 236).

Descriptions from the period indicate that natives were using European cloth and clothing obtained in trade. In 1674, Daniel Gookin (quoted in Welters et al. 1996, 201) observed: "They sell the skins and furs [which was their clothing in former times] to the English, Dutch and French, and buy of them for clothing a kind of cloth, called duffils, or trucking cloth . . . made of coarse wool. . . . Two yards make a mantle, or coat, for men and women, and less for children." However, buttons and other cloth- and clothing-related artifacts such as thimbles, lead seals, and straight pins are often the only archaeological evidence of this aspect of the trade, with notable exceptions. Several varieties of cloth were preserved in two seventeenth-century southeastern New England native cemeteries (Welters et al. 1996). A Narragansett Indian cemetery (RI-1000) yielded 80 textile fragments, and 122 samples were excavated from a Mashantucket Pequot cemetery (Long Pond). The fact that few actual textiles and apparel items survive from the seventeenth-century fur trade in North America underscores the importance of these samples. They "provide tangible evidence of international textile trade, physical properties of textiles traded to New England Indians, and use of European cloth in Indian mortuary practice" (Welters et al. 1996, 203).

Several European countries were involved in cloth production in the seventeenth century, though England dominated the woolen cloth industry (Welters et al. 1996, 204–206). While the country of origin cannot be determined for the RI-1000 and Long Pond samples, they do indicate that the Narragansetts and Pequots made use of a variety of European textiles. Analysis indicates that woolens dominate the samples, which range from fine worsteds to coarse plain and twill weaves. The English used an array of terms for their fabrics, making it difficult to match fabric names to the archaeological specimens. The RI-1000 woolens were dyed red, orange, brown, blue, and black, though historical sources suggest a preference for red and blue. A few fabrics of other fibers include cotton from India, evidence of the global reach of the fur trade.

Some textiles were used to wrap the body prior to burial and possibly to wrap grave goods, since fabrics were found adhering to pots, spoons, and other metal artifacts, though this might have been unintentional. Few fragments appear to derive from tailored clothing. Linda Welters and her colleagues (1996, 207, 232) concluded that native New Englanders replaced the furs and skins they once used for clothing and burial with European textiles after deer and other fur-bearing animals were nearly depleted due to the success of the fur trade. The combination of imports and native goods (e.g., woven mats, skins) in the burials is evidence of accommodation to the new social and political circumstances of the seventeenth century and the role of textiles in that process.

European traders used clothing to mark their social position, especially in the context of formal trade negotiations. The objects that comprise our "social skins" are closely linked to identity because people select materials to literally cover their bodies in order to express their identities to the people with whom they interact. A NWC or AFC *bourgeois* or clerk might have worn a suit of pants and coat over a cotton shirt, socks, and European-style shoes, topped with a beaver hat. Less formal attire was fitting at other times, "resulting in a mixture of European [clothing] and clothes made from animal skins" (Wood et al. 2011, 111). This is what hired hands tended to wear. Leather clothing was warmer than cotton or wool in the winter.

Archaeologists, historians, and museologists have noted that imported objects were often combined with indigenous clothing to create styles that were neither native nor European (Kehoe 2000; Loren 2010; Nassaney 2008b; Neill 2000; White 2012). Fur traders in New France, among others, were "known for their predilection for mixing different dress styles" (Loren 2010, 29). The blending of fashion may have been only partly due to the scarcity of manufactured clothing on the frontier; it was also a practical and political statement that blurred social distinctions and allowed for social mobility (29).

The fur trader Charles McKenzie described his attire during his stay among the Cheyennes and Mandans on the Missouri River in 1805. He wore "the Indian costume of that quarter," which he "considered more *suitable* than any other in my situation and circumstances at the time. With this dress I could pass and repass as often as I pleased through the villages unmolested; whereas a Christian or civilized dress would subject me not only to the notice, but often to the gaze and even to the ridicule of the Natives and the attack of all the Village curs" (McKenzie 1809, 167, quoted in White 1982, 123).

Not only traders and voyageurs but also *habitants* and soldiers supplemented imported clothing with attire made locally. Descriptions of the practice of "cultural cross-dressing" appear at Fort Michilimackinac and elsewhere. Moccasins, breechclouts, and leggings were worn with ruffled shirts and waistcoats, presenting a most incongruous image for some (Cangany 2012, 274; Morand 1994, 67–68; White 2012). Moccasins represented a form of footwear "in which Natives and non-Natives combined the most useful and practical elements of different cultural traditions to create distinctive styles" (Cangany 2012, 275).

Catherine Cangany (2012) has recently documented an unspecified number of moccasin factories in Detroit that integrated native and Atlantic technologies from production to distribution. These factories met a growing demand for practical footwear. Her discussion of the production process and the consumer market underscores the broad social and economic implications of this aspect of the fur trade. In the Great Lakes region, native women crafted moccasins from elk skin or deerskin, performing all facets of the tanning process. They stretched fresh hides to dry overnight, often in domestic structures where drying was hastened with cooking fires. Then they scraped the dried skins to remove tissue and hair and thoroughly cleaned them before they soaked and boiled them in a solution of deer brains. They dried and often smoked the tanned skins to complete the process. The result was a very supple product because of the brains that were used for tanning. Leather cured in this fashion was more desirable than hides tanned using chemicals.

Natives supplied a significant quantity of the deerskins used at Detroit in the eighteenth century, though the specific sources have not been documented (Cangany 2012, 285). Local deer may have been exploited; during this period, declining populations of beaver and other species were shipped abroad. The behaviors and reproductive habits of deer may have rendered them better able to withstand higher rates of predation than fur-bearing carnivores and beaver (see Waselkov 1998). It is clear that the development of the moccasin trade in Detroit depended on both native technology and European manufacturing methods for its success (Cangany 2012, 293). What began as a small imperial settlement that was established to collect and package furs was soon producing a commodity for distant markets, an illustration of how the periphery developed more core-like characteristics in the context of the fur trade.

In fur trade society, clothing that was not manufactured in Europe was often produced in households. Thimbles, scissors, straight pins, and needles are present in shipment lists and at archaeological sites (Quimby 1966, 66; Wagner 2011, table 6.1; Wood et al. 2011, 242; see figure 3.2). Nonperishable objects such as buttons, beads, and lead seals have frequently been analyzed from archaeological contexts to provide insight into the operation of the fur trade and social identities in fur trade society. A distinctive type of button with a raised bird design occurs in the northwestern United States at fur-trade-era sites, particularly along the Columbia River, including Fort Vancouver (Pierson 2011a, 77; Sprague 1998; Strong 1975). These so-called phoenix buttons were made in England for uniforms for King Christophe of Haiti. Pierson (2011a, 77) explains that after Christophe's suicide in 1820, an American trader, Nathaniel Wyeth, marketed the buttons in the lower Columbia River Valley in the early 1830s to challenge the HBC's dominance in the trade. Although the HBC eventually bought out Wyeth, these objects are testimony to the global scope of the fur trade and the competition it engendered.

Perhaps the most common type of trade good that was often affixed to clothing is the glass bead. Produced in Italy, Holland, France, Bohemia, Russia, and China, beads appear in a range of shapes, colors, and sizes. Archaeologists use them for typological purposes that involve hundreds of types and varieties (see Blair et al. 2009; Hayes 1983; Kidd and Kidd 1970; Ross 1990). It is unlikely that any fur trader could have stayed in business without a steady supply of beads, prompting Robert Cromwell (2011, 60) to observe that "beads were the currency of the fur trade, and the HBC imported literally thousands of pounds of European and Chinese glass trade beads to Fort Vancouver each year between 1825 and 1850." While archaeologists usually assume that only natives used glass beads, historical sources indicate that the French and other Europeans who interacted closely with native peoples also used them in daily life (Malischke 2009).

Steven DeVore (1992) studied the glass beads from Fort Union, a national historic site in western North Dakota, in order to characterize the assemblage, ascertain consumer preferences, and provide comparative data. He described the beads according to method of manufacture and raw materials used, employing the typologies Lyle Stone (1974a) and Lester Ross (1974, 1976) developed. He discovered that tribal groups had color preferences and that the majority of bone and shell beads were associated with commercial or storage (as opposed to domestic) areas, which implies that they were important in trade (DeVore 1992, 62).

The lead seal is another cloth-related object that has attracted some archaeological interest (Adams 1989; Davis 2014). Merchants, taxing authorities, and inspectors in Europe often attached lead seals to bolts of cloth to provide information about the origins and types of cloth. Once bolts reached the New World, their lead seals were often casually discarded. In North America, lead seals occur in fur trade contexts and have been recovered from French, Dutch, English, Spanish, and Russian trading posts, habitation sites, and shipwrecks (Davis 2014, 12). They are seldom found at native sites because they were likely removed from the cloth prior to trade (cf. Good 1972, 153–154).

Lead seals were attached in various ways (Stone 1974a, 281). They were also marked with distinctive symbols (iconographic and alphanumeric) that can be related to country of origin and cloth production centers (e.g., Lille, Mazamet). Since different locales specialized in the production of different types of cloth (e.g., twill woolen, kersey, linen), seals can provide information about the textiles that were brought to North America (Davis 2014, 69–72). Access to different types of cloth was often a function of social status in European society, because sumptuary laws dictated the way an individual could dress (Loren 2010, 24–29). However, these laws were subject to renegotiation in the context of the fur trade.

Identifying the People of the Trade: Ethnicity, Status, and Gender

Early fur trade researchers noted that natives replaced traditional artifacts with European ones and interpreted this pattern in support of the acculturation process. Subsequent work has called into question a simple correspondence between objects and ethnic groups because of the malleability of the material world in the hands of agents in different cultural contexts. While it is important to determine the origins of artifacts in order to discern trade routes and distribution patterns, origins are seen as less important for understanding cultural dynamics than how goods were used. Similarly, a focus on the context of material goods shifts attention away from distinguishing the objects Europeans used and those that were the currency of the trade (see Kenyon 1986, 27). With this caveat, archaeologists of the fur trade are very interested in deciphering the materiality of the trade and identifying how the participants mobilized local and foreign goods to express ethnic, status, and gender relations.

In their study of the use and depositional contexts of fur trade objects, archaeologists have recognized native uses for imported goods that differed from their intended functions. For example, when copper alloy first appeared in the so-called protohistoric period in the Northeast (sixteenth century) and the Midwest (seventeenth century), natives used it in a decorative manner to produce disc-shaped pendants, tubular beads, spiral ornaments, and clips (Bradley 1987, 70; Ehrhardt 2005). Many natives saw imported goods as raw materials that could be crafted in traditional ways. Indeed, a hallmark of fur trade culture is the creative use of utilitarian objects, such as the use of sewing thimbles for ornamental purposes (figure 4.6). At Fort Vancouver, most brass thimbles recovered had a perforation in the top, which made it

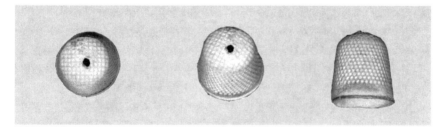

FORT ST. JOSEPH
ARCHAEOLOGICAL PROJECT
WESTERN MICHIGAN UNIVERSITY

CM

IN

Figure 4.6. Perforated thimbles were transformed from tools for clothing production into decorative ornaments. This specimen from Fort St. Joseph was punched from the inside using a nail or similar pointed object. Photo by Katelyn Hillmeyer. Courtesy of the Fort St. Joseph Archaeological Project.

possible to hang them from bags or clothing or incorporate them in neck-laces (Langford 2011, 38; see also Mason 1986, 127, pl. 13.6.7; Quimby 1966, 76; Tottle 1981, fig. 77b). Thimbles and other repurposed objects are symbols of the syncretic nature of fur trade society; people adopted objects but adapted them for new uses (Langford 2011, 38).

Daily practices involving clothing, architecture, ritual activities, and sub-sistence reproduced ethnic relations in fur trade society. Heinz Pyszczyk (1989) compared consumption practices among NWC French Canadians and natives and those among HBC Orkneymen and some native women by using quantitative methods to measure variability in assemblages (223). His analysis revealed significant differences in the consumption of goods be-tween households at company forts in the 1820s, when goods expressed eth-nicity (227). In artifacts that date to the 1850s and 1860s, it is more difficult to distinguish members of ethnic groups based on consumption practices. This is attributable to increased opportunities for upward economic mobility and the practice of emulating the consumption patterns of the upper ranks of the HBC (229).

Pyszczyk (232–233) suggested that certain types of goods are ethnic mark-ers, such as stone smoking pipes, which signal the presence of native peo-ples at fur trade sites. He observed a higher proportion of stone (as opposed to clay) pipes in the NWC assemblages than he did in HBC assemblages. Pyszczyk concluded that this indicated varying proportions of natives liv-ing at the respective company forts before 1821. The decline in frequencies of stone pipes after 1821 corresponds with a significant decrease in the num-ber of native laborers in the HBC. These data suggest that "ethnic groups are identified by very specific forms of artifacts, as well as differentiated by entire assemblages of artifacts" (234). It is also possible to recognize which con-sumption practices articulate specific beliefs and values of an ethnic group. For example, an examination of the goods purchased at inland posts for each ethnic group indicates that the French Canadians were more liberal in their spending patterns: they spent more on goods and purchased a broader range of goods than the Orkneymen. They also consumed significantly more lux-ury items, such as tobacco and alcohol. These patterns are consistent with the personalities, views, and general outlook toward life of the groups; the French Canadians were much more flamboyant and socially oriented than the Orkneymen, who were generally conservative and independent (234). Thus, ethnicity accounts for much of the variability in consumer choice in western Canadian fur trade sites (237). This research helps explain both synchronic and diachronic patterns of material variation and demonstrates that social relations have clear archaeological signatures.

Mann (2003, 2008) sought to demonstrate that French Canadians continued to use traditional architectural techniques after the conquest as a means of asserting their ethnic identity in the Wabash River Valley. Anglo merchants and elites cast French Canadians in the role of fur trade laborers who used familiar traditions as a means of reinforcing a sense of group identity tied to the trade (Mann 2003, 116–117; see also Burley 2000). French Canadian collective identity was inscribed in the material world through Canadian folk housing marked by the use of hand-hewn vertical timbers either set directly in the ground (*poteaux en terre*) or on a horizontal wooden sill (*poteaux sur sole*) (Mann 2003, 128–129). This form of architecture became invested with "meanings that both produced and naturalized *Canadian* fur trade identity" (131). Their houses were easy targets of ridicule for the conquering British, who denigrated them as dilapidated, uninhabitable "huts" (Scott 2001b, 30).

While ethnic boundaries were often maintained through material practices, the relationship between social identity and material outcome is complex because the adoption of mass-produced consumer products across ethnic lines had the potential to mask important social differences. In addition, cross-cultural interaction had the potential to blur distinctions between natives and newcomers. These realities prompted some researchers to emphasize the cultural blending that contributed to the unity of fur trade society, especially in the example of the offspring of mixed parentage (Nassaney 2008b; Van Kirk 1980). An interesting amalgamation of styles, raw materials, techniques, and new forms of material culture and new uses for old objects emerged in the context of the fur trade that reflect the hybridized identities that marked close cultural interactions. The challenge for archaeologists is to use contextual data to ascertain how use practices differed from those intended by their makers.

The most intimate interactions were the sexual unions formed between Europeans and a wide range of native populations that led to creoles and *métis* peoples. New France always had a demographic imbalance; men vastly outnumbered women, despite the Crown's efforts to encourage the emigration of women and the formation of stable nuclear families. For the many voyageurs and *coureurs de bois* (illicit fur traders because they lacked a license) who literally went into the woods to acquire furs and often lived only part-time in settled communities, unions with native women were a practical option that benefited both parties (Brown 1982; C. Gilman 1982, 80; Peterson 1981; Van Kirk 1980; Wood et al. 2011, 112–113). Such close relationships created intimate bonds that led to *métissage* (cultural mixing) and new cultural forms that were neither native nor French (White 2011). These interactions, which are integral to understanding French immigrant life in the western Great Lakes region, left an indelible archaeological imprint.

Archaeologists have begun to use material remains to gain insight into the process of ethnogenesis—the creation, maintenance, and transformation of ethnic identities in the context of intense cultural interaction (Hu 2013). Archaeological and historical evidence associated with French fur trade sites indicates the mutual borrowing of ideas. A melting pot certainly seems to be an apt metaphor. Yet despite the blending of practices, social distinctions of status and gender were not erased (cf. Nassaney 2008b; Nassaney and Brandão 2009).

Architecture and consumption patterns strictly segregated the *bourgeois* from the voyageurs at HBC and NWC posts down to the smallest wintering sites (C. Gilman 1982, 47; Hamilton 2000). Intrasite spatial distributions reinforced Old World concepts of rank and status. For example, Donald Heldman (1991) noted that officers' quarters were located in the northwest corner of Fort Michilimackinac, where they were protected from the prevailing winds and were a safe distance from the powder magazine in the southeast corner of the site. A floor plan of the HBC trading post at Red Lake, Ontario, shows that trading post architecture strictly segregated the gentlemen from the voyageurs (C. Gilman 1982, 47). Alice Kehoe (2000, 174) has posited similar spatial differentiation at a much smaller and less formal peddler's post on the Saskatchewan River, where Francois Le Blanc occupied separate quarters from his men yet "was openly of the same social status."

Charles Ewen (1986) examined archaeological evidence to explore status differences among occupants of the NWC and XYC posts on the Yellow River in the Fond du Lac district in the early nineteenth century. The larger fur returns for 1804, coupled with the experience of the NWC wintering partner, John Sayer, suggests that the NWC post should exhibit evidence of higher social status expressed in: 1) greater meat consumption; 2) more "delicacy" items, such as beaver and evidence of removal of deer tongues; and 3) a higher proportion of preferred deer elements (Ewen 1986, 17). A comparison of the two posts by species and elements indicates that the NWC post occupants had more meat, better cuts of meat, and more delicacy items than their XYC post rivals (21). Ewen also compared the contents of Sayer's domicile (thought to be Cabin 1) with the building the voyageurs occupied (Cabin 2). He found that they contained evidence of essentially similar grades of meat. This prompted other comparisons that showed that Cabin 2 had evidence of far more delicacies such as beaver and deer tongues. It had a subterranean storage pit for concealing valuables similar to the pit found at the house of another *bourgeois* in Minnesota. It also yielded fragments of refined earthenwares (pearlware, stoneware), glass tumblers, and wine bottle glass (25). Thus, faunal, architectural, and artifact data suggest that Sayer and his family actually occupied Cabin 2, not Cabin 1, as was initially thought.

The authority of company officers could be tenuous on the frontier. Consequently, rank distinctions in the NWC were reinforced symbolically and practically through imported wealth items and privileges made available at locations that ranged from the large depots, such as Fort William and Grand Portage, down to the smallest outposts that were occupied by only a few men for short periods of time (Hamilton 2000, 243). The imposing built environment of Fort William, Grand Portage, Ross Colony, Fort Clark, Fort Union, and similar sites was deliberately designed to reinforce social hierarchy. Native peoples were often relegated to neighborhoods outside the palisade walls. These walls were constructed to serve as symbolic and physical barriers for both the laborers and the native population (Culpin and Borjes 1984; Hamilton 2000, 244).

The women and children of the fur trade are often underrepresented in historical sources, but their daily activities contributed to the formation of the archaeological record, prompting some researchers to examine the materiality of gender roles and relations (e.g., Rotman 2015). Elizabeth M. Scott's (1991b) work on gender roles at Fort Michilimackinac has demonstrated that we cannot identify the presence of women in households by looking solely at evidence of activities because men, servants, or slaves might have performed activities attributed to women such as food preparation. However, objects of personal adornment associated with clothing and sewing such as buttons, buckles, cufflinks, thimbles, awls, straight pins, and other accessories may be linked with men and women of various socioeconomic and ethnic affiliations (Kerr 2012).

Native women were active participants in a gender-based division of labor that was profoundly influenced by the fur trade. For example, the transition from the commercial exploitation of beaver to the exploitation of deer in central New York had major effects on how native peoples organized labor along gender lines. With the development of the deerskin trade, Seneca men were able to hunt locally. This meant that they could stay closer to home than in "the beaver-based trade, which had forced them into lengthy and dangerous extra-regional travel and warfare" (Jordan 2008, 299). At the same time, the deerskin trade resulted in a net increase of work for Seneca women because of the intensive processing that was necessary to maximize exchange value of hides (soaking, scraping, softening, soaking a second time in a solution of water and animal brains, drying, softening again, and smoking). Kurt Jordan (300) noted how similarities between processing bone grease and processing deer hides allowed Seneca women to overlap the two processes and engage in both industrial (i.e., commercial) and household production.

After men on the Plains adopted the horse to hunt bison, the mode of production among Plains groups changed. Men and women collaborated to drive game into a pound or over a cliff. As Plains men dominated horse ownership, they controlled buffalo hunting, and women's labor in the traditional collective hunt became unnecessary. Women subsequently lost status as their role was increasingly tied to hide and pemmican production (Klein 1993, 141–142).

The production of goods (e.g., processed hides) and provisions (e.g., wild rice, maize, pemmican) to meet the demands of the fur trade often affected labor relations. In southeastern New England in the seventeenth century, women's labor may have been reallocated toward the production of wampum after demands for surplus increased and new tools were introduced (Nassaney 2004). Similarly, the importation of large quantities of cloth in the western Great Lakes region in the eighteenth century meant that women no longer needed to produce clothing from hides, which freed up their labor for new tasks, many of which were likely tied directly or indirectly to the fur trade (Anderson 1994).

Changes in how labor was allocated may have produced tensions along gender lines as male kin appropriated the surplus goods their sisters, daughters, and wives produced. While women were not excluded from the trade, men often dominated interactions with European traders and accrued the benefits of direct exchange ([Fort St. Joseph Archaeological Project] 2011, 10). The combination of the wider availability of some European goods, such as white clay smoking pipes, and other social and political disruptions may have also strained gender relations as cultural taboos about practices previously reserved for men were relaxed. Native women in southeastern New England adopted the custom of smoking and invented effigy pestles to establish "lines of communication with the supernatural" (Nassaney 2004, 134).

Thus, native women were active agents, just as their male counterparts were. They engaged with the fur trade and challenged its ill effects in various ways. In southeastern New England in the seventeenth century, they mobilized pots, pestles, peague (wampum), and pipes to assert their autonomy, restore physical and spiritual well-being to their communities, and reestablish the importance of their roles in nurturance and biological reproduction in the context of the changing political and economic conditions colonialism and the fur trade brought about (Nassaney 2000, 2004; Nassaney and Volmar 2003). Kehoe (2000) has also argued that women had agency in practices as simple as daily attire. She noted that "Western Indian women wore cloth dresses in original styles—neither cut like hide clothing nor copying Euro-Canadian costumes" (183). Their willingness to wear foreign clothing represents an adoption of innovations they desired rather than a rejection of their culture. Native women often selected objects that were suitable substitutes for goods that already existed in their own societies or modified unfamiliar goods to satisfy their own needs. They were not drawn to frivolous ornaments and other trifles.

The Material Legacy of the Fur Trade

Objects associated with the fur trade era are ubiquitous in archaeological sites throughout much of North America. They are evidence of the exchange relations that took place between natives and newcomers. Archaeologists have interrogated the material goods that literally and figuratively mediated these exchanges to make inferences about the nature of fur trade society and its variation over time and space. Their analyses relate to broad anthropological and historical concerns about chronology, spatial relations, political economy, culture change and continuity, relations of power, symbolic meanings, and the material expressions of social identity. The archaeological record provides new insights into the history and culture of the fur trade era. The following chapter examines in greater detail several fur trade systems and subsystems in North America to highlight the contributions of archaeology to our understanding of animal exploitation, the identities of fur trade agents, and the material outcomes of fur trade interactions in the formation of the American experience.

5

Regional Fur Trade Systems in Archaeological Perspective

The literature examined thus far clearly demonstrates "the interlocking nature of the fur trade" (St-Onge 2008, 21). It connected distant markets with local consumers in a series of overlapping systems that began in coastal regions and penetrated into the heart of the continent through arterial waterways. No groups were untouched in this global process. This chapter examines in greater detail the legacy of the fur trade from the perspective of a number of regional systems and the material record that has been mined in conjunction with other lines of historical evidence to provide insight into the interactions and outcomes of fur trade activities.

Southern New England: The Fur Trade as Prelude to English Settlement

When Giovanni da Verrazzano distributed blue beads, bells, and other trinkets to the Narragansetts in coastal Rhode Island in 1524, his offerings provided the basis for the development of reciprocal trading relations (Trigger and Swagerty 1996, 334–335). Though trade was limited over the next century, Europeans recognized the economic potential of the region. The English settlement at Plymouth, Massachusetts, in 1620 and Dutch excursions from New Amsterdam after 1614 made European goods available to native groups such as the Narragansetts, Pequots, and Wampanoags. Because of the close proximity of the Wampanoags to the early English settlement at Plymouth and the Pequots to the settlement at Hartford, they had more immediate access to goods than the Narragansetts and consequently enjoyed the benefit of new alliances. To obtain their own supply of European goods and a potential ally, the Narragansetts allowed the banished Puritan minister Roger Williams to settle at Providence, Rhode Island, in 1636. They also quickly understood the possibilities the rivalry between the Dutch and the English presented (Turnbaugh 1993, 136). Williams soon established a trading post at nearby Cocumscussoc that operated for nearly four decades (Rubertone 2001, 14).

The limited investigations that have been done at Cocumscussoc have provided only an incomplete inventory of the types of goods Williams and his successors traded to the Narragansetts (Rubertone 2001, 135). Half of a lead seal is evidence of a market for fabrics (see Welters et al. 1996). Glass beads, latten spoons, tin-glazed earthenware sherds, clay pipe stems, and broken glass bottles were also found. Examples of all of these have also been found in Narragansett cemeteries (Robinson et al. 1985; Simmons 1970). The Narragansetts participated in a triangular trade in which they provided some furs but mostly wampum and maize in return for a variety of Old World products such as those found at Cocumscussoc (Ceci 1977; Turnbaugh 1993, 141). The English used the wampum and maize to obtain more furs from interior groups. Natives used many imports in daily life, while they saw others as suitable accompaniments in the afterlife.

Although few foreign objects have been recovered archaeologically at domestic native sites, they have been found in mortuary contexts. These goods, their impact on native society, and their meanings in native hands have attracted considerable archaeological interest, particularly since the discovery and exhumation of some fifty individuals and their associations at a place known as RI-1000 in Wickford, Rhode Island (Nassaney 1989, 2000, 2004; Robinson 1990; Robinson et al. 1985; Rubertone 2001; Turnbaugh 1984, 1993; see also Gibson 1980; Simmons 1970). This Narragansett cemetery was in use from about 1650 until King Philip's War in 1675. It contained valuable biological and cultural information about a group that was perhaps reluctantly entangled in the fur trade.

The mortality profile and skeletal pathologies of these burials are indicative of a population under stress (Robinson et al. 1985, 114–119). There are an inordinate number of adolescents in the cemetery and much of the population suffered from tuberculosis, arthritis, osteoporosis, carious dentition, and other endemic diseases. Poor dental health may be related to dietary changes such as the consumption of refined sugar and molasses or increased consumption of starches (maize and flour) that were coincident with the onset of the fur trade. Yet despite these chronic conditions, the placement and orientation of individual graves was in keeping with traditional beliefs regarding the afterlife.

Particularly intriguing is the incorporation of European objects as grave goods. These can inform us about both continuities and creative accommodations to the economic, social, and political circumstances the fur trade brought about in post-Contact southeastern New England (Nassaney 2004; Rubertone 2001). A broad range of goods was placed in the graves. Careful examination allows us to decipher their meanings in the context of the turbulent seventeenth century. Consistent with the conduct of various native groups discussed in this book, the Narragansetts were discerning consumers who exercised restraint and selectivity in acquiring manufactured goods (Turnbaugh 1993, 141–143). European traders such as Roger Williams needed to learn their customers' preferences if they wanted to do well. Cloth was beginning to replace skin clothing in the seventeenth century (142; Welters et al. 1996). Analysis of textile fragments from RI-1000 led to the identification of five different types of wool, including coarse napped woolens, fine worsteds, and cotton calico (Welters et al. 1996). Their contexts suggest that they were used in place of traditional fur robes to cover the body in burial, as wrappers for grave goods, and in clothing that was often modified through the addition of seed beads, copper or brass tubes, or hoop-type rings resembling broaches. Cloth was well integrated into daily use, yet the Narragansetts did not completely adopt European apparel because they found it constricting, hard to keep clean, and expensive (Turnbaugh 1993, 142). Natives preferred blankets to tailored clothing; they especially liked dark colors made of thickly woven cloth. Heavy woolens, like many of the fragments recovered from RI-1000, were manufactured expressly for trade (Welters and Smith 1985, 4)

Some products replaced native counterparts, while others were used to expand native culture along well-established traditional lines in southeastern New England. For example, iron drills facilitated the production of wampum, while iron files and knives made possible an elaborate lapidary industry that produced goods such as intricate effigy pipes that were used in sacred rituals (figure 5.1; Nassaney 2000). The Narragansetts prized small bells, blue beads, and other decorative items that they could use as ornaments, particularly objects made of copper and brass, raw materials that

Figure 5.1. This effigy pipe featuring a wolf or mountain lion figure is a classic example of the elaborate lapidary industry, made possible by imported European goods, in which natives participated in southeastern New England. It was recovered from Burr's Hill, a seventeenth-century Wampanoag burial ground in Warren, Rhode Island. Drawing by Pamela Rups. Courtesy of Western Michigan University.

native peoples throughout North America esteemed highly (Bradley 1987; Ehrhardt 2005; Waselkov 1989, 122). They also acquired mirrors, nails, medicines, iron spears and harpoons, kettles, awls, pins, needles, hatchets, hoes, guns, and liquor (Turnbaugh 1993, 142). It is important to carefully consider the distribution of grave goods within the cemetery to gain insight about their cultural significance, their relationship to the deceased, and their meaning to the living.

The Narragansetts expressed their creativity and craftsmanship in their treatment of kettles and sheet brass. Patricia Rubertone (2001, 136) notes how they deftly repaired kettles with patches and rivets of their own production and transformed broken pieces of brass into rings, combs, beads, bracelets, and spoons through a variety of metallurgical techniques, including annealing and brazing. They also cast lead to make ammunition and buttons and decorative ornaments, often in effigy forms of totemic significance (138). Although the French often provided guns to native allies, along with a gunsmith for regular repair, the English "attempted to block the trade in martial weapons" and "banned selling, exchanging, or loaning guns to Indians." Thus, natives were forced to obtain "guns by trading with the French to the north, the Dutch to the west, and in the black markets of the English colonies" (Wilder 2013, 38). Because the English also forbade the repair of native guns, the Narragansetts were obliged to master their upkeep (Wilder 2013, 38). The association of a blacksmith's tool kit with one of the males interred at RI-1000 is evidence of the development of metallurgical skills in Narragansett society.

As readily as natives embraced and transformed these foreign objects, they purposely avoided others and limited the distribution of some goods of their own manufacture to certain segments of their population, as in the case of pestles and smoking pipes (Nassaney 2004; Nassaney and Volmar 2003). Rubertone (2001, 140–164) has examined the material symbols of age and gender as Narragansetts struggled with the perplexities of their lives in the face of English intrusion in the late seventeenth century. Children between the ages of three and four years were among the most lavishly buried at RI-1000. Yet they lacked the finger rings that adorned the hands of adolescent women; these were symbolic of dexterity (149). Similarly, necklaces were part of the decorative code of puberty that marked the neck as the locus of communication, just as headbands and combs were linked to cultural understanding. Two totemic symbols that were also associated with young women—one of a bear and one of a turtle—marked their importance in reckoning descent and the continuance of society.

While the mortuary remains literally embodied elements of group solidarity and cultural persistence, the act of commemorating the dead and its associated materiality allowed for multiple messages to the living about the present, the past, and the future. Gender was a particularly volatile locus of struggle in native society as labor was reallocated and roles became redefined in the context of the fur trade. Two traditional artifact forms—pestles and smoking pipes—were transformed to contest the loss of power and control in an unpredictable colonial world. Pestles, cylindrical stones that women used to pound corn and other grains into meal, began to exhibit sculpted representations of otherworldly beings during the seventeenth century and often lacked evidence of utilitarian use. The fact that they were recovered from the graves of women suggests that effigy pestles were a new way of communicating with forces beyond this world in an effort to rectify social instability (Nassaney and Volmar 2003, 89–90). Women and children also adopted smoking pipes as a way to connect with the cosmic realm. While tobacco smoking was confined to men in earlier times, after the onset of the fur trade, other members of native society adopted the practice. They used white clay tobacco pipes obtained in trade. Expanded use signaled a more democratized shamanism as more members of the community "had the potential to acquire spiritual power" (91). Men responded by revitalizing the production of stone pipes, which they carved with intricate designs made possible by imported iron knives and files (figure 5.1). Native men's continued preference for stone pipes is an indication of their desire to reappropriate tobacco smoking for their own ritual use in communicating with the supernatural (88).

English settlement eventually led to disruptions in native life everywhere, though relations generally began somewhat amicably. The English moved in from the coast in 1636, when eight men and their families took up residence in the middle Connecticut River Valley at Springfield and obtained a claim to the surrounding land (Thomas 1985, 135). Trade bound the interests of the English with local natives; they bartered wampum, cloth, and other goods obtained from the coast for maize and beaver pelts. So long as the colonists depended on natives for provisions, relatively peaceful relations prevailed (142).

In an effort to understand the fur trade in the interior, where "English settlements were small and isolated," Peter Thomas (1985, 132; Thomas 1979) examined historical sources and conducted excavations at the site of Fort Hill, a fortified Squakheag village in southern New Hampshire that was occupied from the fall of 1663 to the spring of 1664. His analysis focused on the types of goods the Squakheags consumed, how they incorporated them into their culture, and how the trading system was maintained. Account books indicate that a broad range of goods was available for native consumption, but the monetary value of the cloth that was exchanged was twenty-five times that of glass, iron, brass, and copper (Thomas 1985, 146). Among the goods recovered archaeologically were several pieces of brass that had been reworked into projectile points (148). Thomas (148), who calculated the average annual consumption rates for goods such as cloth, knives, scissors, awls, fishhooks, needles, and pipes, made a convincing case that Native Americans in the region were by no means dependent upon European goods or colonial traders to meet their material needs. However, indebtedness and declining fur returns forced native leaders who relied on the fur trade to seek out an alternative resource to pelts and horticultural produce. That resource was land. By 1660, land had become the collateral for goods that were received on credit, with the promise that pelts would be forthcoming the following spring. Failure to deliver the pelts under increasingly stressful political and economic conditions led to dispossession and its attendant consequences. This was coupled with Mohawk raids from the west that heightened political instability.

That the tension had become palpable is evidenced in the faunal remains recovered from the Squakheag site. Local exploitation seems to have been the practice, as is indicated by the fact that entire large mammals such as deer and bears were butchered at village sites (154). These carcasses were nearly complete, suggesting that villagers chose to hunt closer to home instead of at distant camps, as they had in the past. The rest of the 1660s was marked by contentious court battles over land claims, leading to a reversal that forced natives to purchase goods from those they once provisioned. During this decade, natives often petitioned the Massachusetts colony for relief (155). The fur trade in the Connecticut Valley had effectively ended by 1670, the eve of King Philip's War, which ushered in the final disruptions to the fragile economic alliances the New England natives and the English had managed to maintain for only one or two generations. By then, the English and their French competitors had reached into the North American interior to acquire furs directly from new producers.

Pays d'en Haut and the Northwest Territory: The Heartland of the Fur Trade

While the English were confined to the eastern seaboard and the icy shores of Hudson's Bay in the seventeenth century, the French penetrated the interior of the continent from settlements along the St. Lawrence River at Quebec and Montreal. In their search for a northwest passage, the French had explored Lake Superior by 1634 and had established a mission and trading post at the Straits of Mackinac by the 1660s. The latter proved to be a strategic location for moving furs and goods along water routes in and out of the heart of the continent, and it was a transshipment site for the French, followed by the NWC, and finally the AFC into the nineteenth century.

European goods trickled into the midcontinent through indigenous exchange networks prior to the establishment of settlements at Green Bay, the Straits of Mackinac between the upper and lower peninsulas of Michigan, Fort St. Louis at the western end of Lake Superior, Fort St. Joseph in southwest Michigan, and Detroit (figure 3.1). Natives were responsible for moving their own furs to distribution centers in the east at Montreal and Albany. In addition to furs, some western goods such as red pipestone (catlinite?) and other lithic sources made their way to the Onondaga Iroquois in western New York, evidence of traffic along an east-west axis (Bradley 1987, 130). In the seventeenth century, the Seneca Iroquois' role in the fur trade was "based on beaver pelt procurement; warfare ensured access to productive hunting territories, which became increasingly distant over time" (Jordan 2008, 343). By the second quarter of the eighteenth century, the Senecas had come to rely on locally available animals (deer and smaller fur-bearers) and on goods acquired from western natives seeking passage to British trading posts. The Senecas selectively adopted some of the technologies Europeans introduced and followed subsistence practices that fit into their own lifeways (Jordan 2008, 343–344). James Bradley (1987, 167) came to a similar conclusion with regard to material culture change among the Onondagas.

Natives in the western Great Lakes region and upper Mississippi River Valley were by no means dependent on Europeans in the early phase of the fur trade. The volume of imported goods found at seventeenth-century native sites is negligible, suggesting that native groups adopted new goods selectively and gradually. This changed in the next century. Considerable information about exchange relations comes from the Straits of Mackinac area, the crossroads of the fur trade for nearly two centuries.

Around 1715, after they had established a mission and staged their trading activities from the north side of the Straits of Mackinac, the French constructed Fort Michilimackinac across the straits on the Lower Peninsula in order to thwart incursions from the English at Albany, keep local natives from trading with the English colonies to the southeast, and wage war against the Fox Indians (José António Brandão, personal communication, 2014). Licensed traders, craftsmen, missionaries, and *coureurs de bois* occupied the fort, and the Odawas and Ojibwes were frequent visitors (Stone 1974a). The fort was under French control until 1761, when the French ceded most of their North American territories to the British. The British allowed French fur traders to remain at the fort until 1779, when the fort was dismantled and moved to Mackinac Island.

Fort Michilimackinac in Mackinac City, Michigan, is the site of the longest continuous excavation in North America. Work began in 1959 as archaeologists collected architectural data so the site could be reconstructed for public interpretation. Archaeological and historical evidence document several expansions and two rebuilding episodes in the life of the fort (figure 5.2; Hauser 1982, 19). Thousands of artifacts associated with fur trade activities have been recovered, as have objects associated with daily crafts that supported the trade (Morand 1994; Stone 1974a). Reconstructions of a powder magazine,

FORT MICHILIMACKINAC
MASTER MAP

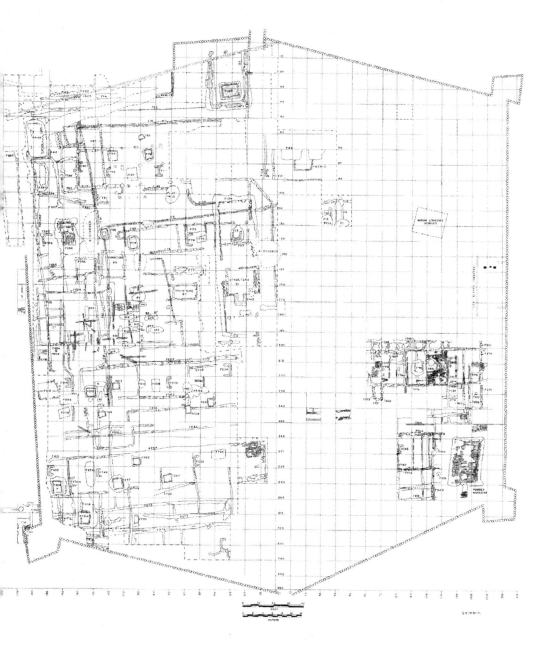

Figure 5.2. Plan view of Fort Michilimackinac. Courtesy of Mackinac State Historic Parks Collection.

a number of row houses, a chapel, and other special-purpose buildings sur-
round a parade ground inside the fort (figure 4.2).

A number of artifact classes have been the focus of archaeological analysis, including iconographic rings (Hauser 1982), lead seals (Adams 1989),
religious paraphernalia (Rinehart 1994), glass (Brown 1971), nails (Frurip et
al. 1983), firearms (Hamilton 1976), and ceramics (Miller and Stone 1970).
The contents of the houses and evidence of subsistence have also been examined in detail (Carlson 2012; Evans 2001; Scott 2001a). It is often possible to
identify which deposits on the site were French and which were English, and
comparisons between the two point to significant dietary differences. While
the French relied more heavily on wild animal species, particularly fish,
the British preferred domesticated animals such as cows, pigs, and chicken
(Scott 1991a). Interhousehold variations were also important. For example,
the British residents of House D of the Southeast Row House ate considerably more fish than anticipated, prompting Scott (2001a, 65) to remark that
if one relied exclusively on these subsistence data, they might suggest that
French Canadians of modest means occupied House D. Yet documentary
and material evidence indicate that English soldiers and officers "who did
not seem to have access to the kinds of domestic meats often associated with
their military rank" lived in this dwelling in the 1760s and 1770s (65).

These data suggest the extent to which the French and the English were
dependent on local resources in daily life. It is this reliance that ultimately
contributed to an American identity; the immigrant population was forced
to interact with new groups of people and adjust to raw materials, subsistence practices, and clothing styles that were foreign to their Old World
cousins. Lynn Evans (2007) has discussed how Native Americans played
a role in which local materials Europeans used. The newcomers obtained
birch bark canoes from the natives at Michilimackinac to carry furs to Montreal because fur required more cargo space than the trade goods that were
shipped back to the fort (Evans 2007, 32). Other goods that sustained the
fur trade were snowshoes, moccasins, maple sugar products, and the Micmac pipe, which was used in cross-cultural diplomacy (Morand 1994, 48–
53).

The nature of interethnic relations in the fur trade dictated the extent to
which Europeans and natives borrowed cultural traits from each other. Smaller
trading posts often had irregular access to goods from the homeland and experienced less oversight. These two conditions facilitated significant material

mixing, borrowing of dress styles, and intermarriage (Nassaney 2008b). Considerable archaeological work was conducted in the 1970s at the French site of Fort Ouiatenon, a trading post along the Wabash River that straddled the Upper Country and the Illinois Country (Martin 1986, 1991a, 1991b; Noble 1983, 1991; Tordoff 1983). Michigan State University archaeologists have examined the outcomes of the close relationships between French Canadians and local native groups. They have recovered data related to settlement patterns, subsistence, and daily life. Native groups such as the Miamis, Piankashas, and Weas lived in immediate proximity to the fortified settlement of Ouiatenon, reflecting the amicable relationships that existed between the French and their allies (Trubowitz 1992a). Analyses of animal remains revealed a subsistence strategy based predominantly on wild animal species, although domesticated animals were present (Martin 1986, 1991a, 1991b). In addition, the presence of a significant number of modified animal remains suggests that the French Canadian residents of the fort and their native relatives and trading partners were using local raw materials for utilitarian and recreational purposes (e.g., turtle carapace bowls; bone and antler projectile points, handles, and perforators; a hide-stropping tool made from a black bear mandible; a bone paintbrush; bone dice; bird bone tubes and whistles).

Following Great Britain's acquisition of New France, King George III issued the Royal Proclamation of 1763, which sought to limit settlement west of the Appalachians. The goal was to improve relations with Native Americans and regulate trade, settlement, and land purchases on the western frontier. Many independent French traders remained in the region, and in the 1770s some of them organized to form the North West Company. Their posts were coordinated by a strict hierarchy of personnel and were spatially divided into districts and departments. The size and shape of the departments were based on environmental and demographic factors, and each filled a specialized role in addition to collecting and transshipping furs (Birk 1984, 51).

To facilitate the movement of goods into and out of the interior, the NWC established its inland headquarters at present-day Grand Portage, Minnesota (Birk 1984, 52; Veit 2011, 27), which is currently owned by the National Park Service. Archaeologists have conducted limited investigations at the site since the 1930s. These have led to the reconstruction of the Great Hall, a kitchen, a warehouse, a gatehouse, and the palisade (Woolworth 1982). Several buildings have been located through geophysical survey inside the palisade and are identified for visitors. Numerous artifacts have been recovered from excavations that shed light on the appearance of the site, the functions of the buildings, and the lifestyles of the area's inhabitants (115).

This transshipment site on the western shore of Lake Superior was linked to Fort Charlotte on the Pigeon River some 8.5 miles away by a portage that the French had used decades earlier and the natives thousands of years before them. The NWC successfully monopolized the portage to secure this strategic location and prevent competitors from using it (see below). Many portages had a long history of use, and traces of human activity can still be identified along or adjacent to these carrying places.

Grand Portage refers to both the transshipment site and the 8.5-mile trail that bypassed the 130-foot falls on the Pigeon River. The site is the terminus for the *canot du maître* (literally master's canoe but also known as a Montreal canoe, often reaching lengths of 36 feet or more) and the *canot du Nord* (north canoe, used on the smaller rivers and lakes west of Grand Portage), where furs were exchanged for imported goods destined for natives in the interior (Innis 1962, 226). Voyageurs carried heavy loads of trade goods (two or more 90-pound packs) from the depot to Fort Charlotte and returned with bundles of furs, pausing at frequent rest stops called *posés*. Some sixteen *posés* evolved, where men would drop their burden and enjoy a quick smoke before resuming the portage. An archaeological survey provided information about changes in the route, and subsurface testing confirmed journal accounts of the use of horse- and oxen-drawn sledges in the wintertime (Veit 2011, 30). Archaeological remains of objects left or lost at the *posés* include fur-trade-era buttons, ice chisels, muskrat spears, awls, brooches, tinkling cones, musket balls, lead shot, and "an assortment of French and English clasp knives, a silver gorget produced by Montreal silversmith Narcisse Roy (active around 1785–1814), and a pair of Jesuit rings fastened together with a twisted cord" (30).

Even more significant losses occurred when voyageurs had accidents. In treacherous white water, daring canoe men would sometimes run the rapids in an attempt to save precious time and energy instead of using a safer portage to bypass them. Capsized canoes frequently dumped precious cargo into icy waters that were too cold and dangerous to permit rescue. Similarly, canoes under sail in larger lakes might be difficult to maneuver in unexpected harsh weather. Finally, portages were often constructed over uneven terrain, where a canoe man could slip and fall under a heavy load (Wheeler 1985, 93–95). One nineteenth-century observer referred to the Savannah Portage, which connected the St. Louis and Mississippi rivers, as "the worst carrying place in the Northwest, judging from the great number of canoes which lie decaying along a part of it" (30).

A unique project was initiated in 1960 when three scuba divers began searching for metal artifacts lost during early fur trade canoe accidents "beneath the waters of the old Grand Portage trade route along what is now the boundary between the state of Minnesota and the province of Ontario" (Wheeler 1975, 7). Guided by firsthand accounts of accidents in the fur trade, archaeologists discovered a remarkable collection of seventeen nested brass kettles. This discovery prompted continued investigations over the next thirteen years in what became the Quetico-Superior Underwater Research Project (Wheeler et al. 1975; Woolworth and Birk 1975, 57). The survey area was soon expanded to other areas, including the French River, which flows into Lake Huron in Canada. The project made three main contributions to the underwater archaeology of the fur trade (Wheeler 1975, 11–13). First, it led to the recovery of actual artifacts that were destined to be exchanged in the fur trade. These objects could be used for interpretive purposes. Second, discoveries provided information about which travel routes the French and NWC and HBC traders used or avoided. Third, the findings could be linked to specific recorded canoe accidents, particularly in locations where canoe men tried to shoot the rapids. A systematic underwater search demonstrated that accidents often occurred in "westward-flowing streams which combined a heavy volume of trade with good bottom conditions and a high proportion of accident-producing features," such as boulders and swift currents (13).

During the project a wide variety of objects was recovered that provides insight into both the goods that were being transported for trade and activities associated with transshipment. Many of the objects are documented in trade lists, but additional information can be obtained from the objects themselves, such as where they were manufactured. Makers' marks appear on files and other artifacts, identifying the workshop where they were produced. Though the ice chisels that were found generally lacked makers' marks, they were recovered from several locations. Nineteen were recovered from the Basswood River in northern Minnesota (Woolworth and Birk 1975, 70–72). Chisels were essential for survival in northern areas, where they were used for ice fishing, cutting ice to obtain water in the winter, and chopping into beaver huts. Another common tool was the double-barbed iron spear, which was used to take muskrat, beaver, and large fish such as sturgeon. Although spears seldom preserve in terrestrial archaeological sites, six have been found in the Basswood River. Their uniformity suggests that they may be the product of the same smith. Seth Eastman depicts nearly identical specimens in his ca. 1850 painting that shows hunters using metal spears mounted on long wooden handles (72; see also C. Gilman 1982, fig. 57).

Other items that were submerged were not likely intended for trade. For example, along the French River between Lake Nipissing and Georgian Bay divers found six northwest trade muskets, two that were loaded when they were lost. This was determined from X-rays of the two barrels. One of the weapons was loaded with bird shot, and the other had a single musket ball (Kenyon 1975, 54). Game was often scarce along well-traveled canoe routes, and voyageurs often loaded their muskets in anticipation of shooting unsuspecting deer, waterfowl, or other wild animals (Wheeler 1985, 69). Other loaded muskets have been found in the Granite and Winnipeg Rivers (Wheeler 1985, 69; Woolworth and Birk 1975, 81–82).

One of the more productive locations for the recovery of fur trade artifacts was the area adjacent to Fort Charlotte along the Pigeon River in northeast Minnesota. Fort Charlotte was the site of the depots of the XYC and the NWC at the western terminus of the Grand Portage. Underwater investigations recovered information about the location and construction techniques of a dock along the shoreline. They also recovered an array of artifacts that provide insight into shifting settlement patterns on the river. Perhaps most notable are the numerous organic artifacts that were preserved in their aquatic resting place, such as wooden and birch bark elements of canoes, parts of wooden kegs, and leather shoe fragments (Woolworth and Birk 1975, 85–87). The canoe parts include a complete canoe thwart, or crossbar, that was retrieved immediately south of the NWC dock structure at Fort Charlotte. Wooden toggles, or rope cleats, which were attached to the lines on a canoe sailing rig, have also been found. Also notable was the recovery of several nearly complete and well-preserved canoe paddles (figure 4.4).

The project also recovered oak keg parts, including staves, head panels, a tapered stopper, and a spigot for containers that must have held liquid such as high wine, though kegs also contained gunpowder, flour, wild rice, and other products (87). The spigot required a special key, indicating that the contents of the keg were controlled by its owner or a trusted person.

Last, leather shoe parts were found, including several thick heels and one shoe with a soft leather sole likely from a type of double-layered moccasin referred to as a *soulier de boeuf* (literally beef shoe) (figure 5.3). Moccasins

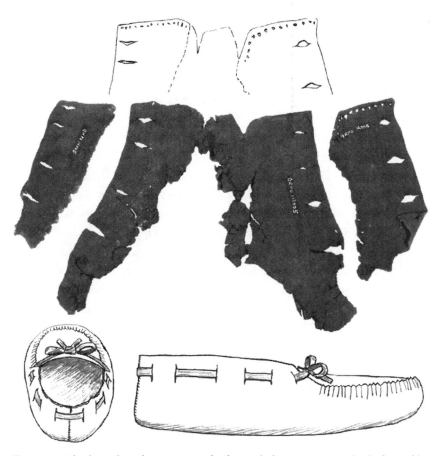

Figure 5.3. A leather sole and two associated side panels from a moccasin that had an ankle-high draw cord to secure it to the wearer were recovered from the Pigeon River near Fort Charlotte. Drawing and photograph by Douglas A. Birk. Courtesy of the National Park Service, Grand Portage National Monument, GRPO 14005.

were common footwear in canoes because they were so comfortable. Heeled shoes were perhaps destined for someone of higher rank. The shoe buckles that were recovered were consistent with more formal European attire. This may suggest that imported shoes were more often transported in canoes than moccasins, which were made in native villages, wintering posts, and other settlements deep in the North American interior (cf. Cangany 2012). Moccasins are a distinctive form of American footwear—an intercultural artifact that became widely available when native technology and European production methods were combined (300–301).

Despite the popularity of the Grand Portage route, the NWC built Fort William on the Kaministiquia River about forty miles to the north in what would become Canada between 1801 and 1807, after the border between the United States and Canada had been established at the Pigeon River by the Treaty of Paris in 1783 (Innis 1962, 228–229; Wheeler 1985, 78). The fort, which was named for William McGillivray, chief superintendent of the NWC, served as the company's headquarters until it merged with the HBC in 1821. After the merger, the fort declined in importance. Fort William was located to meet all the requirements of an entrepôt because of the distance involved in travel between Montreal and the northwest in one season (Morrison 2007, 27). The fort operated as both the NWC's major transshipment point for goods and furs and as the headquarters for its "annual business meeting between wintering partners and Montreal agents," just as Grand Portage had previously done (27). The fort was symmetrical in appearance; its structures were arranged in a balanced way that was characteristic of eighteenth-century architectural styles. It "featured an imposing main building facing a front gate set in high walls surrounding the complex" (25; see Hamilton et al. 2005, fig. 24). The architecture had clear symbolic meaning, similar to the architecture at other forts of the period (see Culpin and Borjes 1984; Monks 1992).

A modern facsimile of Fort William is billed as the "the world's largest fur trade post" (Fort William Historical Park 2008). Fort William Historical Park, which contains forty-two replicated buildings, is located on the Kaministiquia River about nine miles from the original location of the fort. In 1902, the Canadian Pacific Railway removed the last post buildings to make room for its expansion (Morrison 2007, 131). In 1968, Kenneth Dawson (1970) sought below-ground evidence of buildings to verify their locations, dimensions, and methods of construction. Excavations between the tracks in the railway yard exposed the foundations of the Great Hall, the palisade, and the remains of other NWC activities. However, the combination of modern impacts upon the original site and urban developments persuaded officials to select a better location to "convey the ambience of the fur trade era" (Morrison 2007, 134).

While the site lacks authenticity of place, the completeness of the replication based on historical sources communicates a number of messages about the fur trade to tens of thousands of visitors annually. As Laura Peers (1998, 116) has noted, because the park has attempted to reach both scholarly and public audiences, the interpretations it offers are fraught with contradictory messages. Site interpreters make no effort to mask the power of the NWC or its relations of dominance in interactions with the native producers, whose roles are dwarfed in comparison. Only recently has the site become a place for native peoples to explore their own histories. This has led to the communication of more inclusive messages to the public.

Visitors to the Fort William Historical Park learn that life in the NWC was structured by Scottish hierarchical traditions (Morrison 2007, 32). Personal living space, unequal access to preferred foods and clothing, and differential disposal practices created and reproduced the distinctions in rank associated with the NWC (Hamilton 2000). But unlike the HBC traders who were given fixed salaries and "no inducement for 'extra exertion,'" employees of the NWC were motivated by opportunities for social mobility (Morrison 2007, 36).

Alexander Mackenzie's description of the dining practices at Grand Portage in the early 1790s would also pertain to Fort William. The proprietors, clerks, guides, and interpreters dined together at several tables in the Great Hall. Seating at dinner was according to station, and differing ranks of personnel had access to different qualities of tea, teapots, and sugar (32). Those of higher rank consumed "bread, salt pork, beef, hams, fish, . . . venison, butter, peas, Indian corn, potatoes, teas, spirits, wine, . . . and plenty of milk, for which purpose several milch cows are kept" (Alexander Mackenzie n.d., lxxx, quoted in Innis 1962, 224). In contrast, the canoe men ate only maize and melted fat, a dish called hominy in the United States. David Thompson, the British-Canadian fur trader, surveyor, and mapmaker, noted that when the north men or *hivernants*, who had wintered in the interior, arrived at Grand Portage they had access to bread, pork, butter, liquor, and tobacco (Innis 1962, 228). This system of differential access contrasted markedly with the more egalitarian style of the AFC.

An individual's social station could be easily inferred by his clothing, as was the case in nearly all segments of fur trade society throughout the continent (Morrison 2007, 47; see also Wood et al. 2011, 111–112). Gentlemen donned the beaver hat that had found its way back from England to the source of its felt. Genuine London beaver hats could be obtained at Fort William for men, women, and children, whereas the London plated hats that voyageurs and Indian chiefs wore were of inferior quality; they consisted of only a thin layer of beaver felt glued over the foundation of the hat (Morrison 2007, 47).

Consumer choices, the built environment, and subsistence practices have been examined at a number of NWC sites, including several in the Fond du Lac district in Minnesota and Wisconsin (Birk 1984, 1989, 2008; Deseve 2009; Ewen 1986; Gibbon and Wynia 2010; Oerichbauer 1982). Fond du Lac was the largest trade district the NWC organized south of the present international border; its high ecological diversity provided plentiful habitat for beaver (Birk 1984, 52, 54). Its gateway facility, Fort St. Louis, was located at the head of Lake Superior and served as the collection point for furs from areas to the south and west (figure 3.1). Traders were required to visit native villages (*en dérouine*) in the winter in order to obtain quality furs from Ojibwe producers. Natives also collected and processed wild rice, "a storable aquatic grain *above all else* that allowed the population to flourish" in this area (Jenks 1977, quoted in Birk 1984, 54; emphasis in the original). Traders constructed their wintering posts in locations that were convenient for local natives, typically along navigable waterways (Wheeler 1985, 42). These settlements were often short-lived. Two early nineteenth-century wintering posts that have been examined archaeologically are John Sayer's Snake River post and the Forts Folle Avoine. Both were located on small rivers in the Fond du Lac district and operated for one or two seasons, and both have been reconstructed for interpretive purposes.

Douglas A. Birk (1984, 1989) has conducted considerable research on the Snake River post, including archaeological investigations there in the 1980s (figure 4.3). John Sayer was a principal agent and wintering partner for the NWC when he first visited the Snake River in the spring of 1804. He had operated in the Fond du Lac Superior region since about 1780 and chose to remain there after the Treaty of Paris in 1783, when the French ceded the western Great Lakes area, including the Straits of Mackinac and the settlement at Detroit, to the United States. In 1793, Sayer supervised the building of Fort St. Louis and ordered NWC personnel to various locations in the district to open new posts (e.g., Sandy Lake, 1794; Leech Lake, 1798). In 1803, after spending several winters at Leech Lake in northern Minnesota, he moved to Folle Avoine (literally "wild oats," a reference to the wild rice found there), a trade area that included the Yellow River in Wisconsin in 1803.

Joseph La Prairie had established a palisaded fort for the winter trade there the year before with a crew of seven or eight men, some of whom were married to Ojibwe or *métis* women (Deseve 2009, 7–8). The XYC was also scouting the area and chose to establish its trade house less than 100 feet south of

La Prairie's fort, likely so the two companies could cooperate in efforts to defend themselves from the Dakotas. But perhaps the location was chosen merely as calculated advantage to the NWC fur traders, who had already established trade relations with the Ojibwes (9). The purpose of Sayer's arrival the following year was to increase the NWC's returns from the district since he believed that La Prairie was too generous in extending credit and too lavish in distributing gifts to the Indians (10). Two XYC journals provide details of daily life at Forts Folle Avoine, including the names of Ojibwe trappers and information about the quality of the wild rice crop, fears about native attacks, and defiance within the ranks. Soon after the site was abandoned in 1805, fire destroyed all of the wooden structures (15).

Local residents began searching for the site in 1969, and limited excavations in 1970 found material traces (16). Work conducted by Edgar Oerichbauer (1982) under the auspices of the State Historical Society of Wisconsin and the Burnett County Historical Society led to the recovery of thousands of artifacts and architectural remains from the fur trade era. Oerichbauer's goals were to document nineteenth-century fur trade activities in northwest Wisconsin and recover architectural evidence for public interpretation. Archaeology led to the identification of the NWC post, which consisted of three cabins surrounded by a palisade, and the nearby XYC post. His preliminary report described the types of construction techniques used (*poteau sur sole* and *poteau en terre*), identified the gunflints as English varieties, and summarized the faunal remains as consisting of those of deer and animals that were pursued for their fur (180, 197, 228–230).

Charles Ewen's (1986) analysis of the faunal remains from the site showed differences in the types of animals XYC and NWC employees consumed. He also conducted an intrasite analysis to evaluate the extent to which a *bourgeois* such as Sayer had unequal access to desirable food resources and other goods. His study demonstrated that faunal, architectural, and material differences reinforced the rank Sayer and his family enjoyed, though the conditions were by no means luxurious by modern standards.

Sayer shifted his trading activities to a new site along the Snake River in east-central Minnesota in October 1804, where he stayed until the following spring (Birk 1989, 15). Sayer's journal recorded that his men were hard at work building a fort for the first month. Excavations have revealed that the size and layout of the fort were more spacious and more enterprising than the Forts Folle Avoine on the Yellow River. According to Birk (16), the principal building at the Snake River Fort was a row house built of logs that measured 18 × 76 feet (figure 4.3). The exterior walls were built with horizontal logs mortised into upright posts, a style called *pièce-sur-pièce*. The interior partitions and the palisade used *poteau en terre* construction. The palisade measured up to 60 × 100 feet and had bastions at the north and south corners. The main entrance was located opposite the river, facing the row house. Archaeological evidence and entries in Sayer's journal indicate that the six rooms in the row house served as dwellings, a storeroom, and a shop. Remarkably, Sayer and his Ojibwe wife commanded four of the six rooms, three of the four fireplaces, and two concealed subfloor cellars that were used to store high wine and wild rice. The reconstructed row house has the voyageurs and other *engagés* occupying two rooms with a shared fireplace (to the far left in figure 4.3). Sayer used the two rooms on the far right for storage and trade. The storeroom was unheated.

Collectors found the remains of Sayer's Snake River Fort in a cultivated field in the mid-twentieth century. They gathered artifacts there for several years before reporting their discoveries to professional archaeologists (Douglas A. Birk, personal communication, 2014). Following excavation of the site in the 1960s, the Minnesota Historical Society reconstructed the log fort to its original configuration. A sizeable collection of metal, glass, ceramic, lithic, bone, and birch bark artifacts from the site are linked with subsistence practices, craft and construction tools, architecture, and household activities of participants in the fur trade. In quantity, type, and range, the artifacts are consistent with items from an 1804 to 1805 NWC wintering post occupied by a noted *bourgeois*. The excavated artifacts with known provenience have helped researchers determine how space was organized for leisure and commercial activities on the basis of ethnicity, status, and gender. Interestingly, a comparison of the fur trade materials found during excavation with the inventory John Sayer compiled of the trade goods he took to the Snake River shows that archaeologists have recovered physical evidence of only about 25 percent of the items in Sayer's list. The recovered items, made mostly of glass, stone, and metal, survived largely because of their durability. Organic and consumable materials such as cloth blankets and liquid beverages did not survive. The artifacts have provided examples for reproductions used today in the site's public interpretations and ongoing living history programs.

Traders such as Sayer were not completely self-reliant on imported goods or their own provisions; they often depended on native producers. Ojibwes along the south shore of Lake Superior provisioned traders with sturgeon, whitefish, and maple sugar in lieu of furs in order to obtain manufactured goods (Kay 1977, 290). The cultural practices of many native groups were remarkably resilient under all but the most disruptive pressures. The seasonal round of the Ojibwes continued until at least 1836 (284). They continued to plant in the spring in traditional agricultural fields and hunt and gather in the summer. In the late summer, they harvested wild rice and other crops in preparation for a fall deer hunt. In the winter, they hunted smaller fur-bearers such as muskrat. Groups returned to maple sugaring camps in the late winter and early spring. Were it not for the persistence of these practices, white traders would have suffered. Throughout the region they depended on wild rice and other resources obtained from natives in the eighteenth and early nineteenth centuries (332).

While canoes were important for the transportation of many of these goods, overland movement also occurred, particularly in the region between the Middle Missouri area and the western Great Lakes region, where the products of the Plains were linked to markets in the East. For example, by 1869, an annual caravan of some 2,500 Red River carts connected Pembina and St. Paul, Minnesota (fig. 3.4; Peterson 1990, 59). Each cart hauled nearly 1,000 pounds of pemmican, buffalo robes, grease, quilled moccasins, and jackets for the tourist trade (59). When they returned, the carts carried various foodstuffs, tobacco, cloth, whiskey, nails, guns, and ammunition (59).

By the end of the War of 1812, the AFC had filled the gap created by the withdrawal of the NWC to Fort William. Mackinac was now in American hands and the AFC was able to extend its reach throughout the Great Lakes region. Adopting an organizational structure that was similar to that of its predecessor, the AFC placed traders throughout the territory to maximize the exploitation of furs. From small wintering posts, traders obtained furs from native hunters as they had for nearly two centuries, though the types of furs they accepted in the early nineteenth century had changed since the heyday of beaver in the seventeenth and eighteenth centuries. By 1806, fur trade credits were figured in muskrat (Kay 1977, 251). Despite heavy trapping pressure, muskrats were plentiful because of a high reproduction rate and a decreasing mortality rate as predators such as foxes were eliminated. Nineteenth-century inventories document shifts in the types of furs collected from many small, ephemeral sites that have not garnered much archaeological attention (Clayton 1964, fig. 4; Wagner 2011, tables 6.2, 6.3).

In 2000, U.S. Forest Service archaeologists initiated a program to locate sites associated with the early nineteenth-century fur trade on Michigan's Grand Island near the shore of Lake Superior (Franzen 2004). Maps that predate 1840 and other accounts indicate a single trading post on the island that became known as Little Island Rock Post. Henry Levake and his Native American wife likely occupied the site. The first reference to a post in this area of Grand Island is associated with the settlement of the AFC there in 1816–1818. The location was selected because there was a long history of trading there with the Ojibwes and "it was most 'suitable and convenient' for both traders and Indians" (223). By the early nineteenth century, "every group of Indians [in the western Great Lakes and elsewhere] had its own trader" as Euro-American population and competition between traders increased (Gilman 1994, 324, quoted in Franzen 2004, 223).

Survey and test excavations at the site led to the recovery of material culture that revealed the site's chronological placement, the types of activities it supported, and the ethnic identity of its occupants (224–234). A comparison of a small sample of glass beads from the site with large nineteenth-century samples from numerous sealed contexts at Forts Union and Vancouver indicates that the assemblage was consistent with occupation in the 1820s. Two U.S. military buttons date to the period 1812–1815. Pearlware ceramics date to the first quarter of the nineteenth century and represent bowls that may have been used for drinking tea. A case knife with a brass inlay handle resembles specimens found at other early nineteenth-century sites in the region. Other less temporally diagnostic artifacts included a mix of hand-wrought and machine cut nails, a gunflint, lead scrap, lead shot, fragments of white clay pipes, flat glass, curved glass, and a straight pin.

These objects were found in association with two log structures with partially standing walls and several pit features and activity areas (234–239, figs. 9–10). The horizontal log walls had V-notches on log bottoms that matched hewn surfaces to form locking joints that appear to have been chopped with an ax rather than sawn. This building technique contrasts with the *pièce-sur-pièce* method of the French Canadians that diffused from the St. Lawrence Valley to the Pacific Coast at fur trade sites (see Mann 2008). As Anglo-Americans entered the region, they brought the notched horizontal log technique, which requires less time and skill than *pièce-sur-pièce*. The white cedar selected for building construction is particularly decay resistant, which explains why elements have survived some two centuries after abandonment. The large concentration of clay near the chimney in Structure A is indicative of repeated repair in a residential function, whereas the fireplace in Structure B, which was probably used mainly for storage, had little maintenance. The chimneys were located opposite the entry from Lake Superior at the south-southeast area, where outdoor activities occurred. Five distinctive pits have been interpreted as cache pits that were used to store and conceal goods underground.

The relatively small size and ephemeral nature of Little Island Rock Post reminds us that considerable activity at wintering posts was related to subsistence and shelter rather than trade (Franzen 2004, 240). This site and others like it highlight the functional variation that existed in fur trade settlements and contrast with the larger and more diverse trading post complexes that characterize much of the fur trade literature, with their "commercial depots, military garrisons, missions, and agricultural operations" (240). Site investigations revealed information about architecture and spatial organization, and the material culture has implications for ethnicity and gender. The specific method of clay chimney construction used at the site (clay cats) is tentatively attributed to French Canadians, the horizontal log style reflects Anglo-American influence, and the cache pits are traditional Native American storage facilities (240–241). The material assemblage is indicative of a division of labor consistent with a European male and a Native American woman, based on the presence of sewing and beadwork near the fireplace and other widely scattered items. The evidence points to the mixing of cultural practices at a small fur trade site where gender and ethnicity were negotiated in a private arena with little public scrutiny.

The Territorial Expansion of the Hudson's Bay Company

For much of the late eighteenth and early nineteenth centuries, the Hudson's Bay Company vied for control of the fur trade from its factories in the far north. Not content with enticing natives to visit the shores of the bay to trade and thus risking the loss of profitable furs to their southern competitors, they moved inland to establish scores of trading posts on the lakes and rivers of what would become central and western Canada as far south as the Columbia River and as far north as the Yukon River (figure 3.1; Arndt 1996; Innis 1962, 283–338; Morton 1973; Ray 1988, fig. 1). A number of these posts have been the focus of archaeological investigations (e.g., Carlson 2000; Hamilton 2000; Karklins 1983; Klimko 2004).

Though much of the archaeological work conducted at HBC fur trade sites through the 1970s was predominantly descriptive (Klimko 2004, 165–166), the data generated can be used for comparative purposes to gain an understanding of the material similarities and differences within and between sites. One site that has been examined closely is Nottingham House in the Athabasca region at the western end of Lake Athabasca, near the present community of Fort Chipewyan, Alberta (Karklins 1983). In 1802, Peter Fidler, the chief surveyor of the HBC, established the site in an effort to break the rival NWC's monopoly in the area. Over the next four years, the HBC tried but failed to compete successfully with the NWC, who had been in the area since 1788 (Allen 1983, 284). The site was excavated in 1972–1973 and again in 1977. This work exposed two HBC structures (a main house and a storehouse), two NWC watch houses, a garden area, and four trash pits. The goals of the investigation were to confirm the historic identification of the site; determine the layout of and the construction techniques used at the site; and obtain a representative sample of material culture and subsistence remains.

Excavations determined the location of the main house and the function of four contiguous rooms, which researchers labeled A through D. Room A was Peter Fidler's chamber; room B was the cook room; room C was the warehouse/trading room; and room D was the men's quarters. All but room C had fireplaces along an exterior wall. The building resembles the contemporaneous NWC Snake River post in east-central Minnesota (figure 4.3; Karklins 1983, figs. 7, 8, 24). Artifacts were classified into six functional categories: personal, domestic, subsistence and defense, tools and hardware, business, and transportation (67). Among the objects directly implicated in the fur trade were two moose metatarsal fleshers used to remove flesh and fat from hides in preparation for tanning (160). Interestingly, these were associated with room A in the main house (Rick 1983, 251) and suggest that someone in Fidler's household was processing hides. However, much of the processing likely took place beyond the site limits since the faunal assemblage includes only one or two individuals from species classified primarily as fur-bearers (246). A single muskrat represents a species that was abundant in the trade.

The most common species found at Nottingham House were hare and moose. These were probably subsistence remains; the cut marks observed on the bones were consistent with butchering and meat removal. In contrast, "all cuts found on the furbearing red fox, wolverine, and lynx can be interpreted as relating to skinning rather than butchering" (248). Though they were not numerous, these "non-edible" species that were primarily valued for their fur were concentrated in the storehouse and in pit features (260).

Very little bone of any type (fish, bird, or mammal) was recovered from Room A of the main house, indicating that Fidler's room was kept cleaner than other rooms (232, 243, 259). These data, combined with information from historical sources, indicate that the post was dependent on local rather than imported animal foods. This is consistent with the HBC strategy of locating posts in areas where employees could be generally self-sufficient in order to minimize the costs associated with provisioning. Of course, foods such as dried meat and pemmican that were obtained from local natives at various times during the site's occupation would have left no archaeological trace, making it difficult to quantify their contribution to the diets of post residents (257).

The ambitions of HBC directors drove the company to expand into the Yukon River region in the north and to the Pacific Coast in the west. In both locations, various native groups were willing to incorporate Europeans into well-established trading networks. The native peoples along the Northwest Coast, whose economy was based on abundant salmon that could be harvested throughout the year, were among the most complex hunter-gatherer societies in the world (Ames and Maschner 1999). Northwest Coast peoples from northern California to southern Alaska maintained a stratified society characterized by hereditary leadership, an enslaved class, and well-instituted concepts of wealth and status (Wilson 2011, 5). Obsidian, marine shell, salmon, and furs were among the goods that native societies traded prior to European commerce.

By the late eighteenth century, native peoples along the Columbia River were obtaining European goods indirectly from Europeans and Americans in coastal waters and from inland sources as far away as the Plains. After 1825, "goods were brought from England by Cape Horn to Fort Vancouver, then up the Columbia to various posts and up the Okanagan to Kamloops" (Innis 1962, 297). This route was used until 1846, when the boundary line between the United States and Canada was established and goods began being shipped up the lower Fraser River to the HBC's New Caledonia department (British Columbia).

In 1811, the first fur traders into the southern interior plateau in British Columbia set up seasonal trading posts at the confluence of the North and

South Thompson Rivers in Kamloops. In 1821, the HBC erected the Thompson's River Post as a permanent trading establishment. This was the area's first year-round trading post, and native peoples began to settle immediately adjacent to the post, although many native villages already existed in the vicinity. Prior to archaeological investigations, no historical documentation was available regarding the size, layout, or configuration of the post or its surrounding aboriginal community (Carlson 2000, 2006, 220). The local Secwepemcs (aka Shuswaps) and other Interior Salish peoples provided "furs of all kinds, dressed skins, moccasins, roots and berries, dried meat, fat, dried salmon, and dogs and horses" in exchange for "blankets, cloth, glass beads, steel traps, flintlock muskets, powder, ball and shot, axes, tomahawks, steels and flints, knives, tobacco, iron, copper kettles, brass finger-rings, bracelets, etc." (Teit 1909, 537, quoted in Carlson 2000, 283).

Catherine Carlson (2000, 2006, 208) has conducted site investigations from a postcolonial indigenous perspective at a Secwepemc village in proximity to Thompson's River Post in British Columbia. Her objective was to examine the social continuities and transformations in this nineteenth-century native settlement in the context of the fur trade. In the 1990s, she also investigated several surface anomalies in the area where the post once stood and determined that they are the remains of fur-trade-era structures, both aboriginal and European. Through excavations she recovered material evidence of architectural features, storage facilities, artifacts, and subsistence remains (Carlson 2000, 287). The form and contents of the structures told much about their function and the identities of their occupants. For example, the fact that only two nails were present and that no window glass was recovered from five circular subsurface depressions suggests traditional construction methods consistent with the pit houses nineteenth-century ethnographers described. Cache pits of native design were located in and around the houses. They contained both traditional and adopted items, though most technological objects were consistent with a semi-permanent settlement pattern (e.g., no European ceramics were recovered). In contrast, the contents of a rectangular European-style log structure that is thought to represent a trading post building included "large numbers of machine-cut nails and spikes, medicine and other bottle glass, window glass, hinges, kettle and pot parts, nuts and bolts, tin cans, barrel strapping, lead shot, buttons, wire, and clay pipes, as well as blue willow, whiteware, and earthenware ceramics fragments" (Carlson 2006, 226).

Most of the faunal remains represented wild mammal, fish, and bird species, indicating the continuation of a varied subsistence economy involving many traditional hunting and fishing activities (233). Few bones of animals that were typically trapped for the fur trade were found, probably because they were skinned on traplines. The long bones of animal remains had been fractured to extract marrow, testifying to the continuance of ancient food practices. The faunal remains associated with the fur traders indicate that they ate the same foods as the native residents near the trading post, though they consumed slightly less salmon and more deer and beef. Domesticated species (horse, cow, goat/sheep, and pig) are only minimally represented, underscoring the importance of local food resources to the fur traders.

The archaeological evidence from native sites adjacent to the Thompson's River Post is consistent with a combination of native cultural practices and limited uses of imported objects such as nails, window glass, door hardware, and ceramics (Carlson 2000, 287). The data suggest that the Secwepemcs maintained their cultural autonomy and could operate quite independently from the HBC during the early years of trade and interaction. The strategies they developed in their interactions in the fur trade prepared them to maintain a distinct cultural identity that continues into the present (Carlson 2006, 239).

The HBC recognized the importance of this region in the global fur market. In an effort to compete with Russian and U.S. fur traders, establish a permanent presence along the Columbia River, and gather inland furs before they reached sailors on the coast, the HBC relocated its headquarters in the Pacific Northwest from Fort George in Astoria at the mouth of the Columbia River to Fort Vancouver about 100 miles upriver in 1825 (Wilson 2011, 7). In the 1830s and 1840s, Fort Vancouver became one of the largest British colonial settlements in the Pacific Northwest. In addition to processing furs, activities at the settlement included logging, ship building, farming, and various crafts (Wilson 2011, 8–10). Peoples of diverse backgrounds inhabited Fort Vancouver. While some were of English and Scottish descent, many were French Canadian, Hawaiian, Portuguese, *métis*, or members of one of more than thirty Native American groups that included Crees, Delawares, Haidas, and Iroquois.

In the North American fur trade, identity was bound to ethnicity, gender, and occupation and was reinforced by a rigid, racialized social hierarchy that was manifested in architecture, furnishings, subsistence, personal adornment, and many objects used and discarded in daily life (Langford 2011, 29–

Figure 5.4. Unsigned sketch (ca. 1851) of the north end of the village area outside the walls of Fort Vancouver. Courtesy of the National Park Service.

30; Mann 2003; Sleeper-Smith 2001; Vibert 2010). In the HBC's Columbia district of the Pacific Northwest, clerks and officers occupied buildings inside Fort Vancouver's palisade and owned and consumed goods appropriate to their rank. The *engagés* lived in a multiethnic village of over 600 people located beyond the fort walls (figure 5.4). Their houses were constructed in a vernacular style (Mullaley 2011). The knowledge needed to construct and maintain the built environment was transmitted via nonverbal communication that conveyed important social information essential in the practical activities of everyday life (Nelson 2007, cited in Langford 2011, 31).

The HBC's policy of allowing employees to intermarry with native peoples in order to secure furs and other resources contributed to a diverse society marked by multiethnic families, much like the fur trade culture imported from Canada (Wilson 2014, 22). This colonial system contrasted markedly with the racially exclusive practices and policies of the white American settlers who pushed into the area beginning in the late 1840s.

The Deerskin Trade in Southeastern
North America and Adjacent Areas

In the seventeenth century, the acquisition of deerskins from Native Americans in the Middle Atlantic and southeastern regions of North America was a major commercial activity, and deerskins were one of the most important commodities English and Spanish colonists sought (Braund 1993; Lapham 2005; Pavao-Zuckerman 2007, 7; Waselkov 1989). As in the beaver trade in the north, the deerskin trade was fueled by the desire of New World colonists to find a profitable export commodity and native people who were capable of intensifying production of a resource they had been exploiting for millennia and were willing to do so. Native groups were involved as middlemen who obtained hides from inland groups and as producers who intensified local deer hunting (Blair 2009, 171). Evidence of this intensification appears in the significant increases in deer bones and tools associated with deer processing, along with shifts in the age, sex, and seasonality profiles of deer harvests between the pre-Contact period (prior to ca. 1600) and the fur trade era (Lapham 2005, 9).

As in other areas of North America, natives welcomed manufactured goods in exchange for their carefully processed hides (Braund 1993, 121–130; Lapham 2005, 7–8). Members of the Creek Confederacy, which was located between the Coosa and Chattahoochee Rivers, preferred cloth, guns, and ammunition, although they also welcomed iron tools and metallic ornaments such as silver gorgets and armbands (Braund 1993, 121–125). Deerskins were likely exchanged for some of the 70,000 glass beads that have been recovered in mortuary contexts at Mission Santa Catalina de Guale, a sixteenth- and seventeenth-century native cemetery on St. Catherines Island, located off the coast of Georgia (Blair et al. 2009). As was common elsewhere, beads and other goods exchanged for hides circulated widely in the Southeast and were acquired by groups who had not yet come in direct contact with Europeans.

Heather Lapham (2005) sought to examine how the international demand for deerskins that emerged rather suddenly in the seventeenth century both altered social, political, and economic relations and left recognizable traces in the archaeological record. Her work has documented the impact of the demand for hides and the roles of native peoples in this economic system in the Virginia Piedmont. Government documents record that colonists in Virginia and the Carolinas shipped more than 1.1 million deer hides of varying quality from 1699 to 1715 (Lapham 2005, table 1.1). Hides were graded based on an animal's age, sex, and the season it was taken. Their market value was also based on how completely they were processed (10). Most deerskins found their way to London, which had become the capital of the leather industry by the end of the eighteenth century (Braund 1993, 87). Leather was made into clothing, gloves, and footwear. Buckskin, which had a suede finish, was suited for fashionable breeches that English men of all social classes wore. English harness makers, saddlers, and bookbinders often used lower-quality leather in their crafts (88).

On the basis of ethnohistorical data, Lapham (15–17) developed a "hunting for hides model" of altered strategies for harvesting deer involving procurement of select hides and intensified hide processing. She analyzed faunal remains and tools, features associated with deer processing, and the disposition of surplus generated through hide exchange as revealed in mortuary contexts in order to assess change and continuity in native social and economic organization in the first half of the seventeenth century. She noted (23, 99–101) an increase in bone tools (beamers) used to scrape deerskins during the initial processing stage and an increase in mussel-shell scrapers and smudge pits throughout the region during the early to mid-seventeenth century. More white-tailed deer were harvested in this period compared with earlier (i.e., Late Woodland) periods (72). There was also a slight increase in other fur-bearing animals, although bears declined in importance (74–76). Finally, and perhaps most significantly, Lapham (79–81) observed a "prime-age dominated mortality profile" for deer in which Native American hunters selected larger animals that produced larger hides and more meat. This contrasts with the Late Woodland pattern, which resembles a catastrophic mortality profile that results from indiscriminant hunting "in which successively older age classes contain progressively fewer animals" (79). These archaeological data indicate that selective harvests marked the initial phase of the trade when deer were plentiful. Furthermore, there appears to be regional variation, suggesting that not all groups participated in the same harvesting strategy.

At the intrasite level, the spatial distribution of skinning marks, processing tools, and facilities imply that all households were engaged in processing activities. This may reflect social solidarity at the community level, even though Lapham (140) observed the differential distribution of artifacts in mortuary contexts, which she interpreted as evidence of enhanced prestige and social mobility for young males who benefited from the deerskin trade.

The involvement of native groups in the deerskin trade had profound implications for economic and subsistence strategies throughout the Southeast. Barnet Pavao-Zuckerman (2007) used ethnohistorical and zooarchaeological evidence to demonstrate the impact of intensification of localized resources on the adoption of animal husbandry among the Creeks. As the Creeks became producers of deerskins, furs, and other commodities, they became incorporated into an expanding European market and modified their economic strategies. Their involvement in the deerskin trade suppressed the adoption of animal husbandry until exchange relations collapsed. Pavao-Zuckerman's work illustrates the systemic effects of the trade on native societies in the eighteenth century.

Both the French and the English vied for trade alliances in the Southeast. More skins were shipped from the ports of British colonies than by any other imperial rivals; Charlestown and Savannah shipped over 500,000 pounds of skins annually in the 1750s and 1760s (Braund 1993, 98). Such enormous quantities indicate that the production of furs and skins was an intense activity for natives of the region that likely led to transformation from a kin-based mode of reciprocal exchange to capitalist accumulation (Pavao-Zuckerman 2007, 9). However, Pavao-Zuckerman points out that the Creeks were "active participants in the fur trade, not passive 'peripheries' subject to the whims of European 'cores'" (9).

Zooarchaeological remains from sites occupied over time can be used to infer changes in exploitation strategies related to the intensification of the deerskin trade. Data on the frequency of taxa from sites throughout southeastern North America suggest that Native Americans practiced relatively consistent subsistence strategies from the seventeenth through the nineteenth centuries (10–11). The presence of deer remains in assemblages at the Fusihatchee site in east-central Alabama increased nearly sixfold from the seventeenth to the eighteenth centuries, demonstrating a significant increase in Creek involvement in the deerskin trade. Skinning marks consistent with hide removal (see Lapham 2005) using metal knives date to the eighteenth century. Such marks are nearly absent in earlier assemblages. This type of direct evidence of skinning was observed on 30 percent of the astragali (ankle bones) and 22 percent of the proximal phalanges (toe bones) (Pavao-Zuckerman 2007, 21). These data indicate that deer hunting and processing was intensified to meet demands for exchange. Over time, heavy exploitation diminished deer herd sizes and hunting time increased to meet demand. The demands placed on hunters and on land use practices associated with the deerskin trade delayed native people's adoption of domesticated animals. By the nineteenth century, overhunting, white encroachment on native lands, the rise of the slave-based cotton industry, and the use of cow leather as a suitable substitute (e.g., in book binding) had contributed to the collapse of the deerskin trade. As a consequence, beginning in the nineteenth century the Creeks of central Alabama were forced to produce new commodities— baskets, pottery, and domesticated animals and their products (meat, milk, leather, eggs, butter) for local and regional markets—to exchange for the goods such as cloth and guns they had relied on for nearly two centuries (31; Gregory Waselkov, personal communication, 2014). Though they continued to hunt and process deer into the nineteenth century, they likely did so for domestic use rather than for trade.

Colonial traders in Charlestown, Savannah, Mobile, and New Orleans obtained deerskins from native groups throughout the Southeast, including the Chickasaws, Choctaws, Creeks, and Cherokees. Both the French and the English attempted to create and maintain formal alliances with the Chickasaws, who were eager to gain "a reliable source of guns and ammunition," at first for the purposes of warfare and raiding for slaves and later for hunting deer (Johnson 1997, 217).

Recent study of a series of Chickasaw archaeological sites provides insight into the ways the Chickasaws met the demands of an expanding colonial economy in the late seventeenth and early eighteenth centuries (Johnson et al. 2008). Jay Johnson and his colleagues developed a fine-grained chronology based on ceramic seriation to define four temporal periods marked by changing frequencies of stone and metal tools and animal remains. In the Early period (1650–1700), chert tools dominate the assemblages. These include thumbnail scrapers, a specialized type of scraping tool used to process the hides of deer and other fur-bearing animals (figure 5.5). The small working edges of these tools would have made it possible to concentrate considerable force in a small area in the final stage of hide preparation (Johnson 1997, 225). Deer bones predominated in the assemblages Johnson and his colleagues analyzed, although the remains of other fur-bearing animals such as raccoon, mink, fox, beaver, skunk, bobcat, cougar, and wolf were also present. Rabbits and squirrels, which were more common in earlier sites in the region, were absent. Though spall-type gunflints were not present in the Early period at these sites, the authors suggest that an increase in bear bones from the number found at pre-Contact sites indicates that the Chickasaws had likely acquired access to guns (Johnson et al. 2008, 19). Metal scrap first appeared at these sites in the Early Middle period (1700–1730). End scrapers were still common in this period. The most dramatic changes occur in the Late Middle period (1730–1740), when the Chickasaws adopted Natchez refuges, according to historical sources. This is supported by the presence on Chickasaw sites of Natchez ceramics produced with a distinctive paste. The refuges heightened Chickasaw tensions with the French, who were in conflict with the Natchez. In this period, the number of arrow points and scrapers found in assemblages decreased and the number of European tools increased. The number of deer bones increased significantly, "reflecting the fact that the deerskin trade had become a major focus of the Chickasaw economy" (21). By the Late period (1740–1750), the deer that were being taken show a considerably younger age profile, indicating lower numbers of available deer and/or an increase in demand (Waselkov 1978, cited in Johnson et al. 2008, 18).

The archaeological and ethnohistorical data suggest several important historical trends. The Chickasaws were located in Mississippi at the west-

0   4 cm

Figure 5.5. Thumbnail scrapers were specialized stone tools used by natives in the eighteenth century to process deer hides in Mississippi and adjacent areas in southeastern North America. Photo by Jay Johnson.

ern extreme of the British exchange network, and their spatial and social isolation as a result of their hostilities with the French meant that they had only limited access to metal tools prior to 1730 (Johnson 2003). In contrast, contemporaneous Creek sites contain iron axes, chisels, knives, hoes, kettles, gorgets, armbands, bells, buttons, a large variety of glass beads, scissors, swords, and guns (Smith 2000, 112, 115, cited in Johnson et al. 2008, 22). Goods diffused slowly from distant English Atlantic ports and had not fully penetrated to the far western edge of the British Empire until after 1730. However, all segments of society experienced the changes in economic activities associated with the fur trade. For instance, in the 1730s, Chickasaw women and children shifted their attention away from hunting rabbits and squirrels for subsistence and began processing more hides after Chickasaw men began harvesting deer at unprecedented rates (Johnson et al. 2008, 18). The fur trade remained a potent force in the economy of southeastern North America until it was eclipsed by the production of cash crops with enslaved labor in the nineteenth-century plantation system. This increased the demand for native lands, which in turn led to the removal of the primary producers and effectively ended the large-scale commercial exploitation of deer. At the same time, familiar and new fur-bearing species became the focus of mercantile ventures in places even more distant from the markets of Western Europe.

The Maritime Fur Trade along the Pacific Coast

As the deer and beaver trades were beginning to decline in the late eighteenth century, the maritime fur trade was ramping up along the Pacific Coast (Gibson 1988; Whitner 1984). The Russians, British, Spanish, Americans, and other seafaring peoples all converged on this region in a quest to profit from the dark, thick, and lustrous coat of the sea otter (*Enhydra lutris*). The habitat of this aquatic mammal extended from Japan to Mexico, though it was most plentiful from the Gulf of Alaska to Vancouver Island. Because sea otters have a low fertility rate and female pelts were more valuable than male pelts, the species was vulnerable to overexploitation (Vaughan 1982a, 18). Valued by Chinese nobility more for their appearance than their warmth, sea otter furs earned considerable profits on an initial investment. One sea otter pelt was worth the same as ten beaver pelts in 1829, although over the years, the kinds and prices of trade goods that traders and natives accepted in exchange fluctuated widely (Gibson 1988, 375; Gibson 1992, 240).

Native hunters were the primary producers of sea otters and had developed the technology to capture them. The Aleuts were especially proficient predators. They clubbed or netted their prey on shore or used harpoons at sea. They used *baidarkas*, indigenous watercraft that could take a year to construct (Black 2004, 71; Vaughan 1982a, 19). Russian missionary priest Ivan Veniaminov wrote that "not even a mathematician could add very much or scarcely anything to the perfection of its nautical qualities" (Vaughan 1982a, 19). The Russians often captured male Aleuts and their families and forced them to provide tribute (*iasak*) in the form of skins as a way of harvesting this resource. Harsh treatment, accidents, and sickness took a toll on local populations as early as the late eighteenth century (19) and exacerbated social tensions.

In March 1812, a Russian schooner arrived along the north California coast with the goal of establishing a new settlement that would serve as a staging area for hunting sea mammals and raising crops and livestock to provision the North Pacific colonies (Lightfoot et al. 2003, 2–3). On a cliff overlooking a small cove about 100 kilometers north of San Francisco Bay, twenty-five Russian men and eighty native Alaskans cut and shaped redwood timber for a palisade that would "enclose administrative offices and dwellings, barracks, warehouses, a kitchen, and other service buildings" (3). The colony was called Fort Ross.

The population that lived and worked inside the palisade walls at Fort Ross is known primarily through eyewitness accounts from Russian elites or visiting dignitaries. We know little about the significant numbers of non-European laborers at the site, which included creoles of mixed Russian and native ancestry, native Alaskans, Athabascans, and local California natives. These groups, which occupied spaces beyond the walls, accounted for nearly 90 percent of the settlement's population (3). Since the early 1950s, most of the archaeological fieldwork done at this site has focused on Russian architecture at the expense of the people without history.

In the 1980s, the Fort Ross Archaeological Project was initiated to examine how Pacific Coast hunter-gatherers responded to the mercantile policies of the Russian-American Company. Project staff investigated the archaeological remains outside the stockade walls (2, 4). They were also interested in how native practices influenced European lifeways. The goal was to examine how participation in the fur trade precipitated changes in material culture, settlement and subsistence patterns, gender roles, and social and political organization (5; Swagerty 1988, 351). The project was broadly comparative; particular attention was paid to the material remains of marginalized employees so they could be compared with the material remains of the Russian elite (Lightfoot et al. 2003, 4). Analysis focused on how the interactions of native labor with market forces and the emergence of multiethnic communities influenced cultural change.

Kent Lightfoot, Thomas Wake, and Ann Schiff (2003, 8) used a holistic and diachronic approach in their research design, which included ethnohistory, ethnography, native voices, and archaeology. Their analyses suggest that Russian colonization had significant consequences for indigenous groups (115–119, 150). Major residential sites shifted from pre-Contact locations as populations aggregated toward Fort Ross. This indicates that the Russians were successful in recruiting native peoples, sometimes using coercive tactics to ensure ample labor during the agricultural season. Small coastal camps and seafood processing stations were abandoned as a consequence of labor recruitment. This likely reflects changes in processing loci and/or a decline in the use of some maritime subsistence resources as new foods became available. Archaeologists have observed a decrease in firecracked rock that may have been the result of new methods of food preparation, just as the presence of cow and sheep bones in site assemblages reflect changes in diet. Nearby native groups still used obsidian to produce edged tools, but its source changed dramatically. Obsidian from the Napa Valley became dominant, perhaps as a result of Spanish interventions that disrupted the flow of obsidian from previously accessible sources (Farris 1989, 492). Natives used bottle glass in place of obsidian for tools. Despite these changes, there is little evidence that the RAC actively pushed native workers to adopt European ways. This is supported by the noted ambivalence of local natives toward European technology, which Russian observers interpreted as conservatism in adopting foreign customs:

> Their inattention and indifference to everything goes to extremes. They look at our watches, burning-glasses, and mirrors, or listen to our music without attention and do not ask how much or why all this is produced. Only such objects as might frighten them make some impression, but that probably more because of their timidity than thirst for knowledge. (Kostromitinov quoted in Lightfoot et al. 2003, 150)

The Kashaya Pomos generally avoided most cultural innovations and integrated few material objects from other cultures (e.g., bottle glass for making projectile points) into their daily lives. They even avoided the sophisticated technology for exploiting marine resources that native Alaskans had developed; the historical record makes no mention of their use of *baidarkas*, harpoons, darts, throwing sticks, or fishing equipment, and no evidence of these items has been recovered archaeologically at Pomo sites. The coastal Pomos were content to hunt sea mammals from "crude rafts of redwood driftwood" using clubs as weapons instead of imitating the hunting methods of their more northerly cousins (Loeb 1926 quoted in Lightfoot et al. 2003, 151).

Whereas the RAC obtained furs through forced labor and tribute, the Americans and British offered a wide range of goods dictated by native tastes in exchange for furs (Wolf 1982, 183). Shipmasters generally selected a suitable place to drop anchor and waited for native canoes to bring furs on board. This practice, called sojourning, was deemed to be better than cruising in terms of both yield and crew safety (Gibson 1992, 207–208). Regulatory measures, such as limitations on the number of natives allowed aboard at one time, were needed to ensure a smooth exchange. Unlike other areas of North America, few permanent settlements were established on the Pacific Coast for year-round trading, and traders seldom wintered with the natives to collect their furs (127).

In addition to furs, sojourning shipmasters obtained provisions from natives, primarily venison, fish, and potatoes (210). HBC Forts McLoughlin, Simpson, Stikine, and Taku in British Columbia and the Russian settlement of Sitka could obtain these foods at reasonable rates, indicating that the native economy was underwriting the fur trades in this region. In the early days of the trade, natives may have been less discriminating in the items they chose to receive. But by the 1820s, declining stock and competition made it incumbent upon coastal traders to offer the proper trade goods of the best quality, though this was complicated by changing demands of the Haidas, Tlingits, and other groups (214). A decrease in sea otter also led to a shift to land furs after 1820 (240).

Generally natives wanted goods for practical and aesthetic purposes that could be readily counted and compared in anticipation for use in the potlatch, a ceremony of competitive display that reinforced social status. Natives initially preferred metals. Iron was fashioned into ornamental necklets; utilitarian chisels were used to plane and carve wood in their iconic and intricate formline designs (see Brotherton 2000, fig. 13.4). They also used metals for fishhooks, arrowheads, lance tips, adze blades, and knives in place of stone and organic materials (Gibson 1992, 218). From Spanish sources, Northwest Coast groups obtained sheets of copper that measured 26 × 22 inches and as thick as a Spanish real (218). They used it for ornamental purposes; a one-quart copper kettle was worth five skins among the Nootkas in 1786. By the end of the century, metals were superseded by textiles and provisions as desirable trade goods, followed by firearms and spirits, although textiles remained important (215–216).

Natives quickly adopted European cloth and clothing styles to replace the skins they often traded right off their backs; woolen frocks of red and blue were favored (219–220). Europeans also traded firearms as shipmasters' greed exceeded their fear of arming natives, thereby relinquishing any military advantage they may have had. Both the Americans and English were suppliers of firearms to inland tribes, who must have used them on occasion to counter HBC, NWC, and AFC expansion from the east. Most of the lead from musket balls found on lower Columbia River sites appears to have come from English sources, perhaps because the NWC dominated the early terrestrial fur trade (Wilson et al. 2009). Interestingly, the Sitkan Tlingits and Chinooks, among others, preferred to continue to use spears, even after they had acquired muskets, because of the reliability of the former compared to guns, which sometimes fail to hit their targets (Gibson 1992, 222; Douglas Wilson, personal communication, 2014; see also C. Gilman 1982, 25). Nevertheless, natives mastered the use of firearms and often turned them on the traders, though they remained dependent on white armorers to repair their guns and produce custom-made items such as iron collars and chisels (Gibson 1992, 222–223). While there is some debate about the impact of guns on Northwest Coast society, they undoubtedly had become a part of systems of exchange and warfare by the early nineteenth century, and groups who lacked or had unreliable access to munitions were at a decided disadvantage among their neighbors.

Shipmasters introduced alcohol to induce natives to trade less cautiously. Alcohol was initially used ceremoniously to open trade relations, but its consumption soon led to drunkenness and indolence (224–226). Rum, often diluted, was the trade item whites preferred because it returned the highest yields owing to its cheapness.

Guns and textiles remained the mainstay of the trade, even though considerable quantities of trinkets—beads, buttons, holed Chinese coins, finger rings, mirrors, combs, and sundry other consumables—circulated as gifts that Europeans used to initiate trade and barter for provisions (228; Wolf 1982, 187). Natives also continued to use traditional local exchange goods such as shells, ermine skins, hides, fish oil, and slaves as literal and figurative currencies of the trade. For example, coastal and inland groups coveted dentalium shells, which found their way east as far as the Plains, where they were used in necklaces and hair ornaments (Ewers 1954). As a form of shell money, this medium was portable, durable, and quantifiable.

The Tlingits, whom the Russians described as "completely independent," were generally shrewd traders and would often wait for competing ships so they could play one trader off another and ensure the best return on their furs (Vaughan 1982a, 22). In 1791, an officer on a French merchant ship remarked on the commercial aptitude of the Tlingits of Sitka Sound: "They examined with the most scrupulous attention, turned about in every way, all that was presented to them, and they knew very well how to discover defects and point them out: on the other hand, they employed art and cunning in setting off their merchandise" (Gibson 1988, 383). Even before contact there was a strong tradition of barter between coastal and interior groups, and Northwest Coast Indian society was accustomed to the accumulation, display, and redistribution of material goods (Ames and Maschner 1999; Gibson 1992, 8; Hajda and Sobel 2013).

Both declining fur yields and the deterioration of American and Native American relations threatened trade beginning in the 1820s (Gibson 1992, 153). Greed and misunderstanding often contributed to conflict between newcomers and natives, not to mention the arrogance of Euro-Americans who presumed that their customs and manners were superior. James Gibson (155) summarized this attitude succinctly: "prejudice rationalized abuse." As transient traders who did not live among natives, the Americans were prone to treat natives more brutally than did terrestrial fur traders (158). They sold defective goods, seized skins, and kidnapped leaders to improve their bargaining advantage. William Sturgis, an enlightened shipmaster, acknowledged the ways white traders abused power (158): "should I recount all the lawless & brutal acts of white men upon the Coast you would think that those who visited it had lost the usual attributes of humanity. . . . Some among them would have shot an Indian for his garment of Sea Otter skins with as little compunction as he would have killed the animal from whom the skins were originally taken."

When natives felt cheated, they might try to obtain their due in ways that angered traders and often escalated into bloodshed and permanent animosity. In their efforts to level the playing field, natives were not above their own form of deceit. They were known to dilute fish oil with water and blacken sea otter skins to enhance their appearance and get a better price. They also sought revenge for wrongdoings, even if they had to wait for years to obtain satisfaction. They might visit retribution on unsuspecting traders, since they grouped together all white traders as Boston men. But the visitors usually outdid natives by cheating and adulterating their products (159–160).

Gibson (268–296) has explained that the maritime trade affected five different regions with varied populations: the Northwest Coast, the Hawaiian Islands, South China, New England, and Russia. The economic stimulus of the trade had wide ramifications. Because Northwest Coast society was decidedly mercantile before white contact, the inhabitants adopted new goods and ideas on their own terms in ways that suited their own needs. For instance, they used imports to supplement rather than supplant local products, and the imports they adopted were not revolutionary the way the horse and gun were among the Plains Indians. Some objects increased their productivity, for example guns for hunting. They used technological innovations such as metal tools in ways that stimulated monumental art. In addition, the presence of European trade goods led to increased trade between coastal and interior groups, which may have promoted more alliances and more lavish potlatch ceremonies.

The sea otter trade changed settlement patterns (271). Whereas small, independent groups inhabited pre-Contact sites on Vancouver Island, fewer and larger villages emerged after contact so they could benefit from seasonal trading vessels. Native populations also aggregated around interior trading posts and the occasional coastal post such as Fort McLoughlin (Hobler 2000, 8, cited in Carlson 2006, 201). These changes in settlement patterns disrupted subsistence patterns such that coastal groups had to supplement their diets with nonlocal food resources from inland neighbors.

Contact with the world at large also brought a host of negative consequences that natives were powerless to control. Alcohol and firearms were potent ingredients that heightened tensions, exacerbated conflicts, and impaired health and general well-being. Epidemic diseases such as smallpox and yellow fever reduced populations and had long-term effects for the survivors that were difficult to overcome. The last of a series of plagues in the 1830s killed one-third of the population north of Fort Simpson near the mouth of the Nass River in present-day British Columbia, "broke the back of northern Indian resistance to Euroamerican encroachment, both territorial and cultural" (Gibson 1992, 276), and decreased fur returns. The epidemic, which likely started at Fort Vancouver, also decimated the lower Columbia River populations (Boyd 2013). By the 1840s, the sea otter was well on its way to demographic collapse along much of the Northwest Coast. However, at the same time the desire of Euro-Americans for fur declined and the China trade was disrupted, so the sea otter was never completely annihilated (Gibson 1992, 277). The maritime trade in the Pacific Northwest was the arena where representatives of mercantile interests that encircled the globe met face to face. The legacy of the Russian fur trade persists in Alaska and in the physical traces of its presence in places such as Fort Ross. For the Americans, the trade "enriched Boston ship owners [and merchants] and contributed to the formation of capital that enabled New England to evolve from an agrarian to an industrial society" (296), an enduring legacy indeed.

The maritime and interior fur trades had effectively ended by the 1840s in the Northwest, following the arrival of agriculture-based immigrants from the United States. After the boundary between the United States and Canada was finally set at the 49th parallel in 1846, Fort Vancouver operated on foreign soil. This change in political circumstances forced the HBC to relocate its headquarters from Fort Vancouver to Fort Victoria, British Columbia. At the time of the move, the HBC had exterminated "so many animals that large-scale trade could not be sustained" (Langford 2011, 32).

From Beaver Pelts to Bison Robes in the Missouri River Valley

The Missouri River drainage area covers an expansive area that rivals the Mississippi watershed in size. Much of the valley provided suitable habitats for a range of fur-bearing animals, including beaver, bison, and numerous smaller mammals such as otter and mink. By the mid-eighteenth century, the French had penetrated the Middle Missouri (Krause 1972, 12; Wood and Thiessen 1985, 22). The tribes in this area were connected to a continental trade network that existed long before the arrival of Lewis and Clark (Wood et al. 2011, 18). The first Euro-American goods generally entered the area in the 1780s from NWC and HBC trading posts in the north through commerce with distant tribes, since direct contact with Europeans was sporadic until after the Lewis and Clark expedition of 1803 (Rogers 1990, 46). Canadian traders were the principal sources for these goods until the third decade of the nineteenth century, when St. Louis–based traders working for the AFC extended their reach northward to compete for furs (Wood et al. 2011, 25). The arrival of traders in person gave native groups greater access to Euro-American material goods.

Mandan, Hidatsa, and Arikara villages along the Missouri River and its tributaries from northeast Nebraska to Montana were major centers of intertribal trade (Wood et al. 2011, 18) because of their strategic location along the "horse and gun frontier" (Secoy 1953). Horses were obtained from the Spanish colonies in the southwestern part of the continent through nomadic tribes. Although horses were plentiful, "the Spanish prohibited the sale of guns to Indians" (Wood et al 2011, 24). Canadian traders had few horses but were willing to distribute guns to natives so they could harvest more fur-bearers. By the end of the eighteenth century, tribes in the Middle Missouri had obtained horses through intertribal trade and were hunting bison on horseback (Wood et al. 2011, 16). By the middle of the nineteenth century, the horse and the hide trades were central to the economies of a vast majority of Plains Indian groups (Klein 1993, 144). While men traded horses and guns, women exchanged ample supplies of corn for household goods such as kettles, awls, and glass beads. The Middle Missouri was the only place between the Mississippi and the Rio Grande where corn could be procured. Nomadic tribes to the west were happy to exchange their quarry for maize (Wood et al. 2011, 24).

During periods of initial trade, Europeans and their material offerings were seen from the perspective of aboriginal peoples, and traders were compelled to operate within that framework. Nevertheless, natives were fascinated by British (NWC and HBC), Spanish, and American traders, who cultivated an "appetite for new goods, especially guns, metal kettles, and . . . steel awls" (Wood and Thiessen 1985, 70). An increasing volume of foreign goods in native villages and the appearance of new artifact forms support this observation. For example, imported metals were fashioned into blades that were hafted into narrow slotted handles made of bone (Toom 1979, 117; see also Hamilton and Nicholson 2007). These cutting tools may have been used for processing bison, which intensified over the course of the late eighteenth and nineteenth centuries, until industrially manufactured skinning knives began to replace them in the 1830s and 40s (see Nassaney and Abel 2000; Woodward 1970).

Although European traders initially sought beaver, by the late eighteenth century American bison (aka buffalo) were in demand. Bison habitat extended from the Rio Grande to the Canadian Subarctic and from the foothills of the Rockies to the margins of the eastern woodlands. Males weighed as much as two tons, and bison were the staple protein for generations of Plains Indians. Men harvested the animals and women prepared the hides and meat for transport. Women also dried the meat to make pemmican. Voyageurs traveling on water and land were eager consumers of this native-made product. It made the expansion of the fur trade possible by sustaining the brigades that traveled from Hudson's Bay and the Rainey River to the Athabasca-Mackenzie country in the Northwest Territories, Canada (Ray 1996, 296). Supply depots such as Forts Clark and Union on the Missouri River (fig. 3.1) depended on this ideal food resource and on fresh bison meat. The technology associated with making pemmican involved the many grooved, slightly oval-shaped stone mauls recovered archaeologically that resemble the pounding tools found in many ethnological collections (Krause 1972, 62–63). These implements were hafted to flexible, rawhide-wrapped wooden handles and sewn rawhide covers that left only the pounding surface exposed. Their ubiquity at Middle Missouri village sites testifies to the importance of pemmican in the fur trade and the role natives played in provisioning the trade.

J. Daniel Rogers (1990, 49–76) discusses the attitudes of the Arikaras and Euro-Americans toward each other in the context of trade, the changing physical settings of exchange, and the types of goods that changed hands before and after Euro-American arrival. The Arikaras did not see imported goods as simply interchangeable elements; instead, they interpreted them within their own frame of reference. According to their belief system, the power of Europeans derived from the strange objects they possessed that could be obtained as presents or through trade. Thus, for them, trading was structurally similar to purchasing knowledge as a source of power (Rogers 1990, 51). Trade also fit into native notions of the social obligations associated with material possessions. European transgressions of these conventions led to misunderstandings, often with dire consequences. The Arikaras were understandably perplexed and frustrated by Europeans' patterns of wealth accumulation. They questioned one trader's motives (quoted in Rogers 1990,

59): "Why do you make all this powder and balls since you do not hunt? Of what use are all these knives to you? Is not one enough with which to cut the meat? It is only your wicked heart that prevents you from giving them to us. Do you not see that the village has none?"

Europeans had formed opinions about the Arikaras and their neighbors long before they entered the region. As Rogers (1990, 62; see also Saum 1965) has noted, Europeans saw native peoples as a collectivity that shared undesirable traits. This belief made it possible for Europeans to locate natives in a racialized hierarchy that served the interests of capitalism and manifest destiny (Nassaney 2012a; Orser 2007). Traders were motivated by the desire for profit, which required shrewd bartering and minimal gift giving (Rogers 1990, 62–63). As fur resources declined in the early nineteenth century and traders sought alternate sources, hostilities increased and many, though not all, traders viewed the Arikaras in an even less favorable light (64–66). Traders who drove hard bargains negatively impacted interactions with the Arikaras. Their behavior contrasted with that of earlier explorers, who were "more willing to participate in the social obligations of interaction, as defined by the Arikaras" (67).

The movement of the physical setting of exchange from native villages to forts in the late eighteenth century also affected relations between natives and Euro-Americans (67). Traders were integrated more fully into native life when they lived in native villages, where they were expected to present gifts in exchange for the food they were given. Beginning in the 1790s, the British established trading posts among the Mandans in present-day North Dakota, and American forts soon followed. These centralized sites forced natives to travel in order to participate in trade and shifted control over the process to Euro-Americans. Larger groups of Euro-American immigrants occupied these fortified sites. They had their own gardens and conducted their own bison hunts, thus reducing their dependence on the Arikaras for food (68). This spatial separation further diminished the quality of social relations and reinforced the concept that trading was an economic rather than a cultural activity.

People of the Middle Missouri villages produced an agricultural surplus that they exchanged widely with other native groups for foodstuffs and nonperishable goods prior to contact. This served to create alliances that were mobilized in times of localized subsistence stress. Nomadic groups traded wild plant and animal resources (e.g., bison, berries) for agricultural products such as maize and tobacco (Rogers 1990, 72). Raw materials of shell, stone, and wood were also exchanged. Euro-American goods from HBC and NWC traders easily entered this network well before native peoples of the Middle Missouri had direct contact with Europeans. After Lewis and Clark, the source of the influx of goods shifted to the south, to St. Louis (Rogers 1990, 73).

It is instructive to examine the goods obtained and how they were used so we can understand the changing manifestations of the fur trade in this region. Many of the objects native consumers obtained from American posts were typical trade goods, such as ammunition, knives, spears, tomahawks, blue beads, framed mirrors, white blankets, vermilion, hoes, combs, and tobacco. However, like other native groups, the Arikaras used many of these goods in distinctive ways. For example, they sought blue glass beads but then melted and molded them into pendants of their own design (Rogers 1990, 74). Glass pendants were also produced or recovered at other contemporaneous sites on the Plains and in the Mississippi River Valley (Good 1972, 83; Krause 1972, fig. 49; Ubelaker and Bass 1970). Euro-Americans thought it odd that these pendants should be considered more valuable than the beads themselves (Rogers 1990, 75). The Arikaras and neighboring groups may have used these pendants in ceremonies that validated status, and their color likely evoked symbolic meanings. More importantly, the transformation of European beads into a native form marks an effort to use Euro-American power within an indigenous cultural frame of reference (76) that speaks to cultural autonomy and creativity.

To gauge social change among the Arikaras and their use of European and American trade goods, Rogers (79–88) developed a six-part chronological framework that begins in the late sixteenth century and ends in the 1860s. This framework is probably applicable with some modification to neighboring groups. Trade relations were generally good until the early nineteenth century, as the Arikaras became steadily incorporated into the economy of the trade and goods shifted from luxuries to necessities. The early nineteenth century was marked by increasing hostilities brought about by the depletion of beaver resources and a decrease in demand for buffalo robes, leaving the Arikaras unable to maintain their role in the trade. This occurred as the international market for American furs declined due to the War of 1812; this decreased demand persisted until 1819 (Orser 1980, 161–164, cited in Rogers 1990, 85–86). Soon after, fur companies began employing whites to trap small fur-bearing animals, further marginalizing native groups. However, demand for bison hides rose sharply in the 1830s and '40s, and the Arikaras resumed their participation in the trade, although their role as middlemen was no longer viable. When the U.S. government started doling out annuities in the 1860s, the Arikaras were recipients of "the largess of the powerful," a far cry from the reciprocal exchange the earlier trade had brought (Rogers 1990, 88).

In the narrative created by the dominant society, that persisted into the later twentieth century, the Arikaras were seen as gradually and inevitably succumbing to grand market forces that left them powerless dependents. However, the patterns of material culture use in Arikara archaeological sites shed a different light on the relationships between the Arikaras and Euro-Americans in the eighteenth and nineteenth centuries (Rogers 1990, 153). A careful analysis of the frequencies of objects reveals that the presence of Euro-American goods did not increase steadily in native contexts. Sometimes native peoples rejected these goods because their attitudes toward traders and toward the interaction process itself had changed, perhaps as "a strategy for mitigating the effects of European contact" (220). It is interesting to note that elsewhere in the early nineteenth century, native advocates of traditional values such as followers of the Shawnee prophet Tenskwatawa attempted to regain some degree of economic and political autonomy by returning to non-European forms of subsistence patterns, material culture, and clothing and prohibiting other European practices (Wagner 2011, 25). These revitalization efforts occurred as hostilities increased before the balance of power finally shifted away from indigenous peoples and their institutions.

A major change in Arikara mortuary practices occurred in the early nineteenth century. Before 1800, European goods did not play a significant role in status distinctions in mortuary assemblages; by the second decade of the nineteenth century, imported goods were "having an impact on the material expressions of Arikara social categories" (Rogers 1990, 222–223). The Mandans, Hidatsas, Arikaras, and neighboring groups did not experience the severe negative impacts of the fur trade until the second quarter of the nineteenth century. As relations soured with Euro-American traders, groups in the Middle Missouri River Valley responded by building palisades to enclose their villages. Groups aggregated for mutual protection in an environment of conflict and contestation brought about by guns, horses, and rampant warfare. Demographic decline due to several major epidemics in the period 1780–1838 contributed to loss of autonomy (Wood and Thiessen 1985, 72). The effects included population amalgamation that disrupted the roles of Middle Missouri groups as middlemen and the elimination of proprietary rights to pottery designs; the latter is reflected in changes in ceramics assemblages (73–74). Thus, data from both domestic and mortuary contexts indicate changing social processes related to the fur trade.

When British traders began to withdraw from the Middle Missouri River Valley region in the early nineteenth century, the AFC rushed in to fill the vacuum. Fort Clark, located near present-day Stanton, North Dakota, and Fort Union, located near the border of present-day North Dakota and Montana, were major settlements that distributed goods to and collected furs from natives throughout the region. Architecture at posts such as Fort Clark and Fort Union was designed to impress customers and provide their occupants with a sense of security, particularly against theft (Culpin and Borjes 1984; Wood et al. 2011, 43). Though they were also clearly defensive structures, they seldom came under native attack. The palisade and buildings inside and out were whitewashed (Wood et al. 2011, 79–81), which presented an artificial appearance that distinguished these sites from the natural tones of local earth lodges that natives inhabited. Such formidable facades would have been unfamiliar to Native Americans (Culpin and Borjes 1984, 136).

Frontier posts of the early nineteenth century shared architectural characteristics that some claim derive from feudal manors or castles dating to the late twelfth century in England (135–136; see also Monks 1992). The manor house was typically located opposite the main gate, and adjacent structures were built around an open courtyard. Over time, bastions were added for greater security. This style has also been attributed to France's foremost military engineer, Sébastien Le Prestre de Vauban (1633–1707), who formalized defensive architectural design in the late seventeenth century (see Keene 1991, 35–36). High-status dwellings, offices, and rooms for guests were located opposite the main entrance, though sometimes these buildings were sited differently to take local topography into account. Artisans' shops, stables or animal sheds, and Indians' quarters were located on either side of the front gate (Wood et al. 2011, 77). Stores and low-status housing also bordered the courtyard, though employees sometimes occupied one of two blockhouses. Prince Maximilian of Wied-Neuwied, a German explorer who traveled in the Plains in the 1830s, left a detailed description and plan view of Fort Clark as it appeared in 1833 (figure 5.6; 74, 82). Maintenance and rebuilding necessitated by deteriorating timbers led to changes in the size and internal configuration of the fort over time.

Fort Union has been reconstructed on the basis of archival and archaeological evidence. The Bourgeois House is opposite the main gate and domi-

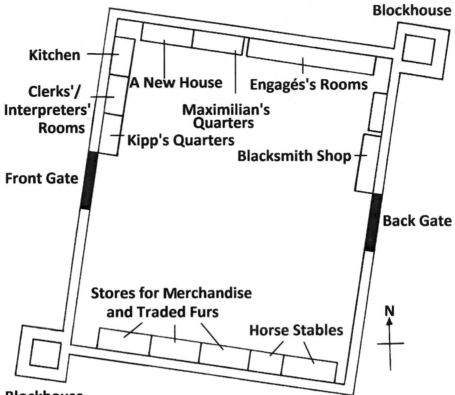

Kitchen

Clerks'/
Interpreters'
Rooms

A New House

Blockhouse

Engagés's Rooms

Maximilian's
Quarters

Kipp's Quarters

Blacksmith Shop

Front Gate

Back Gate

Stores for Merchandise
and Traded Furs

Horse Stables

N

Blockhouse

Figure 5.6. Plan view of Fort Clark along the Missouri River near present-day Stanton, North Dakota, as it appeared in 1833. Adapted from Wood et al. 2011, 74. Drawing by John W. Cardinal.

nates the fort, just as the fort commands the confluence of the Missouri and Yellowstone Rivers (Culpin and Borjes 1984, 137–139). Adjacent structures flanking the Bourgeois House were designated for cooking, storage, and housing support personnel. A log palisade wall was set on a foundation of dry-laid stone that was designed to inhibit deterioration. The palisade enclosed the entire fort, which had stone bastions at opposite corners. Inside the fort was a central plaza or parade ground. This blueprint is replicated at numerous eighteenth- and nineteenth-century sites from the western Great Lakes region to the Pacific Northwest (see Hamilton 2000). It is likely that it was used repeatedly because of its functionality and relative ease of construction.

The Bourgeois House was originally built in the French Canadian *poteau en terre* style, which involved upright posts and stone and plaster to fill the interstices (Culpin and Borjes 1984, 137). The French Canadian influence was common in the Old Northwest because traders, trappers, and company officials moved about the region. Mann (2008) has argued that architecture was a visible sign of Canadian identity that was used in the Wabash River Valley well into the nineteenth century. These vernacular buildings contrasted with the less-imposing Greek Revival style that accompanied westward expansion (Culpin and Borjes 1984, 137). The builders of Fort Union and other fur trade posts created an imposing built environment in an effort to intimidate and psychologically subjugate Native Americans (140).

Fort Clark was constructed in a similar style. This fort, the nearly undisturbed remains of a palisaded native earth lodge village, and another American trading post, Fort Primeau, constitute the Fort Clark State Historic Site in North Dakota. The Mandans first occupied the village (1822–1837), followed by the Arikaras (1838–1861). A sequence of trading posts, principally Fort Clark (1831–1860) and Fort Primeau (1846–1861), were constructed to serve these tribes (Wood et al. 2011, xii). Fort Clark was an important commercial enterprise that was the only American settlement of any significance along the 680-mile stretch of the Missouri River between Fort Pierre, near present-day Pierre, South Dakota, and Fort Union near the border between present-day North Dakota and Montana (7).

The site complex has been the focus of extensive historical and archaeological research that W. Raymond Wood, William J. Hunt Jr., and Randy H. Williams (2011) have summarized. They underscore the untapped potential of the archaeological record, which can be expected to grow with the passage of time in both detail and accuracy, in contrast to historical documents and collective memories of living people (xii). They have used an ethnohistorical approach to provide a comprehensive picture of the appearance of the fort; the activities, personal adornment, health, and hygiene of the occupants; and a host of other details pertaining to fur trade life.

Excavations have been conducted sporadically in the area of the fort and adjacent native village for nearly a century, though not without protests from native groups (216–217). The State Historical Society of North Dakota purchased the site in 1931, affording it some degree of protection. Efforts to study the site systematically began in the 1980s. Geophysical survey provided excellent details about subsurface features in the Mandan village, including the locations of earth lodges, hearths, pits, and artifact concentrations (227).

Archaeological investigations at Fort Clark since 2000 have included microtopographic mapping, a geophysical survey, and small-scale excavations (221–238). The mapping recorded elevations across the site and produced a contour map that shows the locations of palisades, buildings, and other topographic features. A suite of geophysical techniques revealed various landscape features, including the outline of the fort, the trash dump outside the post, some relatively open areas, and a cemetery south of the fort. Excavations within the fort and in the adjacent trash dump provided data about construction sequences and discarded artifacts.

Many of the objects that have been recovered relate to subsistence and provide insight into the diets of the employees at the post (238–241). Animal bones include those of various fish, bird, and mammal species. Most of the bones of mammals were those of wild animals, and the bones of animals used in the fur trade, such as beaver, fox, and bison, appeared frequently. The bison elements that were recovered are consistent with a preference for fleshy parts of the animal, indicating that entire carcasses were not carried to the fort. Plant remains are similar to collections from pre-Contact sites in the region, indicating a reliance on local food sources such as maize, beans, and squash and various wild plants. Food-related artifacts were concentrated in domestic and living areas in the northeast and northwest corners of the post.

Objects that can be linked to their sources demonstrate connections to domestic (New York, Philadelphia, Connecticut) and foreign (England, France, Spain, Italy, Belgium, Slovenia) markets. Some of these goods (e.g., buttons) demonstrate the prevalence of European-style clothing at the fort, which was generally reserved for high-status traders. The large numbers of rat bones recovered in excavation indicate that poor sanitation conditions prevailed at the fort (289). Leisure activities are represented by ceramic gaming pieces that Mandan women used in a popular gambling diversion and the ubiquitous white clay pipe (242). Some red stone pipes, likely made of catlinite, were also found. Numerous artifacts have been recovered that relate to food preparation (e.g., ceramics, tin milk pans), architecture (e.g., hand-wrought and machine-cut nails, window glass), and transportation (e.g., horseshoes, harness buckles). Firearms are represented by flintlocks, percussion cap hardware, and gunflints of various sizes. The lead shot that was recovered was likely used for muskets, rifles, and large-caliber military weapons (244).

A broad range of durable trade goods destined for native hands provides evidence of the fur trade. These include metal gun parts and ammunition, gunflints, brass tacks, glass beads, animal traps, objects of personal adornment such as bracelets and finger rings, fish hooks, and wood working tools such as chisels, files, and augers among others. Beads are by far the most numerous. Analysis reveals that variation in bead color, variety, and size reflects sampling, the length of site occupation, and the relative wealth of the traders (245). The Mandans and Arikaras preferred different types of beads indicating that consumer choice also influences the composition of an assemblage. In sum, archaeology expands on the historical documentation available for places such as Fort Clark and provides comparative data for other fur trade sites in North America.

The Fur Trade in Microcosm

When the histories and archaeological remains of various fur trade systems in North America are juxtaposed, patterns of similarity and difference emerge. To a great extent, each region exhibits in broad outline the phases that C. Gilman (1982) proposed for the Old Northwest. The French, English, Russians, and Americans tapped into different native systems to acquire fur-bearing animals for various uses, motivated by the drive for profit. Natives aimed to benefit from the newcomers and the materials they offered by creating alliances to obtain goods that would serve their purposes and reproduce the structures of their daily life. Of course, unintended consequences ensued as Euro-American populations increased, conflicts arose, fur resources decreased, and natives were weakened by disease and other cultural disruptions. The result was a power imbalance that left Europeans less dependent on natives for provisions and natives more reliant on Europeans for manufactured goods. This was neither a linear nor an inevitable process. Interpretations of the trade, especially in public perception, tend to highlight aspects that existed in the later phases in order to explain the negative outcomes of the process. As a result, the close relations of interdependence that existed when natives and Europeans first encountered each other in the trade are often overlooked. Recent work being conducted at the French trading post of Fort St. Joseph in the western Great Lakes region is exploring a time when the region was still contested and the future of the fur trade was undecided. That is the focus of the next chapter.

6

The Fur Trade in the Western Great Lakes Region

The View from Fort St. Joseph

Fort St. Joseph, located near present-day Niles in southwest Michigan, was one of a string of trading posts the French established in the late seventeenth century to secure the interior of the continent by creating alliances with native groups (figure 6.1; Idle 2003; Peyser 1992). The fur trade was essential for reinforcing those alliances, and fur extraction and the introduction of imported goods in the western Great Lakes region are well documented archaeologically (e.g., Mainfort 1979; Martin 2008; Mason 1986; Quimby 1966; Stone 1974a). Fort St. Joseph was a relatively small but intensely occupied mission, garrison, and commercial center for much of the eighteenth century. It has become the focus of a long-term, multidisciplinary research and service learning project in historical archaeology that is investigating the fur trade and colonialism in southwest Michigan (Nassaney 1999, 2012b; Nassaney et al. 2003, 2007). The Fort St. Joseph Archaeological Project, which began in 1998, was established as a community partnership between Western Michigan University and the city of Niles (Nassaney 2011). I have served as the project's principal investigator since its inception. Investigations conducted regularly since 2002 have provided information about interactions between the French and native peoples and the process of ethnogenesis that led to the creation of a fur trade society on the frontier of New France (Nassaney 2008b).

In this chapter, I use a perspective that builds on earlier humanistic ap-

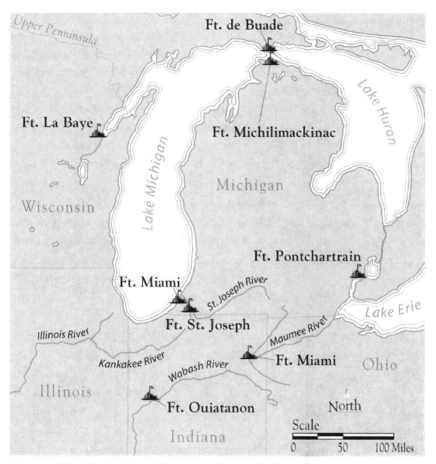

Figure 6.1. The Western Great Lakes region showing the locations of Fort St. Joseph and other French sites. Map © Jan Underwood, Information Illustrated, 2011 for the *Archeological Conservancy Magazine*.

proaches and recent trends in anthropologically oriented fur trade studies to highlight the contributions of the archaeology of Fort St. Joseph and the fur trade to the formation of an American identity. I begin by providing a historical context for the fur trade at Fort St. Joseph and then discuss the research goals, methods, findings of the project and implications of our results for the American experience (see also Brandão and Nassaney 2006, 2008; Nassaney et al. 2002–2004, 2003, 2007). The work conducted at Fort St. Joseph over the past decade demonstrates that the history of the fur trade is significant for public audiences and that engaging the community through public education and outreach is an important process.

Historical Context

The St. Joseph River Valley played a strategic role in French aspirations for the *pays d'en haut* (Upper Country) and consequently has attracted considerable interest among historians (e.g., Ballard 1973; Beeson 1900; Coolidge 1915; Cunningham 1961; Idle 2003; Peyser 1978, 1992). Historians have used oral traditions and documents such as letters, official correspondences, maps, vouchers, and a marriage and baptismal register to provide data about native peoples and the importance of Fort St. Joseph in the history of New France (e.g., see Brandão and Nassaney 2006; Clifton 1977). Documentary, material, and oral evidence indicate that the area had a long history of native settlement prior to the establishment of Fort St. Joseph. Sources suggest that the Potawatomis had moved into western Lower Michigan after they separated from their Ojibwe and Ottawa kin at the Straits of Mackinac sometime before the seventeenth century (Clifton 1977, 1986; Nassaney et al. 2012, 58). Once they were established in their new homeland, they adopted a mixed economic strategy that included maize agriculture.

Sometime in the early seventeenth century, the Potawatomis abandoned their homeland and moved to northeastern Wisconsin. Rock Island appears to be one of several refugee centers brought about by Iroquoian acts or perceived threats of aggression (Mason 1986). The underlying premise of alliance—mediation as a source of influence—emerged in multiethnic communities such as the village on Rock Island, perhaps accompanied by the spread of the calumet, a smoking pipe used in intercultural negotiations. The Potawatomis perfected this essentially Algonquian practice of mediation and showed the French how their role as mediators "made them the most influential group at Green Bay" (White 2011, 35). According to James Clifton (1978, 726), this environment offered the Potawatomis social and strategic advantages by providing temporary security from Iroquois raids, direct access to French trade goods, and a political climate that offered opportunities for expansion and cultural growth.

The Miamis moved into southwest Michigan from LaSalle's Fort St. Louis on the Illinois River in the 1680s, possibly at the insistence of the Jesuit missionary Father Claude Allouez (Myers and Peyser 1991, 12). In 1695, the vanguard of a Potawatomi expansion from their temporary refuge in northeastern Wisconsin, numbering 200 strong, relocated with the support of the French to their former homeland along the St. Joseph River, or River of the Miamis, as it was then known to the French. They soon became the dominant force in the valley (Nassaney et al. 2012, 60). A 1736 census listed 100 Potawatomis, 10 Miamis, and eight Illinois Kaskaskias for the area (Idle 2003, 92). An English surveyor, Thomas Hutchins (1904 [1778]), documented the presence of 200 Potawatomi men immediately across the river from Fort St. Joseph during his visit in 1762 (figure 6.2). Their proximity to the fort suggests that their relations with the French were amicable. For most of the eighteenth century, the Potawatomis occupied the entire lower valley, from the mouth of the St. Joseph River to just above South Bend, Indiana. Although the Potawatomi population gradually declined, there were still 790 in six semi-permanent villages along the river in 1819. Their numbers were surpassed only by the Euro-Americans a decade later, when government treaties made land available to white settlers.

The French recognized the importance of the St. Joseph River Valley in 1679, when LaSalle built Fort Miami at the mouth of the river. In 1686, the Jesuits were granted a tract of land upriver to establish a mission, and in 1691 a garrison and trading post were constructed nearby (Peyser 1992, 43–46). This post "among the Miami," which later became known as Fort St. Joseph,

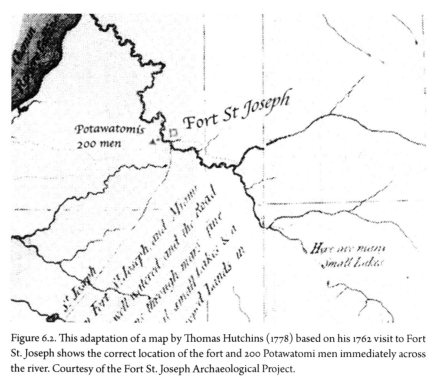

Figure 6.2. This adaptation of a map by Thomas Hutchins (1778) based on his 1762 visit to Fort St. Joseph shows the correct location of the fort and 200 Potawatomi men immediately across the river. Courtesy of the Fort St. Joseph Archaeological Project.

was one of the most important frontier outposts in the North American interior, situated near a strategic portage that linked the River of the Miamis and the Great Lakes basin to the Mississippi drainage area (Idle 2003, 11; Nassaney et al. 2003). It became the keystone of French control of the southern Lake Michigan region and served as a hub of commercial, military, and religious activity for local Native American populations and European colonial powers for nearly a century (Brandão and Nassaney 2006).

This mission-garrison-trading post complex, which was given the name St. Joseph in honor of the patron saint of New France, initially consisted of a palisade, a commandant's house, and a few other structures (Faribault-Beauregard 1982, 175). Governor General Frontenac of New France established it in an attempt to solidify French relations with the local Miami Indians and other native groups west and north of the area. Frontenac also hoped that a permanent French presence supported by the military would stimulate the fur trade in the region and check the expansion and power of the Iroquois Confederacy and its English allies (Brandão 1997; Eccles 1969, 1972; Myers and Peyser 1991). Once the French established Fort St. Joseph, the area again became home to various native groups. By the early eighteenth century, their populations numbered in the hundreds. The fort soon supported eight officers, including a commandant; ten enlisted men; a priest; an interpreter; a blacksmith; and about fifteen fur traders and their French, French Canadian, and native wives (Idle 2003; Peyser 1978, 44). For decades, the site was the locus of a multiethnic population that featured intermarriage between French and French Canadian men and native women and intense cultural interaction. Jesuit priests baptized native women and their mixed-heritage offspring, and native women served as godmothers, testifying to the sincerity of their beliefs and their full integration into the life of the community (Nassaney et al. 2012, 69).

Despite its religious origins, the French establishment on the St. Joseph River was known primarily for its commercial and military functions. It provided a vital link in the colony's communications network and played a major role in the exchange of manufactured commodities for furs. By the middle of the eighteenth century, it ranked fourth among the posts in New France in terms of the volume of furs traded (Heidenreich and Noël 1987). When an oversupply of beaver filled the storehouses in Montreal in the late seventeenth century, many of the posts were closed. However, the French continued to maintain and support Fort St. Joseph and a few other posts by accepting devalued furs in exchange for imported goods, effectively underwriting the fur trade at an economic loss to maintain the loyalty of their native allies. The French also provided the services of a blacksmith for repairing the guns of natives because they did not want the native allies to shift their allegiance to the English (Eccles 1988, 328; Nassaney et al. 2012, 67–68; Peyser 1978, 99). The Crown also paid for some of the musket balls, buckshot, lead, and powder natives needed for hunting and warfare (Peyser 1978, 86).

Fort St. Joseph figured prominently in interactions between native peoples and French and English colonial powers throughout the eighteenth century. It served as a central staging point and supply base for the savage and destructive French wars against the Fox Indians (Mesquakis) in the 1720s and 1730s and later against the Chickasaws (1736–1740). These wars were vital to French expansion to the west and south of the Great Lakes.

Historical documents provide information about the types of imported goods the French at this post supplied to the natives. We can infer related activities from these data. Joseph Peyser (1978) translated a number of French-language manuscripts pertaining to Fort St. Joseph from the 1730s and 1740s that describe the goods and services merchants provided to natives and to those who were conducting official business for the Crown (Peyser 1978, 86). Among these are vouchers that list goods and services associated with the exchange of fur-bearing animals. For example, Louis Hamelin and Louis Gastineau (also Gatineau) were Montreal merchants who hired voyageurs to carry supplies to Fort St. Joseph for the Chickasaw War from 1736 to 1740 (Idle 2003, 86). They paid Antoine De Lestre and Joseph Lepage, Fort St. Joseph residents, with some 500 lbs. of deerskins valued at 875 livres in June, 1739 (see textbox 1). The Crown reimbursed the merchants for these skins, implying that De Lestre and Lepage were owed for goods or services they provided local natives in support of wartime efforts. It is not known if these deerskins were produced at Fort St. Joseph or elsewhere or what their intended use was, but they were likely a medium of exchange. Merchants also provided tallow, an animal product that could have been used for soap or candles, mixed with pigment for face paint, or boiled with pine pitch for sealing birch bark canoes (Michael Zimmerman, personal communication, 2014).

Natives from Fort St. Joseph provisioned France's indigenous allies who were dispatched from the fort to help fight the Chickasaws. They also provisioned voyageurs. For example, Marie Madelaine Réaume, an Iliniwek

Voucher for supplies provided by Hamelin & Co. by order of Coulon de
Villiers, commandant of Fort St. Joseph, June 26, 1739 (from Peyser 1978,
86). The abbreviations for the French monetary units of livre and sol are #
and ^{S}, respectively. There were 20 sols to the livre. The value of a livre varied
across time and space in eighteenth-century New France. A laborer might
earn 5–10 livres per day.

*MEMORANDUM of the supplies furnished for the King by Order of
Monsieur Coulon De Villiers Commandant for the King at the St. Joseph River post.*

TO WIT.

Five ells of cloth at 7# 10^S per ell	*38# 10^S*
Two lbs. of vermilion at 9# per Lb	*18#*
Two and ½ ells of Cloth at 7# 10^S per ell	*18# 15^S*
Two Men's Shirts at 4# each	*8#*
Paid to Antoine De Lestre Two Hundred	
* pounds of deerskins at 35^S per Lb.*	*350#*
To Joseph Lepage ditto	*525#*
For Wampum	*30#*
For ditto	*70#*
Sixteen Lbs of Tallow 10^S per Lb	*8#*
a piece of Meat	*3#*
eight Lbs of Musketballs at 15^S per Lb	*6#*
six Lbs of Lead at ditto	*4# 10^S*
eight ditto of powder at 40^S per ditto	*16#*
a sack of Wheat	*12#*
One Kettle weighing 3 Lb ¼ at 3# 5^S per Lb	*10# 11.3^S*
Two ells ½ of Lyon Cloth at 30^S per ell	*3# 15^S*
Four pounds of Gum at 15^S per Lb	*3#*
Two Lbs of buck-shot at 15^S per Lb	*1# 10^S*
Four pounds of powder at 40^S ditto	*8#*
Total	*1134# 11.3^S*

*At the St. Joseph River Post the 26th of June. Signed Louis Hamelin and
Company. And then is written*

*We Commandant for the King at St. Joseph River certify that Mr. Hamelin with
Mr. Gastineau has provided the Contents of this Memorandum for the service of
His Majesty on the 28th of June 1739. Signed Coulon De Villiers*

woman who lived at Fort St. Joseph in the 1730s, and members of her household supplied grain (wheat, oats, and corn) and vegetables to French traders who wintered in the southern Great Lakes region. This agricultural surplus was central to the success of the St. Joseph fur trade (Sleeper-Smith 1998, 56–57).

Dunning Idle (2003, 82–84) has compiled information on the numbers of canoes sent to the St. Joseph River and the permits that were issued from 1721 to 1745. While they do not specify what types of goods were traded, the data indicate that the French were importing significant quantities of goods for distribution to native allies. Less is known about the types of furs that were collected and shipped back to Montreal from the fort. An undated report claimed that the fort could "furnish four hundred parcels of racoon [sic], bear, wildcat, dwarf deer, [and] elk" (Peyser 1978, 30a). In 1757, the French explorer Bougainville estimated that Fort St. Joseph could produce the same number of "packages of pelts of cats, bears, lynx, otters, deer, and stags" (Idle 2003, 121). No mention is made of beaver.

The English surveyor Thomas Hutchins remarked on the fort's population of fur traders and their economic activities in 1762:

> It is inhabited by about a dozen French families who chiefly support themselves by the trade they carry on with the Indians and notwithstanding the country is very rich about them, they raise nothing more than some Indian corn and make a little hay to support their horses and mules and a few milch cows, which seems to be all the stock they have. (quoted in Cunningham 1961, 72–73)

His remarks betray his disdain for the French. Hutchins clearly implies that the fur trade was not a sustainable livelihood and derides the French for making so few improvements to the land. Indeed, he seems to consider them to be as indolent as the Indians. The French were, after all, a vanquished people.

Commanders at the fort and natives from the region were key players in the events surrounding the Seven Years' War, the first major war for empire in North America, by which France lost Canada to Great Britain (Myers and Peyser 1991; Peyser 1992). Once the English gained control, relationships changed. Lord Jeffrey Amherst discouraged the practice of providing natives with lavish gifts, such as gunpowder and alcohol, in fur trade negotiations, as the French had done, reasoning that it made the natives less industrious about acquiring furs. Native discontent with English practices and attitudes instigated Pontiac's Rebellion in the spring of 1763, in which supporters of the Ottawa leader attacked Fort St. Joseph to remove the English from the area and encourage the return of the French (Widder 2013, 157–159). This forced the English to establish a policy that limited colonial expansion into the interior via the Proclamation of 1763. After 1763, French fur traders were allowed to remain at the fort and continued to practice the trade. Following a daylong raid and occupancy by the Spanish in 1781, the English abandoned the site and the area came under American control. Independent and company traders such as William Burnett and Joseph Bertrand continued trading for furs in the St. Joseph River Valley into the nineteenth century (Cunningham 1967; Johnson 1919, 108–109). In June 1796, Burnett recorded in his ledger that he had sold 99 packs of fur that included "5 bears, 5 pound beaver, 10 fishers, 58 cats, 74 doe, 78 foxes, 108 wolves, 117 otters, 183 minks, 557 bucks, 1,231 deer, 1,340 muskrats, and 5,587 raccoons" (Johnson 1919, 97–98). This list documents the decline of beaver and the importance of deer, muskrat, and raccoon after the fort was abandoned The St. Joseph River Valley continued to provide substantial fur yields into the 1830s (Johnson 1919, 143).

Archaeological Investigations of the Fur Trade in the St. Joseph River Valley

Much is known about the fur trade in the St. Joseph River Valley from historical documents, though information is lacking about some aspects of daily life such as subsistence, settlement locations, the appearance of the built environment, mundane economic activities, and the material outcomes of the relationships and identities that were created and reproduced through cultural interactions. Archaeological investigations can complement and expand on our knowledge of these aspects of the culture and history of the fur trade in the region.

Ruins of the fort were noted as early as the 1820s, when farmers plowed up "relics of the old French and English occupancy" such as flintlock hardware and copper, silver, and iron artifacts (Beeson 1900, 185). Lewis H. Beeson, an avid antiquarian and former president of the Michigan Historical Society, published a legal description of the location of his finds (Beeson 1900, 186), and he may have been responsible for an anonymous sketch map of the fort (Peyser 1992, fig. 6). In the late nineteenth century, Beeson and other amateur historians began amassing significant collections of objects used in the fur trade (figure 2.1). On July 4, 1913, the city of Niles dedicated a 65-ton stone monument to memorialize European settlement there. To mark the event, Judge Coolidge (1915) delivered an address that reflects the dominant narrative of manifest destiny. He praised "the fortitude and heroism of the French" settlers who introduced "Christianity and civilization into the wilds of western Michigan" in the face of "roving savages" (1915, 290–291). His remarks assumed that vanishing Indians had become acculturated to civilized ways or had been displaced to the western frontier, where their culture would gradually die out. While many Potawatomis were removed to Kansas in the 1830s and later to Oklahoma, the Pokagon Band remained in southwest Michigan, having demonstrated that they had become Christian farmers (Secunda 2006). Their history, however, was written out of the dominant narrative that emphasized French exploration and settlement as the prelude to Euro-American cultural domination.

In the 1920s, the city of Niles was nicknamed the City of Four Flags in recognition of the French, English, Spanish, and American presence in the territory; the Potawatomi takeover of 1763 was not accorded a "flag." This version of history further solidified the importance of the fort's European heritage in the collective memory of the community. Despite the historical connection many white residents felt to the fort, its only tangible manifestation at that time was the collection of approximately 100,000 objects from the vicinity of the fort that Beeson and others had donated to museums in Niles (Fort St. Joseph Museum), Kalamazoo (Kalamazoo Public Museum), and South Bend (Center for History) (Hulse 1981). Quimby (1939, 1966, 67) seized on the significance of the Niles collection in defining his Middle Historic period (1670–1760). Since the occupation dates of the fort were well known, he reasoned, its artifacts were good temporal markers. Serious archaeological study did not take place until the 1970s, when the collections were reexamined to ensure their authenticity and chronological placement (Hulse 1977, 1981; Stone 1974b). This work was triggered by the fervor of the nation's bicentennial and a desire to reconstruct the fort for interpretive purposes. However, changes in local hydrology associated with a nearby dam, the establishment of a twentieth-century landfill that partly conceals the area of interest, and the absence of detailed maps or descriptions obscured the exact location of the site and hindered any reconstruction efforts.

Despite the work of avid relic collectors, subsequent commemorative activities, and some scholarly interest, the location of the site eluded modern

archaeologists for most of the twentieth century. Seventeenth- and eighteenth-century maps provided conflicting information or lacked the detail
needed to locate the site on the ground. In 1998, Western Michigan University archaeologists in partnership with Support the Fort, Inc., the Fort
St. Joseph Museum, and the city of Niles conducted a survey to locate the
material remains of Fort St. Joseph, and the Fort St. Joseph Archaeological
Project was born (Nassaney et al. 2003; Nassaney 1999). Using data Joseph
Peyser (1978, 1992) provided from his study of French-language documents
and over 200 maps, a shovel-test pit survey was conducted west of the commemorative boulder on the terrace and into the floodplain adjacent to the
river (Nassaney et al. 2002–2004). Although this produced evidence of eighteenth-century European imports on both landforms, their density was considerably lower on the terrace, where mostly ancient and modern artifacts
were recovered (see figure 6.3; Nassaney 1999). Subsequent work established
the integrity of the floodplain deposits and demonstrated that the location of
Fort St. Joseph had been determined (Nassaney et al. 2002–2004).

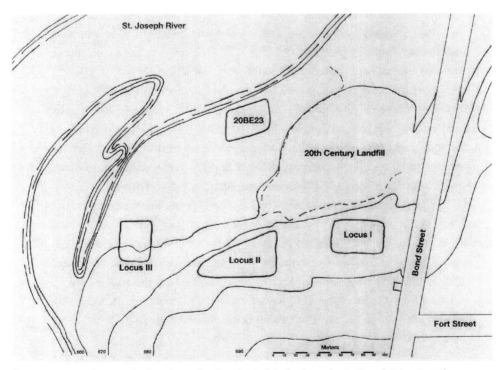

Figure 6.3. Map showing the locations of archaeological finds along the St. Joseph River in Niles,
Michigan, on the terrace (Lyne site) and floodplain (Fort St. Joseph). Drawing by John W. Cardinal.

Native American Sites

In the course of our survey we also collected information on Native American sites that were occupied immediately prior to contact and into the seventeenth and eighteenth centuries (Kohley 2013), though our directive has been to recover architectural data to aid in the reconstruction of the fort (see Berliner and Nassaney 2015, 14). Native American sites in proximity to the fort that are recorded in the state site files maintained in the Office of the State Archaeologist in Lansing have attracted only limited interest among archaeologists. Some sites consist of isolated finds, whereas others are based on historical documents and have not been verified in the field. While most sites cannot be assigned to specific ethnic groups (e.g., Miamis, Potawatomis), the presence of low-fired earthenware ceramics, triangular projectile points, chipped-stone debris, human remains, and associated European imports indicates native occupations immediately prior to and during the time the fort was occupied (Nassaney et al. 2012, 61).

Archaeological evidence of eighteenth-century native activity has been documented across the river from the fort, where the Potawatomis settled after the departure of the Miamis (see figure 6.2). Salvage excavations conducted there in 2000 identified the disturbed remains of an adolescent and an adult female associated with a mid-eighteenth-century brass kettle (Nassaney et al. 2000). The kettle resembles a Type F specimen recovered from a Tunica cemetery in Louisiana (Brain 1979, 178–180). Another native burial was exhumed in the 1950s (Jelinek 1958). Associated silver trade goods date this burial after 1760. The nearby Brandywine Creek 2 site south of the fort has yielded native pottery that may relate it to Miami occupation in the area (Bettarel and Smith 1973, 143). Some of the artifacts in the Fort St. Joseph Museum purported to be "from the vicinity of the fort" might have actually come from eighteenth-century native sites where imported goods were common.

Excavations conducted under the auspices of the Fort St. Joseph Archaeological Project since 2000 have led to the recovery of a culturally and stratigraphically mixed assemblage of artifacts from three loci on the terrace west of the historical marker (figure 6.3). First identified in the 1930s and designated the Lyne site (20BE10), this plowed terrace has yielded triangular Madison projectile points, shell-tempered pottery, copious amounts of fire-cracked rock, several stone smoking pipes, and a range of European imports, including gunflints, flintlock hardware (i.e., a trigger, a sideplate), lead shot

Figure 6.4. Fragment of trade silver perforated for ornamental use. The fragment was recovered from the Lyne site (20BE10) on the terrace near Fort St. Joseph. Photo by John Lacko.

and musket balls, a pewter brooch, numerous copper alloy scraps, hand-blown glass container fragments, and a cut fragment of trade silver that was perforated for ornamental use (figure 6.4).

Because of plowing that took place in the twentieth century, the site contains few undisturbed features. However, Locus II contains two clusters of overlapping pits filled with carbonized corncobs located about 15 meters apart (figure 6.5). Analysis of the contents of four of these pits indicates that corncob remains are dominant, although small amounts of wood charcoal, raspberry, sumac, grape, and carbonized walnuts were also present. Seeds and nuts are possibly accidental inclusions (Hughes-Skallos and Allen 2012; Martinez 2009). These features bear formal similarity to the smudge pits used to tan hides (known as corn holes) that have been noted at several sites in the region, namely nearby Moccasin Bluff (Ford 1973), Rhoads in Illinois (Wagner 2011, 98–100), and Gete Odena on Grand Island in Lake Superior (Skibo et al. 2004, 171–174). A sample of the pit contents has been radiocarbon dated to AD 1710+50 years, indicating probable contemporaneity with the floodplain deposits (Nassaney et al. 2012, 63). A stone scraper found near these pits is similar to Chickasaw end scrapers found in Mississippi, reinforcing the inference that these pits were used for processing fur (see figure 5.5).

To determine if Fort St. Joseph had an influence on the distribution of native settlements in the valley from northern Indiana to the mouth of the St. Joseph River, Alison Kohley (2013) collected and compared distributional data on sites occupied before, during, and after the fort's occupancy. She

Figure 6.5. The remains of a smudge pit from Locus II on the terrace near the site of Fort St. Joseph are evidence of eighteenth-century fur-processing activities. Photo by Stephanie Barrante. Courtesy of the Fort St. Joseph Archaeological Project.

used GIS analysis to demonstrate that Late Woodland sites (AD 1000–1691) were generally small and widely dispersed, reflecting the seasonal round nuclear and extended family units practiced. During the years the fort was occupied (1691–1781), sites tended to cluster close to it and were larger, perhaps indicating aggregations of multifamily units. After the fort was abandoned (post-1781), native sites are again widely dispersed but seem to be located in proximity to new Euro-American sites in the region, perhaps indicating the continued importance of the fur trade and the desire of natives to obtain imported goods. The dispersal pattern suggests that natives maintained their seasonal round and incorporated European sites as just another node in their scheduling of activities, so long as they had access to land and could remain mobile.

The Archaeology of Fort St. Joseph

When we first encountered the presence of eighteenth-century artifacts at the Lyne site, we dismissed their significance due to their low density, despite their proximity to the commemorative boulder. However, subsequent work has suggested that members of the Fort St. Joseph community likely occupied the terrace for special-purpose activities such as hide processing. The 1998 survey of the floodplain led to the discovery of a higher density of eighteenth-century artifacts, undisturbed cultural deposits, and, most significantly, evidence of European-style architecture (Nassaney et al. 2003). Subsequent site evaluation in 2002 involved a geophysical survey (for which magnetometry and ground-penetrating radar were most useful) that detected numerous subsurface anomalies that have potential cultural significance, despite a high ground-water table that inundates the deposits (Nassaney et al. 2002–2004). Subsurface excavation requires the installation of a well-point drainage system even during the dry summer months. Once excavations to evaluate the anomalies demonstrated that the site had integrity, the long-term project goals shifted to obtain historical and archaeological data about the fort's spatial parameters and other architectural details in order to gain a better understanding of the material and social consequences of the fur trade and colonialism in southwest Michigan (e.g., Brandão and Nassaney 2008; Becker 2004; Giordano 2005; Kerr 2012; Malischke 2009; Nassaney and Cremin 2002; Nassaney and Brandão 2009). Investigations have aimed to establish the identities of the site occupants so we can examine their role in creating a fur trade society. The approach recognizes the fluidity of identity and aims to explore the mutual changes that French and natives experienced as a consequence of close cultural interactions brought about by the fur trade. Since 2002, we have recovered over 200,000 eighteenth-century artifacts, samples, and associated plant and animal remains and have identified five European-style fireplaces, sealed pit features, and undisturbed artifact deposits. Analysis of these artifacts, features, and ecofacts provides insights into the fur trade that are unavailable from the written record.

Excavations in the floodplain (figure 6.3) have sampled about 200 square meters, or less than 10 percent of the accessible site area. Although the floodplain has been plowed, undisturbed remains exist below the plow zone. Archaeological materials likely exist beneath the twentieth-century landfill to the east, but current environmental regulations prohibit investigations in this area. Thus, efforts have been focused on locating buildings and inferring their functions, the identity of their occupants, and the activities that were associated with them.

Structures are represented by fireplaces, stone foundations, preserved vertical and horizontal timbers, daub (*bousillage*), mortar-covered stones, and hand-wrought iron hardware including nails, pintles, and hinges. Excavations have been conducted in an effort to delineate the size, orientation, and construction methods of these structures and to recover a sample of their contents. While none of the buildings has been completely excavated, the presence of fireplaces suggests that they are associated with habitations. House 1 is defined by a segment of a stone foundation and two upright posts near the east corner and a fireplace (figure 6.6), whereas House 2 includes a foundation wall along with a hewn wooden architectural element that may be a doorsill marking the building's entry point opposite its fireplace (figure 6.7). This suggests that the builders employed a combination of *poteau en terre* and *poteau sur sole* construction techniques. These two buildings appear to be approximately 5 × 6 meters (15 × 18 feet) in size and were perhaps occupied by nuclear families. Thus, they are modest, stand-alone habita-

Figure 6.6. This stone fireplace (Feature 2) at Fort St. Joseph served as a source of heat and light for cooking and other household tasks. Photo by John Lacko. Courtesy of the Fort St. Joseph Archaeological Project.

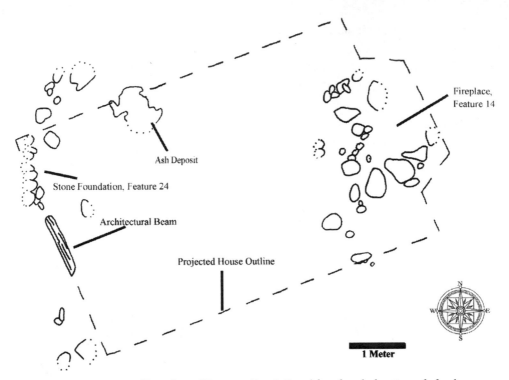

Figure 6.7. Projected boundary of House 2 at Fort St. Joseph based on the locations of a fireplace, a foundation wall, and an architectural beam. Drawing by John W. Cardinal.

tions, unlike the row houses with shared walls at Fort Michilimackinac (e.g., Evans 2001).

Adjacent to the buildings are middens, artifact deposits, and occasional pits suggesting considerable complexity in site formation processes. Objects associated with daily life are scattered inside and outside the buildings. Many are similar to specimens recovered from other fur trade sites throughout the region. These include religious paraphernalia, domestic artifacts (e.g., glass containers, copper kettle parts, faience and other European ceramics, iron knives), weaponry (e.g., flintlock hardware, musket balls, lead shot, gunflints), objects of personal adornment (e.g., glass beads, finger rings, buckles, brooches), and commercial objects directly related to the fur trade (e.g., lead seals, baling needles). It is not always possible to distinguish goods that were used by the occupants of Fort St. Joseph from those that were intended for trade. However, several types of artifacts and features and their associations speak to the social identities of the residents and the daily activities that were conducted at the fort in support of the fur trade.

A particularly interesting cache of artifacts was recovered in proximity to the habitation structures. It contained more than 125 flintlock musket parts, including numerous gun cocks, frizzens, vice screws, lock plates, mainsprings, breech plugs, trigger guards, and other miscellaneous hardware; metal scraps; and a *double sol* silver coin minted between 1709 and 1713 (figure 6.8; Giordano and Nassaney 2004). This feature has been interpreted as a gunsmith's repair kit associated with Antoine Dehaître (also De Lestre), who worked at the fort from

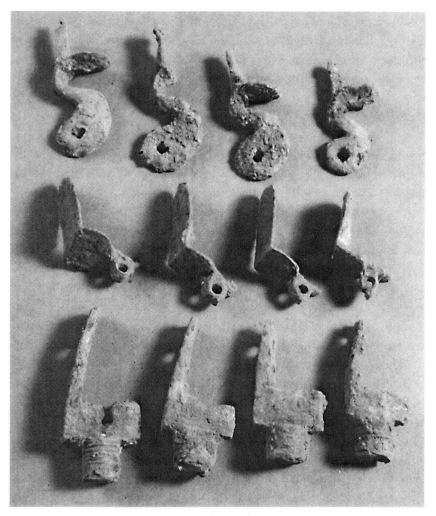

Figure 6.8 A sample of gun cocks, frizzens (the part of the lock mechanism that a gunflint strikes to produce a spark), and breech plugs from the gunsmith's cache at Fort St. Joseph. Photo by John Lacko. Courtesy of the Fort St. Joseph Archaeological Project.

1739 to 1752 (Nassaney et al. 2012, 67–68), or with one of the other documented gunsmiths. The French provided guns to their native allies, who requested them to their own specifications. Often the guns were lightweight and in need of frequent repair, and French gunsmiths were indispensable on the frontier. Documents indicate that resident smiths (e.g., Michel Durivage Baillonjeu, Antoine Dehaître) repaired and inspected native weapons at the Crown's expense for French and Indian combatants before the war against the Chickasaws (Peyser 1978, 99–99/2). Smiths at Fort St. Joseph, Chicago, and Michilimackinac also regularly produced "metal arrowheads" for the Indians; the blacksmith Amiot supplied Le Crapaud (the Toad) with 600 arrowheads in 1746 (Peyser 1978, 121/3, 123). Such large quantities were probably not limited to warfare and also must have been used to hunt prey for food and the fur trade. In addition, numerous gunflints, musket balls, and lead shot and evidence of their production have been found across the site, suggesting the importance of firearms in the fur trade.

Evidence for the processing and shipment of furs consists of a smudge pit, two baling needles (figure 3.2), and an enormous quantity of animal bone recovered from the floodplain. The smudge pit appeared as a shallow, basin-shaped depression, about 20–25 centimeters across and 9 centimeters deep (Cremin and Nassaney 2003, 79–82). It contained some charred oak wood and possible pinecones, ten grape seeds, two cherry stones, three fragments of acorn, and over 200 grams of corn, including cob, kernel, cupule, and stalk fragments. It is similar in form and contents to the pits found on the terrace and provides evidence of hide-processing activities on the floodplain in relatively close proximity to House 2. Whether it represents the work of a native woman, her *métis* daughter, or a French Canadian fur trader, it points to the shared practices that emanated from relations of interdependence in fur trade households at Fort St. Joseph.

Much of the butchering and processing of small fur-bearing animals likely occurred away from the Fort St. Joseph floodplain habitations. The absence of permanent European-style buildings and the paucity of imported ceramics on the terrace suggest a space devoted to the final stages of hide preparation. Once furs were processed, they were bundled in preparation for shipment by canoe. Large baling needles recovered from the floodplain (figure 3.2) were used to secure the bundles with sailcloth to protect them during transport.

The most direct evidence of the fur trade at Fort St. Joseph comes from a remarkably well-preserved assemblage of animal remains, though subsistence certainly played a role in the range of species represented. While analysis is ongoing, nearly 20,000 individual faunal specimens have been examined. Table 3 shows that the vast majority of animal remains recovered derives from a wide variety of wild species, particularly white-tailed deer. Domesticated animals, which included cows, pigs, horses, and chickens, represented a minimal contribution to the diet (Becker 2004; Martin 2008).

Over 4,000 individual specimens (bones, teeth, and bivalve shells) have been identified. They represent fifty vertebrate and invertebrate taxa: twenty bird taxa (order, subfamily, genus, or species), seventeen mammal taxa (genus or species), six fish taxa (family, genus, or species), at least four kinds of reptiles (all turtles), three species of freshwater mussels, and one amphibian (a frog) (see table 3).

Although not abundant, the diversity of bird taxa is consistent with other French faunal assemblages in the Midwest. They included trumpeter swan, sandhill crane, shorebirds, ruffed grouse, a prairie chicken, and domesticated chicken. Fish seem to be underrepresented, although lake sturgeon are more numerous than all the other fish species. The mammals include fur-bearers such as beaver, raccoon, muskrat, marten, bobcat, and gray fox, though all but beaver and raccoon appear in low numbers. Fragmentation makes it dif-

Table 3. Animal remains in the assemblage at Fort St. Joseph
by percent (n = 2,821)

White-tailed deer (*Odocoileus virginianus*)	73.7%
Raccoon (*Procyon lotor*)	5.7%
Beaver (*Castor canadensis*)	4.9%
Wild turkey (*Meleagris gallopavo*)	2.7%
Black bear (*Ursus americanus*)	2.4%
All ducks (minimum of 7 taxa)	2.1%
Swine (*Sus scrofa*)	1.8%
Porcupine (*Erethizon dorsatum*)	1.5%
Canada goose (*Branta canadensis*)	1.5%
All turtles (at least 4 species)	1.5%
Passenger pigeon (*Ectopistes migratorius*)	1.1%
All fish (5 taxa with lake sturgeon most common)	0.4%
All freshwater mussels (3 species)	0.2%
Total	99.5%

ficult to distinguish between large bovid animals such as cattle and bison. Although cattle are present, some bones may be either those of cattle or bison. The assemblage includes sixteen bones/teeth from elk (wapiti) and two horse teeth (Terrance Martin, personal communication, 2014).

The overwhelming frequency of deer bones and other wild species suggests a reliance on local food resources and the adoption of new culinary practices on the frontier. Terrance Martin (2008) has noted that high frequencies of local food resources are often indicative of the close relations that the French cultivated with their native allies, much as we would expect to see at a fur-trading post. Many of the bone and antler specimens that were modified to function as artifacts also reflect this close association with local Native Americans.

Much of the bone analyzed to date appears to derive from animals that were hunted and butchered for subsistence. Although fur-bearers are represented in the assemblage, they constitute a small percentage. However, it is likely that the deer in the assemblage at Fort St. Joseph were also hunted for their hides and were processed for leather goods such as moccasins, as they were at eighteenth-century Detroit (Cangany 2012). The smudge pits identified on the terrace and in the floodplain support this interpretation. This would also help explain the source of the deerskins merchants provided to natives and others that were noted in the vouchers discussed above. Peyser (1978, 123/3) also documented a memorandum of expenses that included "deerskin to make shoes" and "skins smoked (and) to make shoes." These "shoes" are likely *souliers sauvages* (Indian shoes), or what later became known as moccasins (see Cangany 2012, 268).

The high frequency of intentionally fractured deer bones suggests breakage patterns to extract marrow to produce tallow or grease by boiling in the newly imported kettles. Bear grease was a cherished commodity for the French, who used it for frying and seasoning (Ekberg 1985, 302; Ekberg 1998, 217; Surrey 2006, 293), especially since venison was so lean. Tallow appears in the vouchers (e.g., Peyser 1978, 130). In 1750, Jean-Baptist Lefebre provided tallow to natives who were "going down to Montreal to see the general." One of the uses of tallow was as an additive to pinesap to produce pitch for sealing or repairing birch bark canoes (Michael Zimmerman, personal communication, 2014). Adding the tallow during the boiling process made the pitch more easily workable and helped it stay malleable.

Innis (1962, 14) indicated (but without providing a reference) that the inner side of beaver pelts was "scraped and rubbed with the marrow of certain animals." The intensive breakage of deer bones at Fort St. Joseph may have been related to hide processing instead of (or in addition to) culinary practices. At this stage in the analysis, more than 100 bones exhibit cut marks consistent with hide removal, dismemberment, and filleting of meat. These occur on crania, vertebrae, ribs, and long bones of deer and on specimens of cattle, hogs, elk, black bear, beaver, raccoon, Canada goose, and trumpeter swan (Terrance Martin, personal communication, 2014). A demographic profile has yet to be established for deer to determine if hunting practices were selective (see Lapham 2005). Nevertheless, the faunal remains provide data about the types of animals that were being butchered and how bones were being processed for various economic uses. Analysis of intrasite distributional patterns will reveal if animal species are evenly represented in different areas of the site and if frequencies changed over the span of site occupation (Hearns 2015).

In addition to the remains of fur-bearing animals, artifacts have been recovered that facilitated trade or were intended for exchange for furs. Wampum (shell beads) has been found in archaeological contexts at Fort St. Joseph. Purple coloration (sometimes faded to pink) is indicative of quahog shells from the Atlantic Ocean (figure 6.9). The homogeneity of bead size and shape and the absence of biconical perforations suggest that these beads were produced on a lathe, perhaps in Albany or in other eastern workshops. It is likely that wampum made its way to the site as belts, strings, and individual beads, though these cannot be distinguished archaeologically. The merchant Hamelin provided the Corbeau family with "eight strings of wampum" in 1740 (Peyser 1978, 103). Though the quantity is not specified, the value of wampum in two entries in a 1739 voucher was 100 livres (textbox 1). When the cost of deerskins is excluded, wampum accounts for over 38 percent of the rest of the expenditures in this voucher charged to the Crown. Given that the wampum at the site was recovered in midden deposits and was evenly dispersed among households, it was probably used in everyday life in combination with other objects of adornment such as glass beads (see Kerr 2012; Loren 2010; Malischke 2009).

Cloth was one of the most common trade items provided to natives in the western Great Lakes region (Anderson 1994), and there is both documentary and archaeological evidence of its use at the fort. Men's shirts, Lyon cloth, and five ells (a unit of measurement) of nondescript cloth are noted in

Figure 6.9 This wampum recovered from Fort St. Joseph was made from an Atlantic hard-shelled clam or quahog (*Mercenaria mercenaria*). Length: 7 mm. Photo by LisaMarie Malischke.

one voucher (textbox 1). Other vouchers mention blankets, Mackinac coats, women's shirts, a man's work shirt, a hooded jacket, silk edging, and lace (Peyser 1978, 86, 98, 101, 103, 121/2, 121/4, 123/2, 123/3). Material manifestations of clothing appear archaeologically as durable elements such as metal buttons. But other evidence of cloth and clothing production also exists in the form of scissors, straight pins, thimbles, and awls. Scissors were useful for cutting cloth to exact sizes, and awls were used to pierce and produce leather products (e.g., moccasins, pouches, bags, leggings). Straight pins are typically made of copper alloy and are common in the archaeological record at the fort. Although needles frequently appeared in nineteenth-century trade lists (e.g., Wagner 2011, tables 6.1, 6.6, 6.7), only one possible specimen has been recovered from Fort St. Joseph, perhaps because needles were made of iron at this time. But needles and pins were essential for sewing the cloth that was shipped to and distributed from the site. Several thimbles have been recovered from the floodplain and the terrace. Interestingly, those from the floodplain are intact and may have been used with the large baling needles or in clothing repair or construction. In contrast, the thimble found on the terrace is perforated suggesting reuse for a decorative function (figure 4.6; see Langford 2011, 38; Quimby 1966, 76).

While cloth has yet to be recovered at the site, lead cloth seals are common archaeological finds (see Juen and Nassaney 2012, fig. 58). Quimby (1966, 75–76) notes that they are diagnostic of the Middle Historic period (1670–1760) and appear most frequently at forts and trading posts. Lead seals are common at fur trade sites since they were used by various cloth-producing nations, including England and France, both of which dominated the industry in the eighteenth century (Davis 2014, 2, 12). Seals are generally classified according to the markings they bear and the method used to attach them to the bolt of cloth (Adams 1989; Stone 1974a). The iconography that was stamped or etched on the obverse and reverse is critical when attempting to determine their point of origin. Many symbols on seals remain cryptic and unidentifiable, though others can be linked to cloth-producing cities, centers, or regions, some of which specialized in particular types of cloth.

Cathrine Davis (2014, 20–21) recently examined a collection of sixty-six lead seals from Fort St. Joseph, seventeen of which are from excavated contexts. Her study sought to document the collection for comparative purposes and establish the origins of the seals in order to determine the types of cloth that might have been sent to the site. Accounts of cloth imported to Fort St. Joseph are very general and limited in scope (e.g., textbox 1; Peyser 1978). Thus, analysis of seals can complement the evidence from historical documents. Davis (52–55) noted the possible presence of trade cloth from Mazamet (France) and cloth from Montauban, a city in the same region that produced woolens explicitly for trade with Native Americans and uniforms and *capotes* (hooded wool coats) (Dechêne 1988, 152). Some light cotton may have also been imported, but woolens were most common in the collection of identifiable seals, since natives preferred that fabric (Davis 2014, 69–70; see also Welters et al. 1996). Davis's research shows that among the seals identified from Fort Michilimackinac, Nîmes is most frequently represented and that these seals were most likely attached to nonwoolen cloth such as silk. This may suggest that a market for silks, cottons, and other luxury cloth did not extend to Fort St. Joseph, where more practical cloth was likely preferred (Davis 2014, 71).

Another study has focused on the production of tinkling cones at Fort St. Joseph (Giordano 2005; Giordano and Nassaney 2015). Tinkling cones, also referred to as tinklers, bangles, dangles, or jingles (Ehrhardt 2005, 119–120; Good 1972; Jelks 1967; Krause 1972; Odell 2001; Walthall and Brown 2001), are conical-shaped objects with an open apex that are formed by rolling a flat trapezoidal metal blank of cuprous metal cut from sheet metal around a mandrel (Ehrhardt 2005, 120–121). Recycled kettles were often the source of the raw material (figure 4.5; see Bradley 1987, 130–133, fig. 13). The kettle would be cut to produce a desired shape, then the edges would be ground, and the blank would be rolled to form the final cone shape. A thong or some type of hair (often deer or horse) with a knot at one end was threaded through the open tip. The "tinkling" sound comes from individual cones striking one another as they dangle. Tinkling cones are locally crafted objects that were attached to garments, moccasins, earrings, pouches, and bags for visually and aurally aesthetic purposes. These artifacts, which occur in the fur trade era throughout the midcontinent, were not imported from Europe in finished form and do not appear on French or English trade lists. They were typically produced in North America.

A number of tinkling cones (n = 20), preforms, and production debris (i.e., copper alloy sheet scrap) have been recovered from excavations at Fort St. Joseph. These objects provide contextual data that complements the collection of over 350 specimens at the Fort St. Joseph Museum. Brock Giordano (2005) collected data on the formal attributes (i.e., size and production techniques) of the museum specimens to assess the degree to which they were standardized during production (figure 6.10). His analysis demonstrated that tinkling cones exhibit considerable variation in size, techniques of production, and final form, implying the lack of standardization that one would expect if cones had been made by a limited number of specialized producers. Data from excavated contexts, particularly the dispersed spatial distribution of the finished forms and the copper alloy scrap metal that derives from their production, supports the idea that tinkling cones were produced in most households and were possibly used widely in fur trade society (Giordano and Nassaney 2015). Thus, new forms of material culture such as tinkling cones that were made of imported raw materials were probably produced and used by both natives and French residents of the fort. If this is the case, these material remains are an indication of close interactions between the two groups. Site investigations have been confined to a limited area, and more extensive work is needed to determine if the observed pattern is typical of other precincts or if production was confined to the segments of the society who occupied the households examined, such as fur traders, their wives, or others who crafted these intercultural objects.

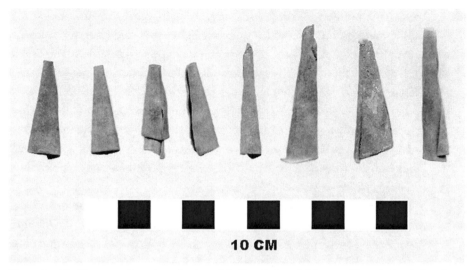

Figure 6.10. Tinkling cones from the collection of the Fort St. Joseph Museum. Photo by Brock Giordano.

In addition to tinkling cones, other artifacts found in association with the habitation structures provide an opportunity to relate their contents to their occupants' identities. Objects of personal adornment are sensitive markers because people consciously chose the clothes and decorative embellishments they placed on their bodies to express their social persona (Loren 2010; White 2005, 9). Ian Kerr (2012), who analyzed the contents of the Fort St. Joseph structures, has demonstrated that there were no significant differences in the sartorial paraphernalia (e.g., rings, buckles, brooches) they contained. He also noted that both military buttons and high-status goods were absent or occurred in very low frequencies, which he interpreted to mean that fur traders, not soldiers, occupied these huts (see Scott 2001b, 30). The materials were similar to those recovered from households at Fort Michilimackinac that were occupied by French and British traders (Kerr 2012). This interpretation of the residents' identities is supported by an analysis of the gunflints from the site. Only 6 of the 109 spall-type gunflints were suitable for large military muskets; the majority were consistent with the fowlers and trade guns most civilians and natives used for hunting (Carvalhaes 2011, 30).

The households at the fort also contain an interesting array of earbobs, wampum, European-style buttons and buckles associated with tinkling cones, and hundreds of seed beads, suggesting that sartorial practices in the multiethnic communities of fur trade society were mixed (Kerr 2012; Loren 2010; Nassaney 2008b). Several other objects indicate flexibility in the use of both native and European-inspired goods and practices. For example, in and among the European-styled houses we have recovered several stone, metal, and bone projectile points. These suggest either the continuance of bow and arrow technology by natives and/or its adoption by French Canadians. This technology must have accrued some benefits to the fort occupants, which would explain why the Crown paid for several gunsmiths who could produce iron arrowheads (e.g., see Peyser 1978, 121/3).

Materials associated with daily activities have been recovered in and immediately adjacent to habitation structures at Fort St. Joseph. Sediments have been wet-screened through 1/8" mesh and flotation has been used with samples from feature contexts. Significant quantities of calcined bone have frequently been recovered near fireplaces, indicating that cooking took place within those structures. These small fragments represent a variety of species that were prepared and discarded over open fires. House 1 also produced an awl, several straight pins, and over 200 seed beads in front of the fireplace. These objects point to leather working and bead embroidery by the light and heat of the fire. Another activity that required an open fire was the production of ammunition. Lead sprue and spatter (solidified pools of once-molten lead from inadvertent spills in the production of musket balls) are common at the site. This is evidence that local ammunition was produced on site, some of which was used in hunting fur-bearing animals.

Efforts to definitively attribute materials and inferred activities to segments of the population are fraught with difficulties. Yet a number of artifact forms that are absent in French culture appear in the context of French Canadian fur trade society, implying peaceful coexistence across cultural lines and the acceptance of new practices. This extends to leisure activities. A modified deer phalanx (Nassaney 2008a, 307) found at the site was probably used in the well-known cup-and-pin game that many natives played. Several gaming pieces made of bone have also been recovered. Two are remarkably similar to specimens Potawatomi women used in a game of chance (Clifton 1978; Nassaney 2008b, fig. 12). One example still has red pigment (vermilion?) adhering to incised surfaces. Finally, both white clay (n = 207) and stone (n = 56) smoking pipe fragments have been recovered. The relative high proportion of stone fragments suggests the importance of ritual mediation in the many exchanges that took place at the site alongside casual smoking (see Nassaney 2008b, fig. 11; Mann 2004). It may also indicate that these types were interchangeable and shared by French and natives alike (cf. Trubowitz 1992b; Wagner 2003).

Another commodity on trade lists and vouchers is vermilion, a red pigment imported from China that "could be rubbed into skin, wood, bone, or hides, or mixed with water or grease for face and body paint" (C. Gilman 1982, 33; Peyser 1978, 77, 86, 94; Wagner 2011, table 6.1). Fort St. Joseph vouchers indicate that vermilion was provided to natives prior to the Chickasaw War (textbox 1). Sometimes tallow is also listed, suggesting that the two could be mixed to make the face paint that was worn during warfare and formal negotiations. A specimen of ocher—hardened clay colored by iron oxide—was recovered from Fort St. Joseph. A scratch test and the facets on its surface indicate that it could have been shaved or ground to produce a suitable bright red pigment. The use of red ocher extends back to the Late Archaic period in much of eastern North America where it may have signified blood and other life-giving properties in ritual contexts (Ritzenthaler and Quimby 1962). Native peoples continued to use red pigments in the fur trade era. The French adopted the practice of face painting, likely in imitation of their native allies (Hackett 1934, 249, cited in Loren 2010, 29; Nassaney 2008b). It may have been used to ease intercultural interactions in contexts of exchange and negotiations, much as the calumet was used.

Even as the French borrowed local raw materials, finished artifacts, and novel cultural practices from their native allies, they imported significant quantities of goods to New France to re-create some aspects of their culture. Glass bottles, windowpane glass, refined earthenware ceramics, religious paraphernalia, and objects of personal adornment testify to the flow of goods (Nassaney 2008b). However, supply lines were not always reliable, and repairs and innovation were both necessary. Numerous fragments of copper alloy sheet scrap from worn-out kettles were cut, scored, folded, snipped, and ground to produce patches and rivets so salvageable kettles could be mended. People on the frontier often crafted their own commodities, as is suggested by the evidence of local production of musket balls and tinkling cones and local deer-hide processing and grease extraction (Nassaney et al. 2007). Members of the Fort St. Joseph community who occupied the terrace and the floodplain liberally borrowed various forms of material culture from different cultural traditions as a strategy for coexistence at particular historical moments. Social identities were fluid and situational in fur trade society and individuals could modify their appearance materially to reflect that. However, some social contexts required more formal behaviors and attire. Certain artifact classes recovered from Fort St. Joseph such as shoe buckles and sleeve buttons (cuff links) suggest that notions of Old World civility and fashion were neither completely ignored nor forgotten, even on the remote frontier of New France (see Nassaney and Brandão 2009). But practicality seems to have been the norm, a value carried forward in the tradition that ironically became known as Yankee ingenuity.

The Legacy of the Fur Trade at Fort St. Joseph

Over a century has passed since Judge Coolidge spoke in the spirit of manifest destiny at the dedication of the boulder to commemorate Fort St. Joseph. The archaeological record challenges his narrative. New readings of historical documents and sensitivity to the concerns of various stakeholders, including descendant communities, make it increasingly difficult to characterize the French as empire builders and native peoples as mere impediments to civilization (Nassaney 2008a). Contemporary archaeology can provide instructive and persuasive stories about interdependence and mutual respect in the fur trade era that can help build trust across the boundaries that divide the descendants of natives and Europeans. Since the archaeological record is underdetermined, multiple interpretations are reasonably consistent with the available evidence (Saitta 2007, 16). Instead of choosing to interpret metal artifacts as evidence of the superiority of European goods, we can examine those same objects to determine how people of different ethnic backgrounds used them in daily life. The occupants of Fort St. Joseph did not find it necessary, desirable, or possible to reproduce many aspects of French culture in the interior of North America. They were members of a fur trade society and that made them different from their forebearers and relatives in Quebec, Montreal, and France. They were laying the groundwork for a culture marked by practicality, inclusiveness, and creativity.

The archaeological record of the activities and identities of the new Americans who lived at Fort St. Joseph suggests that it was a multiethnic community of French *and* Indians in which kin relations and political alliances transcended racial and ethnic categories (Nassaney 2008a, 2008b). While social and cultural differences certainly existed in this pluralistic society (see Nassaney and Brandão 2009), it is increasingly difficult to apply essentialist categories such as "French" and "Indian" to the residents of Fort St. Joseph. Interactions on the frontier led to new cultural forms indicative of ethnogenesis, a product of the culture of colonialism (see Mann 2003, 2008; Silliman 2005). This interpretation suggests that the French were more accommodating and less interested in "civilizing" the groups they encountered than earlier historians were willing or able to admit (Nassaney 2008b). The French were mutually dependent on their native allies, with whom they established close personal, social, and political ties. They likely learned as much from the natives as they taught them (Nassaney 2008a).

Postcolonial theory compels researchers to consider the factors that influence social reconstructions and the implications of those reconstructions (Nassaney 2012a). Contemporary social relations impinge on the stories we tell about Fort St. Joseph because historical conceptualizations of colonial encounters are grounded in current sociopolitical conditions. As archaeologists embrace the value of an indigenous, collaborative, or community-based archaeology, they become receptive to the needs and concerns of a larger group of stakeholders who have a vested interest in the work they do (Nicholas 2008).

The archaeology of Fort St. Joseph blurs the distinctions between the colonized and the colonizers, providing conceptual space to consider the mutual influences that were needed to sustain the fur trade and the outcomes of daily interactions. Sometimes the interests and the experiences of the colonized and the colonizer diverged, while at other times they overlapped. As anthropological archaeologists, it is our responsibility to document this variation to understand the whole of the human condition. Inclusive fur trade archaeologies are poised to make a contribution that accords with both our scientific and our ethical goals.

An emphasis on the mutual exchanges that took place in fur trade society is consistent with multivocal, agent-centered approaches that aim to decolonize the discipline (Nassaney 2012a). Narratives that essentialize the French and native groups fail to acknowledge the material conditions of cultural blending that archaeology has revealed at Fort St. Joseph. By highlighting this unity in fur trade society, archaeologists can rectify their own colonialist practices and work toward a broader reconciliation between their practices and the stakeholders with whom they share an interest. A critical perspective compels us to ask ourselves who is served by a particular interpretation and how it empowers dominant groups and excludes marginalized groups. A reflexive stance will prevent archaeologists from riding roughshod over peoples' histories. Collaboration invites participation from a wide audience with a stake in cultural and historical reconstruction, exposes connections between the past and present, and underscores the importance of the fur trade in forging an American identity.

Public Archaeology at Fort St. Joseph

The Fort St. Joseph Archaeological Project has been a collaborative venture since its inception in 1998. Community concerns have been integral to how the site has been investigated and interpreted (Berliner and Nassaney 2015; Claussen et al. 2013; Nassaney 2011). The outcome has been an award-winning public archaeology program in which archaeologists, community groups, and individuals have held an ongoing dialogue to ensure public participation, outreach, and education in the study of the fur trade.

The partnership developed organically as groups with a vested interest in Fort St. Joseph emerged as stakeholders. Support the Fort, Inc., a local community group interested in the history of the fort, first contacted Western Michigan University (WMU) for help in locating the site. WMU brought the archaeological expertise needed to conduct the 1998 survey and subsequent excavations, analyses, and publications for scholarly and general audiences. The city of Niles owns the site of Fort St. Joseph, and the Fort St. Joseph Museum is responsible for curating artifacts and data collected from the site. WMU and the city entered into a ten-year agreement in 2008 that ensures that the investigation and interpretation of the site will be done in the interest of the public. In 2007, the Niles City Council appointed the Fort St. Joseph Archaeology Advisory Committee, whose members represent diverse interests related to the fort. The committee meets regularly and recommends and promotes the course of action for the investigation of Fort St. Joseph. This ensures that esoteric archaeological goals are not pursued at the expense of work that has a broader public appeal. Various funding agencies, service organizations, private individuals, and volunteers, who share the vision of making the history of the fur trade accessible to a wide audience, have been a source of ongoing support.

Public education and outreach convey the findings of the archaeological investigations, which provide a more inclusive interpretation of the past.

People who were previously written out of history are highlighted, as are the close working relationships that developed between the natives and Europeans. Interpretations often present the French as neophytes with limited knowledge of the landscape, resources, and local customs who were therefore dependent to a considerable degree on their native allies. This outreach demonstrates that archaeology is both a way to see beyond the primary documents that harbor the biases and limitations of their literate authors and a way of revealing the unspoken, lived experience of daily life.

The community has embraced this message, which is disseminated through various channels. The most intense activity takes place during the WMU archaeological field school that brings together graduate and undergraduate students to learn and teach the craft and science of archaeology over a six-week period. A public lecture series is held in conjunction with the field school that hosts nationally renowned speakers, who discuss their research pertaining to a theme selected for the season. Over the past few years we have highlighted the women of New France, the militia on the eve of revolution, eighteenth-century foodways, architecture, and, of course, the fur trade (Juen and Nassaney 2012; [Fort St. Joseph Archaeological Project] 2011). Our chosen theme is emphasized in all of our outreach efforts. In addition to the lectures, the project has offered a popular summer camp program since 2002 that gives middle and high school students, teachers who need continuing education credit, and lifelong learners the opportunity to engage in the archaeological enterprise and obtain hands-on experience. Since 2006, each field season has culminated with the annual Archaeology Open House, when the general public is invited to view ongoing excavations and experience interpretation in the form of artifact displays, presentations by public scholars, informational panels, and living history reenactments. Executed largely by the efforts of the field school students and staff and volunteers from the community, this form of experiential learning provides the interested public with a chance to see archaeology in their own backyard and engage with the process of creating history. Approximately 2,000 people have attended this free event each season, making it one of the most popular educational programs in southwest Michigan.

The project staff and students also use other formal and informal means of communicating about Fort St. Joseph to the community. These efforts have earned the project numerous awards, such as the Historical Society of Michigan's Education Award (2009, 2013) and the Governor's Historic Preservation Award (2007). Each week during the field season, students participate in the Niles French Market, where local farmers sell produce and craftspeople share their work (Berliner and Nassaney 2015). WMU students set up a booth and interact with the public by discussing the project, handing out informational booklets, and selling T-shirts. This forum often prompts discussion of the archaeological process, what we know about the fur trade, the importance of the past for the present, and how the study of the fort enhances community pride. Site investigations have also led to the production and dissemination of a series of four DVDs that examine various aspects of the project, including site discoveries, public archaeology, and student involvement. Finally, the project has a significant and growing online presence (Western Michigan University n.d.). Informational panels and booklets are posted online, including the results of funded research on the fur trade (e.g., Juen and Nassaney 2012). In addition to the website, the project maintains a Facebook page that informs the public about programs and upcoming events. Beginning in 2011, regular blog postings have allowed the public to follow our discoveries in the field and in the laboratory throughout the year. Entries often highlight evidence as it comes to light and discuss what it tells us about the people who participated in the fur trade. Emphasis is placed on how their lives were both similar to and different from ours in the twenty-first century. Archaeology underscores the connections between the present and the past, linking detritus discarded along a riverbank by anonymous people to their contributions to the American experience. Public fascination with these stories indicates a considerable level of interest in topics such as the fur trade at Fort St. Joseph and demonstrates the relevance of archaeological research beyond the community of scholars.

7

The Fur Trade Legacy and the American Experience

For most of human history, people outside the tropics relied on animal furs to clothe their hairless bodies (Ingold 1994). Hunter-gatherer societies worldwide derived much of their protein from the flesh of mammals, and hunting was central to subsistence practices for millennia, especially in cold climates. Domesticated animals were no less important for meat, milk, and blood and by-products such as fur, wool, leather, and bone. While many cultures viewed animals as part of the interconnected web of existence, in the Western tradition animals were generally seen as subservient to humans. Early European explorers and settlers brought that ideology to the New World as they sought to profit from mercantilism.

For many Americans today, furs and other animal products evoke the mastery of humans over other living forms, rightly or wrongly. Although there have been dissident voices in defense of animal rights since the nineteenth century, activism did not galvanize until the 1960s among people who disapproved of the use of animals for food, clothing, experimentation, and entertainment (Sayers 2003). While this may be a growing perspective, it remains the minority one. Meat is consumed by large segments of the population and animal furs continue to be used as luxury goods. Today, 80 percent of the pelts in the multibillion-dollar fur industry come from animals raised on farms. Hunting, capturing, and processing fur-bearing animals in the wild are declining practices of diminished commercial value, though they are still conducted for sport and supplement household economies in many areas across the continent.

The North American fur trade emerged in the sixteenth century and expanded over the next 400 years to include furs from numerous animals that could be sold at a profit. This spatially expansive and enduring enterprise varied considerably according to the nature of the groups involved, their geographic location, resource availability, political motivations, goods exchanged, and numerous other factors. European traders depended upon Native American harvesting and processing techniques and modes of transportation to acquire furs, and the means of subsistence provisioning were based on native cultural developments. Traders and native peoples were forced to communicate and cooperate, at least in the early phases of the trade when power relations were more equitable. Fortunately for archaeologists, the fur trade had a decidedly tangible dimension—the detritus of everyday life. Although historical documents suggest similarities among the processes that took place in New England in the seventeenth century, the western Great Lakes region in the eighteenth century, and the Northwest Coast of North America in the nineteenth century, closer inspection reveals that the similarities are likely to be only superficial. Rigorous comparative analysis is needed to identify the material patterns of the fur trade era.

A phenomenon as broad and all-encompassing as the fur trade is as difficult to characterize as other large-scale processes, such as capitalism or colonialism (see Matthews 2010). The challenge for archaeologists is to examine global forces at local scales to understand their social, economic, and material implications for human agents. For example, the fur trade was experienced differently by various segments of society along lines of gender, status, race, and ethnicity (Pyszczyk 1989; Scott 1991b; Vibert 2010). It is important to interrogate the record at this level of specificity instead of glossing over its impact and assuming homogeneity among men, women, and children; chiefs and commoners; French and English; officers and laborers; and creoles and métis. By drawing upon multiple lines of evidence, historical archaeologists are well positioned to explore the materiality of the fur trades and expose a multiplicity of experiences that contribute to a better understanding of this aspect of North American history and the ways that natives, newcomers, and their descendants intertwined their lives to create a truly new world.

Some of the daily practices of the fur trade reinforced values that have contributed to the formation of an American experience. In this closing chapter I highlight some of the most significant cultural and ecological impacts of the growth, operation, and decline of the trade. I also examine how the trade has been remembered in popular culture and how those portrayals serve to create and perpetuate a particular perspective on nationhood, citizenship, and American identity. I conclude by advocating a revisionist representation of the fur trade that is more consistent with contemporary readings of the archaeological record and useful for building a multicultural and inclusive future.

Ecological and Cultural Consequences

One of the problems with discussing the consequences of the fur trade is the potential for envisioning the outcomes of 400 years of animal exploitation and interactions between Native Americans and Europeans as inevitable. In the early history of the trade, colonists were generally dependent upon native groups for provisions and geographical knowledge. Under these conditions, relatively peaceful relations prevailed, and ways of settling differences, such as the calumet, were developed. Amicable relations among some groups led to the sharing of technologies and the creative amalgamation of language, belief systems, styles of negotiation, and kinship (White 2011).

Cultural interactions were mutually transformative in ways that could be neither predicted nor reversed. The global nature of the fur trade meant that distant events had local impacts for all participants. Those who participated in tea ceremonies in Boston used porcelain cups and saucers made in China. These had been purchased from local merchants who had access to overseas markets in Canton through ship masters who exchanged sea otter skins they acquired from native producers on the Northwest Coast for manufactured goods made in Europe that were obtained as they circumnavigated the globe (Howay 1923). Mandan women skinned buffalos for their robes using knives from the John Russell Cutlery Company, which distributed its products by barge from the Green River down the Connecticut River to steamships in New York, which took them to New Orleans, where they were placed on steamboats to St. Louis and taken up the Missouri to reach native consumers (Woodward 1927). The London gentry wore felt hats that were produced from beaver fur acquired in central New York, which Iroquoian hunters delivered in exchange for wampum produced by coastal Algonquian tribes who traded it to English settlers for goods produced in British workshops (Ceci 1990). The fur trade wove an intricate web that had long-range consequences for everyone in its reach.

The acquisition of furs prompted ancillary activities besides the provisioning needed to sustain traders in the form of intensified production of maize, wild rice, pemmican, and other staples. The increased hunting and warfare stimulated by the trade and competition required more guns and ammunition. The Sauks and the Mesquakis had begun mining and smelting lead in northwest Iowa by 1766. They used molds presumably to make musket balls, which they traded with other nations (Kay 1977, 175). The Winnebagos (Ho-Chunks) of Wisconsin also produced lead, which they exchanged for food provided by the traders. Traders then exchanged lead with other native groups for furs in yet another triangular trade (Kay 1977, 332).

Although Europeans may initially have tried to impose mercantile practices on natives, the trade had to meet the needs and desires of both parties if it was to succeed. While the fur trade opened up possibilities for the circulation of goods and connections with distant groups, such entanglements within a larger world system brought a host of negative consequences that native groups were particularly powerless to control. Disease, warfare, population loss, alcoholism, and loss of land placed natives at a decided disadvantage in terms of their ability to procure furs and participate in exchange relations on an equal basis. Unscrupulous traders sold defective goods, seized skins, and kidnapped leaders to improve bargaining conditions (Gibson 1992). Americans were especially prone to engage in these behaviors, particularly when they gained an upper hand by establishing permanent settlements, monopolizing exchange, and conducting trade on their own terms (see Rogers 1990, 68). As the trade evolved, kinship played a lesser role and exchange relations became capitalist (see C. Gilman 1982, 2).

Yet contrary to models that posit a general and persistent decline in native population as a result of the fur trade, Kay (1977, 164) argued that the native population actually increased in the eighteenth century in Wisconsin "owing to recovery from 17th century dispersal and adoption of refugees from neighboring groups." Moreover, in Wisconsin and in many other places in North America, natives were not a threat to European expansion since they were viewed as customers and suppliers in the economy. Suffice it to say that natives were active participants in the fur trade and not passive victims, as earlier historiography and archaeology suggested.

The resources of the natural world were equally important factors in the long-term success of the fur trade. There is no evidence that natives intentionally implemented conservation measures; the reproductive viability of most species was not threatened by pre-Contact exploitation rates (see Krech 1999). However, unprecedented European demands for furs jeopardized some animal species in localized habitats. For example, Innis (1962, 28) argued that improved hunting equipment rapidly led to the overhunting of beaver in the St. Lawrence River Valley. He (1962, 6) also hypothesized that settlement expansion into the heart of the continent was driven by the destruction of the beaver, though other factors were certainly at play.

The sheer volume of animals taken indicate that their numbers must have declined. In the early nineteenth century, "tribes across the Plains were trading nearly 100,000 bison robes every year, in addition to the thousands they killed for their own use and those that were killed to provide protein for the traders. Hunters at Fort Union alone, for example, annually killed some 600 to 800 bison to feed the fort staff" (Wood et al. 2011, 10). Beavers were extinct by the 1860s in the middle Missouri River region and the great herds of bison had been reduced considerably.

Using historical documents, Kay (1977) examined the ecological impact of the Green Bay fur trade from the seventeenth through the nineteenth centuries to determine if wildlife depletion had occurred and if so, how it influenced native settlement patterns and subsistence practices in the region. She found that big game animals that were important to subsistence (i.e., bison, beaver, elk, deer) had been overharvested but that muskrat and marten were plentiful as late as 1836 (see also Clayton 1964). The earliest records of wildlife depletion in North America refer to beaver. Kay (1977, 157) noted that they were gone from southern Ontario in 1634, from New York state by the 1640s, and near Mackinac by 1700. This general trend appears to be borne out by the archaeological record, which finds that animal remains exhibit shifts in species composition that reflect new exploitation patterns (e.g., Jordan 2008). The presence of beaver bones at Fort St. Joseph in the eighteenth century suggests that beaver continued to be important in the western Great Lakes region at that time. By the late eighteenth century, however, deer and raccoon had replaced beaver as the primary fur resource in the region (Franzen 2004; Gilman 1974; Kay 1977).

In the Pacific Northwest, sea otters were rapidly depleted in coastal waters. Overhunting was driven by the great profits both native and white traders could earn (Gibson 1988, 385). By the 1820s, the low reproductive rate of this animal could not be sustained and it faced extinction. Changing styles that suppressed demand ultimately saved the sea otter. From 1823 to 1841, the

HBC implemented what is known as the fur desert policy in the Columbia River Valley and its tributaries. The HBC designed the policy to leave few live animals for competing traders to harvest and consequently discourage Americans from entering its territory (Langford 2011, 32; Ott 2003).

In her study of the deerskin trade in the southeastern colonies in the seventeenth century, Lapham (2005, 149) claimed that continued depopulation of deer in the east forced merchants to seek hides from settlements farther west. Yet Waselkov (1998, 203–205), who used both archaeological and historical evidence, argued that deer remained plentiful in the same region through the eighteenth century. Animal density must be assessed for each locale, and the fact that populations are capable of rapid rebound when they remain undisturbed for one or two generations must be taken into account in any analysis.

Resource exploitation rates also varied widely over time. Although such short-term fluctuations may not be detectable archaeologically, they can be documented using historical sources. Estimates of game availability and returns on the trade for the AFC's Western Outfit in the tri-state region of Illinois, Iowa, and Wisconsin suggest that "the exploitation of resources was too low to have effectively harmed breeding populations among the Dakota" in the nineteenth century (Whelan 1993, 263–264, quoted in Hannes 1994, 25). Similarly, the quantities of furs collected in northern Minnesota challenge explanations that attribute a decline in the fur trade to overexploitation. The St. Paul firm of Joseph Ullman and Company shipped more than 800,000 pelts in 1870, nearly three times the number collected by the AFC's Western Outfit in 1836 (Gilman 1972, 103–104, cited in Hannes 1994, 26). With these data, Gilman (1972) concluded that the decline in the fur trade was caused by a labor shortage created by the movement of whites further west and the dispossession of Native Americans from their land holdings and not by the depletion of fur-bearing animals, whose populations remained healthy (see Hussey [1957] for a similar argument in the Pacific Northwest).

Animals were not the only casualties of the fur trade. Other resources needed to sustain the trade were also overexploited. For example, after the 1830s, goods were transported into the heart of the continent up the Missouri River by steamboat (Wood et al. 2011, 8). A vessel the size of the *Yellowstone* that made repeated visits to Fort Clark burned ten cords of wood a day, an amount that weighed between twenty-five and forty tons. As a result, the forests surrounding Fort Clark had all but vanished by the late 1850s; their wood was used to fuel the hundreds of steamboats that ascended the river with goods to exchange for furs.

Contrasting Portrayals of the Legacy of the Fur Trade

The history of the fur trade will never be fully known to us because it had various manifestations and meanings even for those who lived it. Our understandings will always be partial. In addition, our reconstructions through history and archaeology differ from public perceptions (Peers 1998). Thus, the fur trade is a study in contrasting portrayals taken from different historical moments to serve shifting national myths. Bruce White (1982, 125) aptly caricatures an earlier myth of the trade as

> [spring] brigades of canoes manned by cheerful, singing, hungover French-Canadian canoemen . . . impelled by a spontaneous spirit of adventure in search of the furs that would make them all rich. . . . European manufactures were so useful and attractive to the simpleminded Indians that they paid enormous prices to traders and quickly abandoned their own material culture, leading them to lose all their native cultural traditions. . . . Fur traders actuated only by greed quickened this inevitable process by "flooding" the Indian country with rum— the very essence of European civilization that drove primitive man to destruction while making the fur trader wealthy.

In this myth, a colorful French voyageur of the Canadian borderlands married a native woman, paddled a birch bark canoe, wore a casual toque with the tassel tossed to the side, and met all sorts of challenges in the north woods to obtain furs in exchange for the precious trinkets and bolts of cloth he provided to his native customers. This myth of ethnic harmony and interaction contrasts with the independent mountain man of the 1840s who led his packhorse up a narrow pass with a knife ready at his side so he could ward off unexpected threats from man and beast. Yet both embody virtues of America—the former as America was and the latter as she would become. When the English defeated the French in the Seven Years' War, the process of reinscribing a new narrative on the land began (Mann 2003) and the mythic voyageur began to be downplayed. He was a likeable character but was too frivolous to be the basis for an Anglo national identity. In contrast, the mountain man was everything America aspired to be—forward looking, energetic, resourceful, and staunchly individualistic. He only needed to be merged with the ruthless, land-hungry pioneer to create an American archetype.

Historical archaeology shows that these imaginings are far too simplistic to fit with the diversity of the material record that was created over the spatial and temporal expanse of the fur trade. Archaeology forces us to challenge the popular mythical figures of the fur trade. In the course of adopting the iconic mountain man for the national narrative, much had to be forgotten that might be worth reclaiming in the twenty-first century. The lessons of the interdependence that developed in the fur trade between unknown but knowable strangers were lost. The practice and possibility of rapprochement was replaced with arrogance, cruelty, and intimidation. A history of interaction and mutual respect across cultural lines and the creative process of crafting a new culture in tandem with (rather than in opposition to) others did not serve the new nation. The native people's creative practice of transforming goods for new purposes was appropriated and renamed "Yankee ingenuity." Older fur trade history became marginalized in the nineteenth century, when evolutionary and racialized ideologies gained ascendency (Orser 2007). Interdependent relations were inconsistent with the concept of manifest destiny and the desire of Americans to transform all peoples into their own likeness (see Camp 2013). Native peoples who had helped nurture new Americans were no longer deemed useful even as food producers or enslaved labor. Natives were moved farther and farther west. Miscegenation was frowned upon and native or nonwhite blood (the one-drop rule) placed all people of color in a subservient class. Limited efforts were made to civilize those who wished to stay in the East, but a belief that biology determined behavior doomed such experiments to failure. In commemorations of Fort St. Joseph in the early twentieth century, the City of Four Flags ignored the contributions of natives to the fur trade and denied the presence of native descendants who clung to their homelands. Ironically, the "removal of American Indians from their land—the worst of the many terrible things done to them—was as much contrary to the interests of the fur trade as it was to the health and cultural well-being of the Indians" (White 1982, 125).

The archaeology of the North American fur trade over the past century reflects the dominant concerns of the broader discipline of archaeology. For much of the twentieth century, archaeology served the interests of colonialism, but there are signs that this narrative is being reversed as the discipline becomes more sensitive to the interests of a larger community of stakeholders. Foremost is a gradual and long-overdue shift toward consideration of the central role of native groups in the fur trade (e.g., Peterson and Anfinson 1984). As archaeologists pay increasing attention to native concerns, they will accord native groups greater agency and recognize them as often equal, if not dominant, partners in a complex set of relationships that extended over much of the North American continent for several centuries.

The process of remembering the fur trade and our collective history can be cathartic because it brings to our attention the good, the bad, and the ugly. Alongside a history of cooperation, ingenuity, and autonomy are practices of reckless individualism, unbridled competition, racialization, and genocide (Camp 2013; Jordan 2008; Orser 2007). Archaeology can provide a means of recovery from the narratives that dehumanize us all (Nassaney 2012a). It can help us identify sites that played a role in the fur trade and provide the opportunity to interrogate and commemorate them in order to come to a new understanding about the meaning of the past for the future. The National Park Service recognizes the importance of fur trade sites and knows that "there are places in our country, such as Fort Vancouver, that are a part of our psyche and represent our spirit" (Fortmann 2011, 109). A movement has begun that seeks to reach an ever-wider audience with the story of the people who contributed to daily life at many fur trade sites. As with most of America, the infrastructure was built from the ground up by people whose lives have not been recorded in documents. Their voices can be heard, however, in the detritus scattered about the smudge pits, vernacular houses, and workspaces of sites that range from large trading posts to small encampments. While not all these sites have the same story to tell, collectively they constitute a narrative that is more complete and compelling than earlier accounts that relied exclusively on written sources about the fur trade. These sites have much to say about the American past and how it resonates in the present.

References

Adams, Diane

1989 *Lead Seals from Fort Michilimackinac, 1715–1781*. Archaeological Completion Report Series, no. 14. Mackinac State Historic Parks, Mackinac Island, MI.

Allen, Robert S.

1983 *Peter Fidler and Nottingham House, Lake Athabasca, 1802–1806*. History and Archaeology series, no. 69. National Historic Parks and Sites Branch, Parks Canada, Environment Canada, Ottawa.

Ames, Kenneth M., and H. D. G. Maschner

1999 *People of the Northwest Coast: Their Archaeology and Prehistory*. Thames and Hudson, London.

Anderson, Dean

1994 The Flow of European Trade Goods into the Western Great Lakes Region, 1715–1760. In *The Fur Trade Revisited*, edited by Jennifer S. H. Brown, William J. Eccles, and Donald P. Heldman, 93–115. Michigan State University Press, East Lansing, and Mackinac State Historic Parks, Mackinac Island, MI.

Arkush, Brooke S.

2000 Improving Our Understanding of Native American Acculturation through the Archaeological Record: An Example from the Mono Basin of Eastern California. In *Interpretations of Native North American Life: Material Contributions to Ethnohistory*, edited by Michael S. Nassaney and Eric S. Johnson, 188–224. Society for Historical Archaeology and University Press of Florida, Gainesville.

Arndt, Katherine Louise

1996 Dynamics of the Fur Trade on the Middle Yukon River, Alaska, 1839–1868. PhD dissertation, University of Alaska Fairbanks.

Ballard, Ralph

1973   *Old Fort St. Joseph*. Hard Scrabble Books, Berrien Springs, MI.

Bamforth, Douglas B.

1993   Stone Tools, Steel Tools: Contact Period Household Technology at Helo. In *Ethnohistory and Archaeology: Approaches to Postcontact Change in the Americas*, edited by J. Daniel Rogers and Samuel M. Wilson, 49–72. Plenum Press, New York.

2003   Discussion. In *Stone Tools in the Contact Era*, edited by Charles R. Cobb, 165–172. University of Alabama Press, Tuscaloosa.

Beaudoin, Matthew A.

2013   A Hybrid Identity in a Pluralistic Nineteenth-Century Colonial Context. *Historical Archaeology* 47(2): 45–63.

Becker, Rory

2004   Eating Ethnicity: Examining 18th Century French Colonial Identity through Selective Consumption of Animal Resources in the North American Interior. MA thesis, Department of Anthropology, Western Michigan University, Kalamazoo.

Beeson, Lewis H.

1900   Fort St. Joseph—The Mission, Trading Post and Fort, Located about One Mile South of Niles, Michigan. *Collections of the Michigan Pioneer and Historical Society* 28: 179–186.

Behm, Jeffrey

2008   The Meskwaki in Eastern Wisconsin: Ethnohistory and Archaeology. *Wisconsin Archeologist* 89(1&2): 7–85.

Berliner, Kelley, and Michael S. Nassaney

2015   The Role of the Public in Public Archaeology: Ten Years of Outreach and Collaboration at Fort St. Joseph. *Journal of Community Archaeology* and *Heritage* 2(1): 3–21.

Bettarel, Robert L., and Hale G. Smith

1973   *The Moccasin Bluff Site and the Woodland Cultures of Southwestern Michigan*. Anthropological Papers, no. 49. Museum of Anthropology, University of Michigan, Ann Arbor.

Bibeau, Donald F.

1984   Fur Trade Literature from the Tribal Point of View: A Critique. In *Rendezvous: Selected Papers of the Fourth North American Fur Trade Conference, 1981*, edited by Thomas C. Buckley, 83–92. North American Fur Trade Conference, St. Paul, MN.

Biggar, Henry P.

1901   *The Early Trading Companies of New France: A Contribution to the History of Commerce and Discovery in North America*. University of Toronto, Toronto.

Binford, Lewis R.

1967 Smudge Pits and Hide Smoking: The Use of Analogy in Archaeological Reasoning. *American Antiquity* 32: 1–12.

Birk, Douglas A.

1982 The La Verendryes: Reflections on the 250th Anniversary of the French Posts of La Mer de L'Ouest. In *Where Two Worlds Meet: The Great Lakes Fur Trade*, by Carolyn Gilman, 116–119. Museum Exhibit Series, no. 2. Minnesota Historical Society, St. Paul.

1984 John Sayer and the Fond du Lac Trade: The North West Company in Minnesota and Wisconsin. In *Rendezvous: Selected Papers of the Fourth North American Fur Trade Conference, 1981*, edited by Thomas C. Buckley, 51–61. North American Fur Trade Conference, St. Paul, MN.

1989 *John Sayer's Snake River Journal, 1804–05*. Institute for Minnesota Archaeology, Inc., Minneapolis.

1991 French Presence in Minnesota: The View from Site Mo20 near Little Falls. In *French Colonial Archaeology: The Illinois Country and Western Great Lakes*, edited by John A. Walthall, 237–266. University of Illinois Press, Urbana.

2008 Lost, Found, and Fading Away: The Archaeology of a North West Company Fort Site at Whitefish Lake, Crow Wing County, Minnesota. *Minnesota Archaeologist* 67: 140–174.

Birk, Douglas A., and Jeffrey J. Richner

2004 *From Things Left Behind: A Study of Selected Fur Trade Sites and Artifacts, Voyageurs National Park and Environs, 2001–2002*. Midwest Archeological Center, Lincoln, NE, and Institute for Minnesota Archaeology, Minneapolis.

Black, Lydia T.

2004 *Russians in Alaska, 1732–1867*. University of Alaska Press, Fairbanks.

Blair, Elliot H.

2009 The Role of Beads on St. Catherines Island. In *The Beads on St. Catherines Island*, by Elliot H. Blair, Lorann S. A. Pendleton, and Peter Francis Jr., 167–178. Anthropological Papers of the American Museum of Natural History, no. 89. New York, NY.

Blair, Elliot H., Lorann S. A. Pendleton, and Peter Francis Jr.

2009 *The Beads on St. Catherines Island*. Anthropological Papers of the American Museum of Natural History, no. 89. New York, NY.

Bodoh, Brad W.

2004 *Mesquaki Flintlocks: Cultural Accommodation and Adaptation during the Early Fur Trade in the Western Great Lakes*. Reports of Investigations, no. 10. Archaeology Laboratory, Department of Religious Studies and Anthropology, University of Wisconsin-Oshkosh.

Boyd, Robert

2013   Lower Columbia Trade and Exchange Systems. In *Chinookan Peoples of the Lower Columbia*, edited by Robert T. Boyd, Kenneth M. Ames, and Tony A. Johnson, 229–249. University of Washington Press, Seattle.

Bradley, James W.

1987   *Evolution of the Onondaga Iroquois: Accommodating Change, 1500–1655*. Syracuse University Press, Syracuse, NY.

Brain, Jeffrey P.

1979   *Tunica Treasure*. Papers of the Peabody Museum of Archaeology and Ethnology, no. 71. Harvard University, Cambridge, MA.

Brandão, José António

1997   *"Your Fyre Shall Burn No More": Iroquois Policy towards New France and Its Native Allies to 1701*. University of Nebraska Press, Lincoln.

2008   Introduction: New France, the Fur Trade, and Michilimackinac. In *Edge of Empire: Documents of Michilimackinac, 1671–1716*, edited by Joseph L. Peyser and José António Brandão, xxiii–xliii. Michigan State University Press, East Lansing, and Mackinac State Historic Parks, Mackinac Island, MI.

Brandão, José António, and Michael S. Nassaney

2006   A Capsule Social and Material History of Fort St. Joseph (1691–1763) and Its Inhabitants. *French Colonial History* 7: 61–75.

2008   Suffering for Jesus: Penitential Practices at Fort St. Joseph (Niles, MI) during the French Regime. *Catholic Historical Review* 94(3): 476–499.

Brasser, T. J.

1978   Early Indian-European Contacts. In *Handbook of North American Indians*, Vol. 15, *Northeast*, edited by Bruce G. Trigger, 78–88. Smithsonian Institution Press, Washington, D.C.

Braund, Kathryn E. Holland

1993   *Deerskins* and *Duffels: The Creek Indian Trade with Anglo-America, 1685–1815*. University of Nebraska Press, Lincoln.

Brotherton, Barbara

2000   Tlingit Human Masks as Documents of Culture Change and Continuity. In *Interpretations of Native North American Life: Material Contributions to Ethnohistory*, edited by Michael S. Nassaney and Eric S. Johnson, 358–397. Society for Historical Archaeology and University Press of Florida, Gainesville.

Brown, Jennifer S. H.

1982   Children of the Early Fur Trades. In *Childhood and Family in Canadian History*, edited by Joy Parr, 199–206. McClelland and Steward, Toronto.

Brown, Jennifer S. H., William J. Eccles, and Donald P. Heldman (editors)

1994   *The Fur Trade Revisited*. Michigan State University Press, East Lansing, and Mackinac State Historic Parks, Mackinac Island, MI.

Brown, Margaret

1971   Glass from Michilimackinac: A Classification System for Eighteenth Century Glass. *Michigan Archaeologist* 17(3–4): 97–215.

Buckley, Thomas C. (editor)

1984   *Rendezvous: Selected Papers of the Fourth North American Fur Trade Conference, 1981*. North American Fur Trade Conference, St. Paul, MN.

Burley, David

2000   Creolization and Late Nineteenth Century Metis Vernacular Architecture on the South Saskatchewan River. *Historical Archaeology* 34(3): 27–35.

Butler, Virginia, and Michael A. Martin

2013   Aboriginal Fisheries of the Lower Columbia River. In *Chinookan Peoples of the Lower Columbia*, edited by Robert T. Boyd, Kenneth M. Ames, and Tony A. Johnson, 80–105. University of Washington Press, Seattle.

Camp, Stacey Lynn

2013   *The Archaeology of Citizenship*. University Press of Florida, Gainesville.

Cangany, Catherine

2012   Fashioning Moccasins: Detroit, the Manufacturing Frontier, and the Empire of Consumption, 1701–1835. *William and Mary Quarterly* 69(2): 265–304.

Carlos, Ann M., and Frank D. Lewis

2010   *Commerce by a Frozen Sea: Native Americans and the European Fur Trade*. University of Pennsylvania Press, Philadelphia.

Carlson, Catherine C.

2000   Archaeology of a Contact-Period Plateau Salishan Village at Thompson's River Post, Kamloops, British Columbia. In *Interpretations of Native North American Life: Materials Contributions to Ethnohistory*, edited by Michael S. Nassaney and Eric S. Johnson, 272–295. Society for Historical Archaeology and University Press of Florida, Gainesville.

2006   Indigenous Historic Archaeology of the 19th-Century Secwepemc Village at Thompson's River Post, Kamloops, British Columbia. *Canadian Journal of Archaeology* 30: 193–250.

Carlson, Jenna K.

2012   *Culinary Creolization: Subsistence and Cultural Interaction at Fort Michilimackinac, 1730–1761.* Archaeological Completion Report Series, no. 18. Mackinac State Historic Parks, Mackinac Island, MI.

Carvalhaes, Cezar

2011   An Examination of Gunflints from the Fort St. Joseph Site (20BE23) in Niles, Michigan. Senior honors thesis, Western Michigan University, Kalamazoo.

Cassell, Mark S.

2003   Flint and Foxes: Chert Scrapers and the Fur Industry in Late-Nineteenth- and Early-Twentieth-Century North Alaska. In *Stone Tool Traditions in the Contact Era*, edited by Charles R. Cobb, 151–164. University of Alabama Press, Tuscaloosa.

Caywood, Louis R.

1967   Post-1800 Sites: Fur Trade. *Historical Archaeology* 1: 46–48.

Ceci, Lynn

1977   The Effect of European Contact on the Settlement Pattern of Indians in Coastal New York, 1524–1664. PhD dissertation, City University of New York.

1990   Native Wampum as a Peripheral Resource in the Seventeenth-Century World-System. In *The Pequots in Southern New England: The Fall and Rise of an American Indian Nation*, edited by Laurence M. Hauptman and James D. Wherry, 48–63. University of Oklahoma Press, Norman.

Chittenden, Hiram Martin

1902   *The American Fur Trade of the Far West.* 3 vols. Francis P. Harper, New York.

Claussen, Erin, Erica D'Elia, and Michael S. Nassaney

2013   How Can Archaeology Help Itself and Others?: 21st Century Relevancy at Fort St. Joseph. *Society for Applied Anthropology Newsletter* 24(4): 27–29.

Clayton, James L.

1964   The American Fur Company: The Final Years. PhD dissertation, Cornell University, Ithaca, NY.

1967   The Growth and Significance of the American Fur Trade, 1790–1890. In *Aspects of the Fur Trade: Selected Papers of the 1965 North American Fur Trade Conference*, edited by R. H. Gilman, 62–72. Minnesota Historical Society, St. Paul.

Cleland, Charles E.

1970   Comparison of the Faunal Remains from French and British Refuse Pits at Fort Michilimackinac: A Study in Changing Subsistence Patterns. *Canadian Historic Sites Occasional Papers in Archaeology and History* 3: 3–23.

1993   Economic and Adaptive Change among the Lake Superior Chippewa of the

Nineteenth Century. In *Ethnohistory and Archaeology: Approaches to Postcontact Change in the Americas*, edited by J. Daniel Rogers and Samuel Wilson, 111–122. Plenum Press, New York.

Cleland, Charles E. (editor)

1971 *The Lasanen Site: An Historic Burial Locality in Mackinac County, Michigan*. Anthropological Series, Vol. 1, no. 1. Publications of the Museum, Michigan State University, East Lansing.

Clifton, James A.

1977 *The Prairie People: Continuity and Change in Potawatomi Indian Culture, 1665–1965*. Regents Press of Kansas, Lawrence.

1978 Potawatomi. In *Handbook of North American Indians*, Vol. 15, *Northeast*, edited by Bruce G. Trigger, 725–742. Smithsonian Institution Press, Washington, D.C.

1986 Potawatomi. In *Peoples of the Three Fires: The Ottawa, Potawatomi and Ojibway of Michigan*, edited by James A. Clifton, G. L. Cornell, and James M. McClurken, 39–74. Michigan Indian Press, Grand Rapids Inter-Tribal Council, Grand Rapids.

Cobb, Charles R.

1993 Archaeological Approaches to the Political Economy of Stratified Societies. In *Archaeological Method and Theory*, Vol. 5, edited by Michael B. Schiffer, 43–100. University of Arizona Press, Tucson.

Cook, Peter

1998 Symbolic and Material Exchange in Intercultural Diplomacy: The French and the Haudenosaunee in the Early Eighteenth Century. In *New Faces of the Fur Trade: Selected Papers of the Seventh North American Fur Trade Conference, Halifax, Nova Scotia, 1995*, edited by Jo-Anne Fiske, Susan Sleeper-Smith, and William Wicken, 75–100. Michigan State University Press, East Lansing.

Coolidge, O. W.

1915 Address at the Dedication of the Boulder Marking the Site of Fort St. Joseph. *Collections of the Michigan Pioneer and Historical Society* 39: 283–291.

Cox, Bruce Alden

1993 Natives and the Development of Mercantile Capitalism: A New Look at "Opposition" in the Eighteenth-Century Fur Trade. In *The Political Economy of North American Indians*, edited by John H. Moore, 87–93. University of Oklahoma Press, Norman.

Cremin, William M., and Michael S. Nassaney

2003 Sampling Archaeological Sediments for Small-Scale Remains: Recovery, Identification, and Interpretation of Plant Residues from Fort St. Joseph (20BE23). *Michigan Archaeologist* 49(3–4): 73–85.

Cromwell, Robert J.

2011 Technology: From Stone Tools to Modern Technology. In *Exploring Fort Vancouver*, edited by Douglas C. Wilson and Theresa E. Langford, 51–68. Fort Vancouver National Trust, Vancouver, WA, in association with the University of Washington Press, Seattle.

Cronon, William

1983 *Changes in the Land: Indians, Colonists, and the Ecology of New England*. Hill and Wang, New York.

Culpin, Mary Shivers, and Richard Borjes

1984 The Architecture of Fort Union: A Symbol of Dominance. In *Rendezvous: Selected Papers of the Fourth North American Fur Trade Conference, 1981*, edited by Thomas C. Buckley, 135–140. North American Fur Trade Conference, St. Paul, MN.

Cunningham, Wilbur M.

1961 *Land of Four Flags: An Early History of the St. Joseph Valley*. William B. Eerdmans Publishing Company, Grand Rapids, MI.

Cunningham, Wilbur M. (editor)

1967 *Letter Book of William Burnett: Early Fur Trader in the Land of Four Flags*. Fort Miami Heritage Society of Michigan, Inc., St. Joseph, MI.

Cusick, James G. (editor)

1998 *Studies in Culture Contact: Interaction, Culture Change, and Archaeology*. Occasional Paper, no. 25. Center for Archaeological Investigations, Southern Illinois University, Carbondale.

Cuthbertson, Stuart, and John C. Ewers

1939 *Preliminary Bibliography on the American Fur Trade*. United States Department of the Interior, National Park Service, Jefferson National Expansion Memorial, St. Louis, MO.

Davis, Cathrine M.

2014 Lead Seals from Colonial Fort St. Joseph (20BE23). Senior honors thesis, Western Michigan University, Kalamazoo.

Dawson, Kenneth C. A.

1970 Preliminary Archaeological Investigation of Fort William in Northwestern Ontario. *Historical Archaeology* 4: 34–50.

Dechêne, Louise

1988 *Habitants et marchands de Montréal au XVIIe siècle*. Les Éditions du Boréal, Montreal.

Dennis, Matthew

1993 *Cultivating a Landscape of Peace: Iroquois-European Relations in Seventeenth-Century America*. Cornell University Press, Ithaca, NY.

Deseve, Jacques

2009 *Voices from Our Past: Telling the Folle Avoine Story*. Burnett County Historical Society, Danbury, WI.

DeVore, Steven Leroy

1992 *Beads of the Bison Robe Trade: The Fort Union Trading Post Collection*. Friends of the Fort Union Trading Post, Williston, ND.

Diamond, Stanley

1974 *In Search of the Primitive: A Critique of Civilization*. Transaction Books, New Brunswick, NJ.

Dolin, Eric Jay

2010 *Fur, Fortune, and Empire: The Epic History of the Fur Trade in America*. W. W. Norton, New York.

Donnelly, Joseph P.

1947 *A Tentative Bibliography for the Colonial Fur Trade in the American Colonies: 1608–1800*. St. Louis University Press, St. Louis.

Doroszenko, Dena

2009 Exploration, Exploitation, Expansion, and Settlement: Historical Archaeology in Canada. In *International Handbook of Historical Archaeology*, edited by Teresita Majewski and David Gaimster, 507–524. Springer, New York.

Douglas, Thomas

1816 *A Sketch of the Fur Trade in North America*. 2nd ed. J. Ridgway, London.

Eccles, William J.

1969 *The Canadian Frontier, 1534–1760*. Holt, Rinehart, and Winston, New York.

1972 *France in America*. Harper and Row, New York.

1979 A Belated Review of Harold Adams Innis, *Fur Trade in Canada*. *Canadian Historical Review* 60(4): 419–441.

1988 The Fur Trade in the Colonial Northeast. In *Handbook of North American Indians*, Vol. 4, *History of Indian-White Relations*, edited by Wilcomb E. Washburn, 324–334. Smithsonian Institution Press, Washington, D.C.

Ehrhardt, Kathleen L.

2005 *European Metals in Native Hands: Rethinking the Dynamics of Technological Change, 1640–1683*. University of Alabama Press, Tuscaloosa.

Ekberg, Carl J.

1985 *Colonial Ste. Genevieve: An Adventure on the Mississippi Frontier*. Patrice Press, Gerald, Missouri.

1998 *French Roots in the Illinois Country: The Mississippi Frontier in Colonial Times.*
University of Illinois Press, Urbana.

Esarey, Duane

2013 Another Kind of Beads: A Forgotten Industry of the North American Colonial Period. PhD dissertation, University of North Carolina, Chapel Hill.

Evans, Lynn M.

2001 *House D of the Southeast Row House: Excavations at Fort Michilimackinac, 1989–1997.* Archaeological Completion Report Series, no. 17. Mackinac State Historic Parks, Mackinac Island, MI.

2007 "Europeans Themselves Would Not Know a Better Way": Native Technology in the Michilimackinac Fur Trade. *Michigan Archaeologist* 53(1–2): 31–39.

Ewen, Charles R.

1986 Fur Trade Archaeology: A Study of Frontier Hierarchies. *Historical Archaeology* 20(1): 15–28.

Ewers, John C.

1954 The Indian Trade of the Upper Missouri before Lewis and Clark. *Missouri Historical Society Bulletin* 10: 429–446.

Faribault-Beauregard, Marthe

1982 *La population des forts français d'Amérique (xviiie siècle).* 2 vols. Éditions Bergeron, Montreal.

Farris, Glenn J.

1989 The Russian Imprint on the Colonization of California. In *Columbian Consequences,* Vol. 1, *Archaeological and Historical Perspectives on the Spanish Borderlands West,* edited by David Hurst Thomas, 481–498. Smithsonian Institution Press, Washington, D.C.

Ferris, Neal

2009 *The Archaeology of Native-Lived Colonialism: Challenging History in the Great Lakes.* University of Arizona Press, Tucson.

Fiske, Jo-Anne, Susan Sleeper-Smith, and William Wicken (editors)

1998 *New Faces of the Fur Trade: Selected Papers of the Seventh North American Fur Trade Conference, Halifax, Nova Scotia, 1995.* Michigan State University Press, East Lansing.

Fitzhugh, William W.

1985 Introduction. In *Cultures in Contact: The European Impact on Native Cultural Institutions in Eastern North America, A.D. 1000–1800,* edited by William W. Fitzhugh, 1–15. Smithsonian Institution Press, Washington, D.C.

Ford, Richard I.

1973 The Moccasin Bluff Corn Holes. In *The Moccasin Bluff Site and the Woodland*

Cultures of Southwestern Michigan, compiled by Richard L. Bettarel and Hale G. Smith, 188–193. Anthropological Papers, no. 49. Museum of Anthropology, University of Michigan, Ann Arbor.

Fortmann, Tracy A.

2011 Why Collections Matter. In *Exploring Fort Vancouver,* edited by Douglas C. Wilson and Theresa E. Langford, 105–109. Fort Vancouver National Trust, Vancouver, WA, in association with the University of Washington Press, Seattle.

[Fort St. Joseph Archaeological Project]

2011 *Women of New France.* Fort St. Joseph Archaeological Project, Booklet Series, no. 1. Department of Anthropology, Western Michigan University, Kalamazoo.

Fort William Historical Park

2008 Fort William Historical Park. http://fwhp.ca.

Foster, H. Thomas, II, and Arthur D. Cohen

2007 Palynological Evidence of the Effects of the Deerskin Trade on Forest Fires during the Eighteenth Century in Southeastern North America. *American Antiquity* 72(1): 35–51.

Fox, Georgia L.

2015 *The Archaeology of Smoking and Tobacco.* University Press of Florida, Gainesville.

Franzen, John G.

2004 Wintering at Little Island Rock: A Fur Trade Site on Grand Island. *Midcontinental Journal of Archaeology* 29(2): 219–248.

Frurip, David J., Russell Malewicki, and Donald P. Heldman

1983 *Colonial Nails from Michilimackinac: Differentiation by Chemical and Statistical Analysis.* Archaeological Completion Report Series, no. 7. Mackinac State Historic Parks, Mackinac Island, MI.

Galloway, Patricia K.

1993 Ethnohistory. In *The Development of Southeastern Archaeology,* edited by Jay K. Johnston, 78–108. University of Alabama Press, Tuscaloosa.

Gibbon, Guy, and Katie Ann Wynia

2010 A Fur Trade Era Row House at Big Sandy Lake. *Minnesota Archaeologist* 69: 97–113.

Gibson, James R.

1988 The Maritime Trade of the North Pacific Coast. In *Handbook of North American Indians,* Vol. 4, *History of Indian-White Relations,* edited by Wilcomb E. Washburn, 375–390. Smithsonian Institution Press, Washington, D.C.

1992   *Otter Skins, Boston Ships, and China Goods: The Maritime Fur Trade of the Northwest Coast, 1785–1841.* University of Washington Press, Seattle.

Gibson, Susan

1980   *Burr's Hill: A 17th Century Wampanoag Burial Ground in Warren, Rhode Island.* Studies in Anthropology and Material Culture, Vol. 2. Haffenreffer Museum of Anthropology, Brown University, Providence, RI.

Giddens, Anthony

1990   *The Consequences of Modernity.* Polity Press, Cambridge, U.K.

Gilman, Carolyn

1982   *Where Two Worlds Meet: The Great Lakes Fur Trade.* Museum Exhibit Series, no. 2. Minnesota Historical Society, St. Paul.

Gilman, Rhoda R.

1972   Last Days of the Upper Mississippi Fur Trade. In *People and Pelts: Selected Papers of the Second North American Fur Trade Conference,* edited by Malvina Bolus, 103–135. Minnesota Historical Society Press, St. Paul.

1974   The Fur Trade in the Upper Mississippi Valley, 1630–1850. *Wisconsin Magazine of History* 58: 3–18.

1982   Foreword. In *Where Two Worlds Meet: The Great Lakes Fur Trade,* by Carolyn Gilman. Museum Exhibit Series, no. 2. Minnesota Historical Society, St. Paul.

1994   Apprentice Trader: Henry H. Sibley and the American Fur Company at Mackinac. In *The Fur Trade Revisited,* edited by Jennifer S. H. Brown, W. J. Eccles, and Donald P. Heldman, 317–330. Michigan State University Press, East Lansing, and Mackinac State Historic Parks, Mackinac Island, MI.

Gilman, Rhoda R. (editor)

1967   *Aspects of the Fur Trade: Selected Papers of the 1965 North American Fur Trade Conference.* Minnesota Historical Society, St. Paul.

Giordano, Brock

2005   Crafting Culture at Fort St. Joseph: An Archaeological Investigation of Labor Organization on the Colonial Frontier. MA thesis, Department of Anthropology, Western Michigan University, Kalamazoo.

Giordano, Brock, and Michael S. Nassaney

2004   An Unusual Artifact Recently Recovered from Fort St. Joseph (20BE23) in Niles, Michigan. *Le Journal* 20(2): 1–4.

2015   Crafting Culture at Fort St. Joseph: An Examination of Labor Organization through a Technological Investigation of Tinkling Cones. Manuscript on file, Department of Anthropology, Western Michigan University, Kalamazoo.

Gladysz, Kevin

2011 *The French Trade Gun in North America, 1662–1759.* Mowbray Publishers, Woonsocket, RI.

Good, Mary Elizabeth

1972 *Guebert Site: An 18th Century Historic Kaskaskia Indian Village in Randolph County, Illinois.* Memoir no. 2. Central States Archaeological Societies, Inc., Wood River, IL.

Gookin, Daniel

1792 [1674] *Historical Collections of the Indians of New England.* Massachusetts Historical Society, Boston.

Gosden, Christopher

1997 *Culture Contact and Colonialism.* Routledge, London.

2002 Postcolonial Archaeology: Issues of Culture, Identity, and Knowledge. In *Archaeological Theory Today,* edited by I. Hodder, 241–261. Blackwell, Malden, MA.

Greenman, Emerson F.

1951 *Old Birch Island Cemetery and the Early Historic Trade Route, Georgian Bay, Ontario.* University of Michigan Press, Ann Arbor.

Hackett, Charles Wilson

1934 *Pichardo's Treatise on the Limits of Louisiana and Texas.* 5 vols. University of Texas Press, Austin.

Hajda, Yvonne, and Elizabeth A. Sobel

2013 Lower Columbia Trade and Exchange Systems. In *Chinookan Peoples of the Lower Columbia,* edited by Robert T. Boyd, Kenneth M. Ames, and Tony A. Johnson, 106–124. University of Washington Press, Seattle.

Hamell, George

1983 Trading in Metaphors: The Magic of Beads. In *Proceedings of the 1982 Glass Trade Bead Conference,* edited by Charles F. Hayes III, 5–28. Rochester Museum and Science Center Research Records, no. 16, Rochester, NY.

Hamilton, Scott

2000 Dynamics of Social Complexity in Early Nineteenth-Century British Fur-Trade Posts. *International Journal of Historical Archaeology* 4(3): 217–273.

Hamilton, Scott, James Graham, and Dave Norris

2005 *If These Walls Could Speak: Using GIS to Explore the Fort at Grand Portage National Monument (21CK6).* Unpublished report prepared for the Grand Portage National Monument, National Park Service. Department of Anthropology, Lakehead University, Thunder Bay, Ontario.

Hamilton, Scott, and B. A. Nicholson

2007 The Middleman Fur Trade and Slot Knives: Selective Integration of European Technology at the Mortiach Twin Fawns Site (DiMe-23). *Canadian Journal of Archaeology* 31(3): 137–162.

Hamilton, T. M.

1976 *Firearms on the Frontier: Guns at Fort Michilimackinac 1715–1781.* Reports in Mackinac History and Archaeology, no. 5. Mackinac State Historical Parks, Mackinac Island, MI.

1987 *Colonial Frontier Guns.* Pioneer Press, Union City, TN. Originally published by Fur Press, Chadron, NE, 1980.

Hannes, Sheri M.

1994 The Faunal Analysis of the Horseshoe Bay Site: A Subsistence Study of a Nineteenth-Century Fur Trading Post. MA thesis, Department of Anthropology, University of Iowa.

Hanson, James A.

2005 *When Skins Were Money: A History of the Fur Trade.* Museum of the Fur Trade, Chadron, NE.

Hauptman, Lawrence M.

1990 The Pequot War and Its Legacies. In *The Pequots in Southern New England: The Fall and Rise of an American Indian Nation,* edited by Laurence M. Hauptman and James D. Wherry, 69–80. University of Oklahoma Press, Norman.

Hauser, Judith Ann

1982 *Jesuit Rings from Fort Michilimackinac and Other European Contact Sites.* Archaeological Completion Report Series, no. 5. Mackinac State Historic Parks, Mackinac Island, MI.

Hayes, Charles F., III (editor)

1983 *Proceedings of the 1982 Glass Trade Bead Conference.* Rochester Museum and Science Center Research Records, no. 16, Rochester, NY.

Hearns, Joseph

2015 Patterns in Faunal Remains at Fort St. Joseph (20BE23), a French Fur Trade Post in the Western Great Lakes. MA thesis, Department of Anthropology, Western Michigan University, Kalamazoo.

Heidenreich, Conrad, and Françoise Noël

1987 Plate 40: France Secures the Interior. In *Historical Atlas of Canada,* Vol. 1, edited by Richard Colebrook Harris. University of Toronto Press, Toronto.

Heldman, Donald P.

1991 The French in Michigan and Beyond: An Archaeological View from Fort

Michilimackinac Toward the West. In *French Colonial Archaeology: The Illinois Country and the Western Great Lakes*, edited by John A. Walthall, 201–217. University of Illinois Press, Urbana.

Holm, Bill

1982   Objects of Unique Artistry. In *Soft Gold: The Fur Trade and Cultural Exchange on the Northwest Coast of America*, by Thomas Vaughan and Bill Holm, 31–168. Oregon Historical Society, Portland.

Howay, F. W.

1923   Early Days of the Maritime Fur-Trade on the Northwest Coast. *Canadian Historical Review* 4: 26–44.

Hu, Di

2013   Approaches to the Archaeology of Ethnogenesis: Past and Emergent Perspectives. *Journal of Archaeological Research* 21(4): 371–402.

Hudson, Charles

1976   *The Southeastern Indians*. University of Tennessee Press, Knoxville.

Hughes-Skallos, Jessica, and Susan E. Allen

2012   Analysis of Feature 21, A Smudge Pit from the Lyne Site, Michigan (20-Be-10). Manuscript on file, Department of Anthropology, Western Michigan University, Kalamazoo.

Hulse, Charles A.

1977   An Archaeological Evaluation of Fort St. Joseph: An Eighteenth Century Military Post and Settlement in Berrien County, Michigan. MA thesis, Department of Anthropology, Michigan State University, East Lansing.

1981   An Archaeological Evaluation of Fort St. Joseph (20BE23), Berrien County, Michigan. *Michigan Archaeologist* 27(3–4): 55–76.

Hussey, John A.

1957   *The History of Fort Vancouver and its Physical Structure*. National Park Service and Washington State Historical Society, Portland, OR.

Hutchins, Thomas

1904 [1778] *A Topographical Description of Virginia, Pennsylvania, Maryland, and North Carolina*. Edited by Frederick Charles Hicks. Burrows Brothers Company, Cleveland.

Idle, Dunning

2003   The Post of the St. Joseph River during the French Regime 1679–1761. PhD dissertation, University of Illinois, Urbana. Reprinted by Fort St. Joseph Museum, Niles, MI. Originally completed in 1946.

Ingold, Tim (editor)

1994   *What Is an Animal?* Routledge, London.

Innis, Harold A.

1962 *The Fur Trade in Canada: An Introduction to Canadian Economic History*. Yale University Press, New Haven, CT.

Jelinek, Arthur

1958 A Late Historic Burial from Berrien County. *Michigan Archaeologist* 4(3): 48–51.

Jelks, Edward B.

1967 The Gilbert Site: A Norteño Focus Site in Northeastern Texas. *Texas Archaeological Society Bulletin* 37. Dallas.

Jenks, Albert Ernest

1977 The Wild Rice Gatherers of the Upper Lakes: A Study in American Primitive Economics. *Reprints in Anthropology*, Vol. 9. J & L Reprint Company, Lincoln, NE.

Jenness, Diamond

1918 The Eskimos of Northern Alaska: A Study in the Effect of Civilization. *Geographical Review* 5(2): 89–101.

Johnson, Ida Amanda

1919 *The Michigan Fur Trade*. Michigan Historical Commission, Lansing.

Johnson, Jay K.

1997 Stone Tools, Politics, and the Eighteenth-Century Chickasaw in Northeast Mississippi. *American Antiquity* 62(2): 215–230.

2003 Chickasaw Lithic Technology: A Reassessment. In *Stone Tool Traditions in the Contact Era*, edited by Charles R. Cobb, 51–58. University of Alabama Press, Tuscaloosa.

Johnson, Jay K., John W. O'Hear, Robbie Ethridge, Brad R. Lieb, Susan L. Scott, and H. Edwin Jackson

2008 Measuring Chickasaw Adaptation on the Western Frontier of the Colonial South: A Correlation of Documentary and Archaeological Data. *Southeastern Archaeology* 27(1): 1–30.

Jordan, Kurt A.

2008 *The Seneca Restoration, 1715–1754: An Iroquois Local Political Economy*. University Press of Florida, Gainesville.

2009 Colonies, Colonialism, and Cultural Entanglements: The Archaeology of Postcolumbian Intercultural Relations. In *International Handbook of Historical Archaeology*, edited by Teresita Majewski and David R. M. Gaimster, 31–49. Springer, New York.

Juen, Rachel, and Michael S. Nassaney

2012 *The Fur Trade*. Fort St. Joseph Archaeological Project, Booklet Series, no. 2. Department of Anthropology, Western Michigan University, Kalamazoo.

Kalm, Peter

1772   *Travels into North America.* 2nd ed. 2 vols. London.

Kardulias, P. Nick

1990   Fur Production as a Specialized Activity in a World System: Indians in the North American Fur Trade. *American Indian Culture and Research Journal* 14(1): 25–60.

Karklins, Karlis

1983   *Nottingham House: The Hudson's Bay Company in Athabasca, 1802–1806.* History and Archaeology series, no. 69. National Historic Parks and Sites Branch, Parks Canada, Environment Canada, Ottawa.

1992   *Trade Ornament Usage among the Native Peoples of Canada: A Source Book.* Studies in Archaeology, Architecture and History. National Historic Sites, Parks Service, Environment Canada, Ottawa.

Kay, Jeanne

1977   *The Land of La Baye: The Ecological Impact of the Green Bay Fur Trade, 1634–1836.* PhD dissertation, University of Wisconsin, Madison.

Keene, David

1991   Fort de Chartres: Archaeology in the Illinois Country. In *French Colonial Archaeology: The Illinois Country and the Western Great Lakes,* edited by John A. Walthall, 29–41. University of Illinois Press, Urbana.

Kehoe, Alice B.

2000   François' House, A Significant Pedlars' Post on the Saskatchewan. In *Interpretations of Native North American Life: Material Contributions to Ethnohistory,* edited by Michael S. Nassaney and Eric S. Johnson, 173–187. Society for Historical Archaeology and University Press of Florida, Gainesville.

Kennedy, Kenneth A. R.

1989   Skeletal Markers of Occupational Stress. In *Reconstruction of Life from the Skeleton,* edited by M. Yaşar İşcan and Kenneth A. R. Kennedy, 129–160. Alan R. Liss, New York.

Kent, Timothy J.

1997   *Birchbark Canoes of the Fur Trade,* 2 vols. Silver Fox Enterprises, Ossineke, MI.

Kenyon, Walter A.

1975   The Quetico Report. In *Voices from the Rapids: An Underwater Search for Fur Trade Artifacts 1960–73,* by Robert C. Wheeler, Walter A. Kenyon, Alan R. Woolworth, and Douglas A. Birk, 45–54. Minnesota Historical Society, St. Paul.

1986   *The History of James Bay 1610–1686: A Study in Historical Archaeology.* Archaeological Monograph 10. Royal Ontario Museum, Toronto.

Kerr, Ian

2012　An Analysis of Personal Adornment at Fort St. Joseph (20BE23), an Eighteenth-Century French Trading Post in Southwest Michigan. MA thesis, Department of Anthropology, Western Michigan University, Kalamazoo.

Kicza, J. E., and R. Horn

2013　*Resilient Cultures: America's Native Peoples Confront European Colonization, 1500–1800*. Pearson, Boston.

Kidd, Kenneth E.

1979　*Glass Bead-Making from the Middle Ages to the Early 19th Century*. History and Archaeology series, no. 30. Parks Canada, Ottawa.

Kidd, Kenneth E., and Martha A. Kidd

1970　A Classification System for Glass Trade Beads for the Use of Field Archaeologists. *Canadian Historic Sites Occasional Papers in Archaeology and History* 1: 45–89.

Klein, Alan M.

1993　Political Economy of the Buffalo Hide Trade: Race and Class on the Plains. In *The Political Economy of North American Indians*, edited by John H. Moore, 133–160. University of Oklahoma Press, Norman.

Klimko, Olga

2004　Fur Trade Archaeology in Western Canada: Who Is Digging Up the Forts? In *The Archaeology of Contact in Settler Societies*, edited by Tim Murray, 157–175. Cambridge University Press, Cambridge, UK.

Kohley, Allison M.

2013　Change and Continuity: Euro-American and Native American Settlement Patterns in the St. Joseph River Valley. MA thesis, Department of Geography, Western Michigan University, Kalamazoo.

Krause, Richard A.

1972　*The Leavenworth Site: Archaeology of an Historic Arikara Community*. University of Kansas Publications in Anthropology, no. 3. Lawrence.

Krech, Shepard, III

1999　*The Ecological Indian: Myth and History*. W. W. Norton, New York.

Lai, Ping, and Nancy C. Lovell

1992　Skeletal Markers of Occupational Stress in the Fur Trade: A Case Study from a Hudson's Bay Company Fur Trade Post. *International Journal of Osteoarchaeology* 2: 221–234.

Laird, Matthew R.

1995　The Price of Empire: Anglo-French Rivalry for the Great Lakes Fur Trade, 1700–1760. PhD dissertation, College of William and Mary, Williamsburg, VA.

Langford, Theresa E.

2011 Identity: Using Objects to "Fit In" and "Stand Out." In *Exploring Fort Vancouver*, edited by Douglas C. Wilson and Theresa E. Langford, 29–50. Fort Vancouver National Trust, Vancouver, WA, in association with the University of Washington Press, Seattle.

Lapham, Heather A.

2005 *Hunting for Hides: Deerskins, Status, and Cultural Change in the Protohistoric Appalachians.* University of Alabama Press, Tuscaloosa.

Leacock, Eleanor

1954 The Montagnais "Hunting Territory" and the Fur Trade. *American Anthropological Association Memoir 78.*

Lebeau, B. Pierre, Lucy Eldersveld Murphy, and Robert C. Wiederaenders

2008 *Plumbing the Depths of the Upper Mississippi Valley: Julien Dubuque, Native Americans, and Lead Mining.* Center for French Colonial Studies, St. Louis, MO.

Lee, Ellen Rose

1984 Fort St. Joseph, Ontario: Settlement Patterns and Building Use at Fur Trade Sites. In *Rendezvous: Selected Papers of the Fourth North American Fur Trade Conference, 1981,* edited by Thomas C. Buckley, 141–154. North American Fur Trade Conference, St. Paul, MN.

Lewis, Oscar

1942 *The Effects of White Contact on Blackfoot Culture.* Monographs of the American Ethnological Society, no. 6. University of Washington Press, Seattle.

Lightfoot, Kent G.

2005 *Indians, Missionaries, and Merchants: The Legacy of Colonial Encounters on the California Frontiers.* University of California Press, Berkeley.

Lightfoot, Kent G., Thomas A. Wake, and Ann M. Schiff

2003 *The Archaeology and Ethnohistory of Fort Ross, California,* Vol. 1, Introduction. Contributions of the University of California Archaeological Research Facility, no. 49. University of California at Berkeley.

Little, Barbara J.

2007 *Historical Archaeology: Why the Past Matters.* Left Coast Press, Walnut Creek, CA.

Loeb, Edwin M.

1926 Pomo Folkways. *University of California Publications in American Archaeology and Ethnology* 19(2): 149–405.

Lohse, E. S.

1988 Trade Goods. In *Handbook of North American Indians,* Vol. 4, *History of Indian-*

White Relations, edited by Wilcomb E. Washburn, 396–403. Smithsonian Institution Press, Washington, D.C.

Loren, Dianna DiPaolo

2010 *The Archaeology of Clothing and Bodily Adornment in Colonial America*. University Press of Florida, Gainesville.

Lyford, Carrie A.

1940 *Quill and Beadwork of the Western Sioux*. Branch of Education, Bureau of Indian Affairs, United States Department of the Interior, Washington, D.C.

Lyons, Natasha

2014 Localized Critical Theory as an Expression of Community Archaeology Practice: With an Example from Inuvialuit Elders of the Canadian Western Arctic. *American Antiquity* 79(2): 183–203.

Mackenzie, Alexander

n.d. *Voyages from Montreal through the Continent of North America to the Frozen and Pacific Oceans in 1789 and 1793 with an Account of the Rise of the Fur Trade*. 2 vols. Toronto.

Mainfort, Robert C., Jr.

1979 *Indian Social Dynamics in the Period of European Contact*. Anthropological Series, Vol. 1, no. 4. Michigan State University Museum, East Lansing.

Malischke, LisaMarie

2009 The Excavated Bead Collection at Fort St. Joseph (20BE23) and Its Implications for Understanding Adornment, Ideology, Cultural Exchange, and Identity. MA thesis, Department of Anthropology, Western Michigan University, Kalamazoo.

Mann, Rob

2003 Colonizing the Colonizers: Canadien Fur Traders and Fur Trade Society in the Great Lakes Region, 1763–1850. PhD dissertation, Binghamton University, Binghamton, NY.

2004 Smokescreens: Tobacco, Pipes, and the Transformational Power of Fur Trade Rituals. In *Smoking and Culture: The Archaeology of Tobacco Pipes in Eastern North America*, edited by Sean M. Rafferty and Rob Mann, 165–183. University of Tennessee Press, Knoxville.

2008 From Ethnogenesis to Ethnic Segmentation in the Wabash Valley: Constructing Identity and Houses in Great Lakes Fur Trade Society. *International Journal of Historical Archaeology* 12(4): 319–337.

Martin, Calvin

1975 The Four Lives of a Micmac Copper Pot. *Ethnohistory* 22(2): 111–133.

Martin, Terrance J.

1986   A Faunal Analysis of Fort Ouiatenon, An Eighteenth Century Trading Post in the Wabash Valley. PhD dissertation, Michigan State University, East Lansing.

1991a   An Archaeological Perspective on Animal Exploitation Patterns at French Colonial Sites in the Illinois Country. In *French Colonial Archaeology: The Illinois Country and the Western Great Lakes*, edited by John A. Walthall, 189–200. University of Illinois Press, Urbana.

1991b   Modified Animal Remains, Subsistence, and Cultural Interaction at French Colonial Sites in the Midwestern United States. In *Beamers, Bobwhites, and Blue-Points: Tributes to the Career of Paul W. Parmalee*, edited by James R. Purdue, Walter E. Klippel, and Bonnie W. Styles, 409–419. Illinois State Museum Scientific Papers, Vol. 23. Illinois State Museum, Springfield.

2008   The Archaeozoology of French Colonial Sites in the Illinois Country. In *Dreams of the Americas: Overview of New France Archaeology*, edited by Christian Roy and Helen Côté, 185–204. Association des archéologues du Québec, Québec.

Martinez, David J.

2009   Dirt to Desk: Macrobotanical Analyses from Fort St. Joseph (20BE23) and the Lyne Site (20BE10). MA thesis, Department of Anthropology, Ohio State University, Columbus.

Mason, Carol I., and Margaret B. Holman

2000   Maple Sugaring in Prehistory: Tapping the Sources. In *Interpretations of Native North American Life: Material Contributions to Ethnohistory*, edited by Michael S. Nassaney and Eric S. Johnson, 261–271. Society for Historical Archaeology and University Press of Florida, Gainesville.

Mason, Ronald J.

1986   *Rock Island: Historical Indian Archaeology in the Northern Lake Michigan Basin.* MCJA Special Paper, no. 6. Kent State University Press, Kent, OH.

Matthews, Christopher N.

2010   *The Archaeology of American Capitalism.* University Press of Florida, Gainesville.

Maxwell, Moreau S., and Lewis H. Binford

1961   *Excavations at Fort Michilimackinac, Mackinac City, Michigan, 1959 Season.* Publications of the Museum, Cultural Series, Vol. 1, no. 1. Michigan State University, East Lansing.

McKenzie, Charles

1809   *Some Account of the Missouri Indians in the Years 1804, 5, 6 and 7.* Rare Book Department, McGill University Library, Montreal.

McLaughlin, Castle

1987   Style as a Social Boundary Marker: A Plains Indian Example. In *Ethnicity and Culture: Proceedings of the Eighteenth Annual Conference of the Archaeological Association of the University of Calgary*, edited by Réginald Auger, Margaret F. Glass, Scott MacEachern, and Peter M. McCartney, 55–66. University of Calgary Archaeological Association, Calgary, Alberta.

Miller, J. Jefferson, II, and Lyle M. Stone

1970   *Eighteenth-Century Ceramics from Fort Michilimackinac: A Study in Historical Archaeology.* Smithsonian Studies in History and Technology, no. 4. Smithsonian Institution Press, Washington, D.C.

Miller, Mark S. Parker

2000   Obtaining Information via Defective Documents: A Search for the Mandan in George Catlin's Paintings. In *Interpretations of Native North American Life: Material Contributions to Ethnohistory*, edited by Michael S. Nassaney and Eric S. Johnson, 296–318. Society for Historical Archaeology and the University Press of Florida, Gainesville.

Monks, Gregory F.

1992   Architectural Symbolism and Non-Verbal Communication at Upper Fort Garry. *Historical Archaeology* 26(2): 37–57.

Moore, John H.

1993   Political Economy in Anthropology. In *The Political Economy of North American Indians*, edited by John H. Moore, 3–19. University of Oklahoma Press, Norman.

Morand, Lynn L.

1994   *Craft Industries at Fort Michilimackinac, 1715–1781.* Archaeological Completion Report Series, no. 15. Mackinac State Historic Parks, Mackinac Island, MI.

Morantz, Toby

1980   The Fur Trade and the Cree of James Bay. In *Old Trails and New Directions*, edited by Carol M. Judd and Arthur J. Ray, 39–58. University of Toronto Press, Toronto.

Morrison, Jean

2007   *Superior Rendezvous-Place: Fort William in the Canadian Fur Trade.* Natural Heritage Books, Toronto.

Morton, Arthur S.

1973   *A History of the Canadian West to 1870–71.* 2nd ed. University of Toronto Press, Toronto.

Mullaley, Meredith J.

2011   *Rebuilding the Architectural History of the Fort Vancouver Village.* MA thesis, Department of Anthropology, Portland State University, Portland, OR.

Mullins, Paul R., and Robert Paynter

2000   Representing Colonizers: An Archaeology of Creolization, Ethnogenesis, and Indigenous Material Culture among the Haida. *Historical Archaeology* 34(3): 73–84.

Murray, David

2000   *Indian Giving: Economies of Power in Indian-White Exchanges.* University of Massachusetts Press, Amherst.

Myers, Robert C., and Joseph L. Peyser

1991   Four Flags over Fort St. Joseph. *Michigan History* 75(5): 11–21.

Nassaney, Michael S.

1989   An Epistemological Inquiry into Some Archaeological and Historical Interpretations of 17th Century Native American-European Relations. In *Archaeological Approaches to Cultural Identity,* edited by S. Shennan, 76–93. Unwin Hyman, London.

1992   Experiments in Social Ranking in Prehistoric Central Arkansas. PhD dissertation, University of Massachusetts, Amherst.

2000   Archaeology and Oral History in Tandem: Interpreting Native American Ritual, Ideology, and Gender Relations in Contact-Period Southeastern New England. In *Interpretations of Native North American Life: Material Contributions to Ethnohistory,* edited by Michael S. Nassaney and Eric S. Johnson, 412–431. Society for Historical Archaeology and the University Press of Florida, Gainesville.

2004   Native American Gender Politics and Material Culture in Seventeenth-Century Southeastern New England. *Journal of Social Archaeology* 4(3): 334–367.

2008a Commemorating French Heritage at Fort St. Joseph, an Eighteenth-Century Mission, Garrison, and Trading Post Complex in Niles, Michigan. In *Dreams of the Americas: Overview of New France Archaeology,* edited by Christian Roy and Hélène Côté, 96–111. Association des archéologues du Québec, Québec.

2008b Identity Formation at a French Colonial Outpost in the North American Interior. *International Journal of Historical Archaeology* 12(4): 297–318.

2009   European Exploration and Early Settlements. In *Archaeology in America: An Encyclopedia,* Vol. 2, *Midwest and Great Plains/Rocky Mountains,* edited by Francis McManamon, Linda S. Kordell, Kent G. Lightfoot, and George R. Milner, 45–52. Greenwood, Westport, CT.

2011   Public Involvement in the Fort St. Joseph Archaeological Project. *Present Pasts* 3: 42–51.

2012a Decolonizing Archaeological Theory at Fort St. Joseph, An Eighteenth-Century Multi-Ethnic Community in the Western Great Lakes Region. *Midcontinental Journal of Archaeology* 37(1): 5–24.

2012b Enhancing Public Archaeology through Community Service Learning. In *The Oxford Handbook of Public Archaeology*, edited by Robin Skeates, Carol McDavid, and John Carman, 414–440. Oxford University Press, Oxford, UK.

2014 The North American Fur Trade in Historical and Archaeological Perspective. In *Oxford Handbooks Online*, edited by James Symonds and Vesa-Pekka Herva.

Nassaney, Michael S., and Marjorie Abel

2000 Urban Spaces, Labor Organization, and Social Control: Lessons from New England's Cutlery Industry. In *Lines That Divide: Historical Archaeologies of Race, Gender, and Class*, edited by James Delle, Stephen Mrozowski, and Robert Paynter, 239–275. University of Tennessee Press, Knoxville.

Nassaney, Michael S., and José António Brandão

2009 The Materiality of Individuality at Fort St. Joseph: An Eighteenth-Century Mission-Garrison-Trading Post Complex on the Edge of Empire. In *The Materiality of Individuality: Archaeological Studies of Individual Lives*, edited by Carolyn L. White, 19–36. Springer, New York.

Nassaney, Michael S., José António Brandão, William M. Cremin, and Brock Giordano

2007 Economic Activities at an Eighteenth-Century Frontier Outpost in the Western Great Lakes. *Historical Archaeology* 41(4): 3–19.

Nassaney, Michael S., and William M. Cremin

2002 Realizing the Potential of the Contact Period in Southwest Michigan through the Fort St. Joseph Archaeological Project. *Wisconsin Archaeologist* 83(2): 123–134.

Nassaney, Michael S., William M. Cremin, Renee Kurtzweil, and José António Brandão

2003 The Search for Fort St. Joseph (1691–1781) in Niles, Michigan. *Midcontinental Journal of Archaeology* 28(2): 107–144.

Nassaney, Michael S., William M. Cremin, and Daniel Lynch

2002–2004 The Archaeological Identification of Colonial Fort St. Joseph, Michigan. *Journal of Field Archaeology* 29(3&4): 309–321.

Nassaney, Michael S., William M. Cremin, and LisaMarie Malischke

2012 Native American-French Interactions in 18th-Century Southwest Michigan: The View from Fort St. Joseph. In *Contested Territories: Native Americans and Europeans in the Lower Great Lakes 1700–1850*, edited by Charles Beatty-Medina and Melissa Rinehart, 55–79. Michigan State University Press, East Lansing.

Nassaney, Michael S., and Eric S. Johnson

2000 The Contributions of Material Objects to Ethnohistory in Native North America. In *Interpretations of Native North American Life: Material Contributions to Ethnohistory*, edited by Michael S. Nassaney and Eric S. Johnson, 1–30. Society for Historical Archaeology and University Press of Florida, Gainesville.

Nassaney, Michael S., Daniel Osborne, and Stacy Bell

2000 *Salvage Excavations near the Junction of French and St. Joseph Streets, Niles, Michigan.* Report of Investigations, no. 108. Department of Anthropology, Western Michigan University, Kalamazoo.

Nassaney, Michael S., and Michael Volmar

2003 Lithic Artifacts in Seventeenth-Century Native New England. In *Stone Tool Traditions in the Contact Era*, edited by Charles R. Cobb, 78–93. University of Alabama Press, Tuscaloosa.

Nassaney, Michael S. (editor)

1999 *An Archaeological Reconnaissance Survey to Locate Remains of Fort St. Joseph (20BE23) in Niles, Michigan.* Archaeological Report no. 22. Department of Anthropology, Western Michigan University, Kalamazoo.

Nassaney, Michael S., and Eric S. Johnson (editors)

2000 *Interpretations of Native North American Life: Material Contributions to Ethnohistory.* Society for Historical Archaeology and the University Press of Florida, Gainesville.

Nassaney, Michael S., and Kenneth E. Sassaman, Jr. (editors)

1995 *Native American Interactions: Multiscalar Analyses and Interpretations in the Eastern Woodlands.* University of Tennessee Press, Knoxville.

Neill, Susan M.

2000 Emblems of Ethnicity: Ribbonwork Garments from the Great Lakes Region. In *Interpretations of Native North American Life: Material Contributions to Ethnohistory*, edited by Michael S. Nassaney and Eric S. Johnson, 146–170. Society for Historical Archaeology and University Press of Florida, Gainesville.

Nelson, Peter

2007 Landscape in the Great Northwest: Investigations of Four Hudson's Bay Company Posts. Ms. on file, Fort Vancouver National Historic Site, Vancouver, WA.

Nicholas, George P.

2008 Melding Science and Community Values: Indigenous Archaeology Programs and the Negotiation of Cultural Differences. In *Collaborating at the Trowel's Edge: Teaching and Learning in Indigenous Archaeology*, edited by Stephen W. Silliman, 228–249. University of Arizona Press, Tucson.

Noble, Vergil E.

1983　Functional Classification and Inter-Site Analysis in Historical Archaeology: A Case Study from Fort Ouiatenon. PhD dissertation, Michigan State University, East Lansing.

1991　Ouiatenon on the Ouabache: Archaeological Investigations at a Fur Trading Post on the Wabash River. In *French Colonial Archaeology: The Illinois Country and the Western Great Lakes*, edited by John A. Walthall, 65–77. University of Illinois Press, Urbana.

Norton, Thomas Elliot

1974　*The Fur Trade in Colonial New York, 1686–1776*. University of Wisconsin Press, Madison.

Odell, George H.

2001　The Use of Metal at a Wichita Contact Settlement. *Southeastern Archaeology* 20(2): 173–186.

Oerichbauer, Edgar S.

1982　Archaeological Excavations at the Site of a North West and XY Company Winter Post (47-BT-26): A Progress Report. *Wisconsin Archaeologist* 63(3): 153–236.

Orchard, Trevor J.

2009　*Otters and Urchins: Continuity and Change in Haida Economy during the Late Holocene and Maritime Fur Trade Periods*. BAR International Series, no. 2027. Archaeopress, Oxford, UK.

Orser, Charles E., Jr.

1980　An Archaeological and Historical Socioeconomic Analysis of Arikara Mortuary Practice. PhD dissertation, Southern Illinois University.

2004　*Historical Archaeology*. 2nd ed. Pearson, Upper Saddle River, NJ.

2007　*The Archaeology of Race and Racialization in Historic America*. University Press of Florida, Gainesville.

Ott, Jennifer

2003　"Ruining" the Rivers in the Snake Country: The Hudson's Bay Company's Fur Desert Policy. *Oregon Historical Quarterly* 104(2): 166–195.

Pavao-Zuckerman, Barnet

2007　Deerskins and Domesticates: Creek Subsistence and Economic Strategies in the Historic Period. *American Antiquity* 72(1): 5–33.

Peers, Laura

1998　Fur Trade History, Native History, Public History: Communication and Miscommunication. In *New Faces of the Fur Trade: Selected Papers of the Seventh North American Fur Trade Conference, Halifax, Nova Scotia, 1995*, edited by

Jo-Anne Fiske, Susan Sleeper-Smith, and William Wicken, 101–119. Michigan State University Press, East Lansing.

Peers, Laura, and Robert Coutts

2010 Aboriginal History and Historic Sites: The Shifting Ground. In *Gathering Places: Aboriginal and Fur Trade Histories*, edited by Carolyn Podruchny and Laura Peers, 274–293. UBC Press, Vancouver.

Pego, Christina, Robert F. Hill, Glenn W. Solomon, Robert M. Chisholm, and Suzanne E. Ivey

1999 Tobacco, Culture, and Health among American Indians: A Historical Review. In *Contemporary Native American Cultural Issues*, edited by Duane Champagne, 245–262. Altamira Press, Walnut Creek, CA.

Peña, Elizabeth S.

2001 The Role of Wampum Production at the Albany Almshouse. *International Journal of Historical Archaeology* 5(2): 155–174.

Pendergast, R. A.

1972 The Economics of the Montreal Traders. *Western Canadian Journal of Anthropology* 3(1): 34–42.

Peterson, Jacqueline C.

1981 The People in Between: Indian-White Marriage and the Genesis of a Métis Society and Culture in the Great Lakes Region, 1680–1830. PhD dissertation, University of Illinois, Chicago Circle.

1985 Many Roads to Red River: Métis Genesis in the Great Lakes Region, 1680–1815. In *The New Peoples: Being and Becoming Métis in North America*, edited by Jacqueline C. Peterson and Jennifer S. H. Brown, 37–71. University of Manitoba Press, Winnipeg.

1990 Gathering at the River: The Métis Peopling of the Northern Plains. In *The Fur Trade in North Dakota*, edited by Virginia L. Heidenreich, 47–64. North Dakota Heritage Center, Bismark.

Peterson, Jacqueline C., and John Anfinson

1984 The Indian and the Fur Trade: A Review of Recent Literature. In *Scholars and the Indian Experience: Critical Reviews of Recent Writing in the Social Sciences*, edited by William R. Swagerty, 223–257. Indiana University Press, Bloomington.

Peterson, Jacqueline C., and Jennifer S. H. Brown, editors

1985 *The New Peoples: Being and Becoming Métis in North America*. University of Manitoba Press, Winnipeg, and University of Nebraska, Lincoln.

Peyser, Joseph L. (editor and translator)

1978 Fort St. Joseph Manuscripts: Chronological Inventory of French-Language

Manuscripts and Their Translations and Abstracts. Compiled for the Four Flags Historical Study Committee. On file in the Niles District Library, Niles, MI.

1992 *Letters from New France: The Upper Country, 1686–1783.* University of Illinois Press, Urbana.

Phillips, Paul C.

1961 *The Fur Trade.* 2 vols. University of Oklahoma Press, Norman.

Pierson, Heidi K.

2011a Globalization: New Iterations of Old Patterns of Change. In *Exploring Fort Vancouver,* edited by Douglas C. Wilson and Theresa E. Langford, 69–78. Fort Vancouver National Trust, Vancouver, WA, in association with the University of Washington Press, Seattle.

2011b Health: Germs, Food, and Medicine. In *Exploring Fort Vancouver,* edited by Douglas C. Wilson and Theresa E. Langford, 79–94. Fort Vancouver National Trust, Vancouver, WA, in association with the University of Washington Press, Seattle.

Podruchny, Carolyn

1998 Festivities, Fortitude, and Fraternalism: Fur Trade Masculinity and the Beaver Club, 1785–1827. In *New Faces of the Fur Trade: Selected Papers of the Seventh North American Fur Trade Conference, Halifax, Nova Scotia, 1995,* edited by Jo-Anne Fiske, Susan Sleeper-Smith, and William Wicken, 31–52. Michigan State University Press, East Lansing.

Podruchny, Carolyn, and Laura Peers (editors)

2010 *Gathering Places: Aboriginal and Fur Trade Histories.* UBC Press, Vancouver.

Pollard, Juliet Thelma

2011 The Making of the Métis in the Pacific Northwest: Fur Trade Children: Race, Class, and Gender. PhD dissertation, University of British Columbia, Vancouver.

Prucha, Francis Paul

1962 *American Indian Policy in the Formative Years: The Indian Trade and Intercourse Acts 1790–1834.* Harvard University Press, Cambridge, MA.

Pyszczyk, Heinz

1989 Consumption and Ethnicity: An Example from the Fur Trade in Western Canada. *Journal of Anthropological Archaeology* 8(3): 213–249.

Quimby, George I.

1939 European Trade Articles as Chronological Indicators for Archaeology of the Historic Period in Michigan. *Papers of the Michigan Academy of Science, Arts, and Letters* 24: 25–31.

1966   *Indian Culture and European Trade Goods: The Archaeology of the Historic Period in the Western Great Lakes Region.* University of Wisconsin Press, Madison.

Rafferty, Sean M., and Rob Mann (editors)

2004   *Smoking and Culture: The Archaeology of Tobacco Pipes in Eastern North America.* University of Tennessee Press, Knoxville.

Ray, Arthur J.

1974   *Indians in the Fur Trade.* University of Toronto Press, Toronto.

1978   History and Archaeology of the Northern Fur Trade. *American Antiquity*
43(1): 26–34.

1980   Indians as Consumers in the Eighteenth Century. In *Old Trails and New Directions: Papers of the Third North American Fur Trade Conference,* edited by Carol
M. Judd and Arthur J. Ray, 255–271. University of Toronto Press, Toronto.

1988   The Hudson's Bay Company and Native People. In *Handbook of North American Indians,* Vol. 4, *History of Indian-White Relations,* edited by Wilcomb E.
Washburn, 335–350. Smithsonian Institution Press, Washington, D.C.

1996   The Northern Interior, 1600 to Modern Times. In *The Cambridge History of
the Native Peoples of the Americas,* Vol. 1, *North America,* part 2, edited by Bruce
G. Trigger and Wilcomb E. Washburn, 259–327. Cambridge University Press,
Cambridge, UK.

Ray, Arthur J., and Donald B. Freeman

1978   *"Give Us Good Measure": An Economic Analysis of Relations between the Indians
and the Hudson's Bay Company before 1763.* University of Toronto Press, Toronto.

Redfield, Robert, Ralph Linton, and Melville Herskovits

1936   Memorandum for the Study of Acculturation. *American Anthropologist* 38(1):
149–152.

Richter, Daniel K.

1992   *The Ordeal of the Longhouse.* University of North Carolina Press, Chapel Hill.

Rick, Anne Meachem

1983   Appendix B. Faunal Analysis of Nottingham House. In *Nottingham House: The
Hudson's Bay Company in Athabasca, 1802–1806,* by Karlis Karklins and Robert
S. Allen, 227–266. History and Archaeology series, no. 69. National Historic
Parks and Sites Branch, Parks Canada, Environment Canada, Ottawa.

Rinehart, Charles J.

1994   Crucifixes and Medallions from Michilimackinac. In *The Fur Trade Revisited:
Selected Papers of the Sixth North American Fur Trade Conference, Mackinac
Island, Michigan, 1991,* edited by Jennifer S. H. Brown, William J. Eccles, and

Donald P. Heldman, 331–348. Michigan State University Press, East Lansing and Mackinac State Historic Parks, Mackinac Island, MI.

Ritchie, William A.

1954 Dutch Hollow, an Early Historic Period Seneca Site in Livingston County, New York. *Researches and Transactions of the New York State Archaeological Association*, Vol. 13, no. 1. Rochester, NY.

Ritzenthaler, Robert E., and George Irving Quimby

1962 The Red Ocher Culture of the Upper Great Lakes and Adjacent Areas. *Fieldiana: Anthropology* 36(11): 243–275.

Robertson, Roland

1995 Glocalization: Time-Space and Homogeneity-Heterogeneity. In *Global Modernities*, edited by Mike Featherstone, Scott Lash, and Roland Robertson, 25–44. Sage, London.

Robinson, Paul A.

1990 The Struggle Within: The Indian Debate in Seventeenth-Century Narragansett Country. PhD dissertation, State University of New York at Binghamton.

2000 One Island, Two Places: Archaeology, Memory, and Meaning in a Rhode Island Town. In *Interpretations of Native North American Life: Material Contributions to Ethnohistory*, edited by Michael S. Nassaney and Eric S. Johnson, 398–411. Society for Historical Archaeology and the University Press of Florida, Gainesville.

Robinson, Paul A., Marc A. Kelley, and Patricia E. Rubertone

1985 Preliminary Biocultural Interpretations from a Seventeenth-Century Narragansett Indian Cemetery in Rhode Island. In *Cultures in Contact: The European Impact on Native Cultural Institutions in Eastern North America, A.D. 1000–1800*, edited by William W. Fitzhugh, 107–130. Smithsonian Institution Press, Washington, D.C.

Rogers, J. Daniel

1990 *Objects of Change: The Archaeology and History of Arikara Contact with Europeans*. Smithsonian Institution Press, Washington, D.C.

2005 Archaeology and the Interpretation of Colonial Encounters. In *The Archaeology of Colonial Encounters*, edited by Gil J. Stein, 331–354. School of American Research Press, Santa Fe, NM.

Ross, Lester A.

1974 *Hudson's Bay Company Glass Trade Beads: Manufacturing Types Imported to Fort Vancouver (1829–1860)*. Bead Journal, Los Angeles, CA.

1976 Fort Vancouver, 1829–1860: A Historical Archeological Investigation of the

Goods Imported and Manufactured by the Hudson's Bay Company. Manuscript on file, Fort Vancouver National Historic Site, Vancouver, WA.

1990 Trade Beads from Hudson's Bay Company Fort Vancouver (1829–1860), Vancouver, Washington. *Beads: Journal of the Society of Bead Researchers* 2: 29–68.

Rotman, Deborah L.

2015 *The Archaeology of Gender in Historic America.* University Press of Florida, Gainesville.

Rubertone, Patricia E.

1996 Matters of Inclusion: Historical Archaeology and Native Americans. *World Archaeology Bulletin* 7: 77–86.

2001 *Grave Undertakings: An Archaeology of Roger Williams and the Narragansett Indians.* Smithsonian Institution Press, Washington, D.C.

Sahlins, Marshall

1972 *Stone Age Economics.* Aldine Publishing, New York.

Saitta, Dean

2007 *The Archaeology of Collective Action.* University Press of Florida, Gainesville.

Saum, Lewis O.

1965 *The Fur Trade and the Indian.* University of Washington Press, Seattle.

Sayers, Daniel O.

2003 Animal Liberation and Praxis: The Challenges of Animal Rights Theory to Our Production of Inclusive Emancipatory Histories in Archaeology. Paper presented at the Radical Archaeology Theory Symposium, State University of New York, Binghamton, October 17–18.

Scott, Elizabeth M.

1991a "Such Diet as Befitted His Station as Clerk": The Archaeology of Subsistence and Diversity at Fort Michilimackinac, 1761–1781. PhD dissertation, University of Minnesota, Minneapolis.

1991b A Feminist Approach to Historical Archaeology: Eighteenth-Century Fur Trade Society at Fort Michilimackinac. *Historical Archaeology* 25(4): 42–53.

2001a Appendix 1: Faunal Remains from House D of the Southeast Rowhouse, British Period (1760–1781), Fort Michilimackinac. In *House D of the Southeast Row House: Excavations at Fort Michilimackinac, 1989–1997,* by Lynn L. M. Evans, 60–66. Archaeological Completion Report Series, no. 17. Mackinac State Historic Parks, Mackinac Island, MI.

2001b "An Indolent Slothful Set of Vagabonds": Ethnicity and Race in a Colonial Fur-Trading Community. In *Race and the Archaeology of Identity,* edited by Charles E. Orser Jr., 14–33. University of Utah Press, Salt Lake City.

Secoy, Frank Raymond

1953 *Changing Military Patterns on the Great Plains.* American Ethnological Society, Monograph 21. J. J. Augustin, Locust Valley, NJ.

Secunda, W. Ben

2006 To Cede or Seed? Risk and Identity among the Woodland Potawatomi during the Removal Period. *Midcontinental Journal of Archaeology* 31(1): 57–88.

Shott, Michael J.

2012 Toward Settlement Occupation Span from Dispersion of Tobacco-Pipe-Stem-Bore Diameter. *Historical Archaeology* 46(2): 16–38.

Silliman, Stephen W.

2005 Culture Contact or Colonialism? Challenges in the Archaeology of Native North America. *American Antiquity* 70(1): 55–74.

Simmons, William S.

1970 *Cautantowwit's House: An Indian Burial Ground on the Island of Conanicut in Narragansett Bay.* Brown University Press, Providence, RI.

Skibo, James, Terrance Martin, Eric C. Drake, and John G. Franzen

2004 Grand Island's Post-Contact Occupation at Williams Landing. *Midcontinental Journal of Archaeology* 29(2): 167–186.

Sleeper-Smith, Susan

1998 Furs and Female Kin Networks: The World of Marie Madeleine Réaume L'archevêque Chevalier. In *New Faces of the Fur Trade: Selected Papers of the Seventh North American Fur Trade Conference, Halifax, Nova Scotia, 1995,* edited by Jo-Anne Fiske, Susan Sleeper-Smith, and William Wicken, 53–72. Michigan State University Press, East Lansing.

2001 *Indian Women and French Men: Rethinking Cultural Encounter in the Western Great Lakes.* University of Massachusetts Press, Amherst.

Sleeper-Smith, Susan (editor)

2009 *Rethinking the Fur Trade: Cultures of Exchange in an Atlantic World.* University of Nebraska Press, Lincoln.

Smith, G. Hubert

1972 *Like-a-Fishhook Village and Fort Berthold, Garrison Reservoir, North Dakota.* National Park Service, United States Department of the Interior, Washington, D.C.

Smith, Marvin T.

1983 Chronology from Glass Beads: The Spanish Period in the Southeast c. A.D. 1513–1670. In *Proceedings of the 1982 Glass Trade Bead Conference,* edited by Charles F. Hayes, 147–158. Rochester Museum and Science Center Research Records, no. 16. Rochester, NY.

2000 *Coosa: The Rise and Fall of a Mississippian Chiefdom.* University Press of Florida, Gainesville.

Sprague, Roderick

1998 The Literature and Location of the Phoenix Button. *Historical Archaeology* 32(2): 56–77.

Stoler, Ann Laura

2001 Tense and Tender Ties: The Politics of Comparison in North American History and (Post) Colonial Studies. *Journal of American History* 88(3): 829–865.

Stone, Lyle M.

1974a *Fort Michilimackinac, 1715–1781.* Michigan State University Anthropological Series, Vol. 1. East Lansing.

1974b A Review of the Fort St. Joseph Archaeological Collections: Niles, Michigan and South Bend, Indiana. Unpublished report on file in the Fort St. Joseph Museum, Niles, MI.

St-Onge, Nicole

2008 The Persistence of Travel and Trade: St. Lawrence River Valley French Engagés and the American Fur Company, 1818–1840. *Michigan Historical Review* 34(2): 17–37.

Strong, Emory

1975 Enigma of the Phoenix Button. *Historical Archaeology* 9: 74–80.

Sudbury, J. Byron

2009 *Politics of the Fur Trade: Clay Tobacco Pipes at Fort Union Trading Post (32WI17).* Historical Clay Tobacco Pipe Studies Research Monograph no. 2. Clay Pipes Press, Ponca City, OK.

Surrey, N. M. Miller

2006 [1916] *The Commerce of Louisiana During the French Regime, 1699–1763.* University of Alabama Press, Tuscaloosa.

Swagerty, William R.

1988 Indian Trade in the Trans-Mississippi West to 1870. In *Handbook of North American Indians*, Vol. 4, *History of Indian-White Relations*, edited by Wilcomb E. Washburn, 351–374. Smithsonian Institution Press, Washington, D.C.

Teit, James A.

1975 [1909] *The Shuswap.* AMS Press, New York.

Thomas, Peter A.

1979 In the Maelstrom of Change: The Indian Trade and Cultural Process in the Middle Connecticut River Valley: 1635–1665. PhD dissertation, University of Massachusetts, Amherst.

1985 Cultural Change on the Southern New England Frontier, 1630–1665. In *Cul-*

tures in Contact: The European Impact on Native Cultural Institutions in Eastern North America, A.D. 1000–1800, edited by William W. Fitzhugh, 131–161. Smithsonian Institution Press, Washington, D.C.

Thompson, David

1916   *David Thompson's Narrative of His Explorations in Western America, 1784–1812.* Edited by Joseph Burr Tyrrell. Champlain Society, Toronto.

Toom, Dennis L.

1979   The Middle Missouri Villagers and the Early Fur Trade: Implications for Archeological Interpretation. MA thesis, Department of Anthropology, University of Nebraska, Lincoln.

Tordoff, Judith D.

1983   An Archaeological Perspective on the Organization of the Fur Trade in Eighteenth Century New France. PhD dissertation, Michigan State University, East Lansing.

Tottle, Terry P.

1981   *The History and Archaeology of Pine Fort.* Papers in Manitoba Archaeology Preliminary Report, no. 7. Department of Cultural Affairs and Historical Resources, Historic Resources Branch, Winnipeg.

Trigger, Bruce G.

1985   *Natives and Newcomers: Canada's "Heroic Age" Reconsidered.* McGill-Queen's University Press, Kingston, ON.

2007   *A History of Archaeological Thought.* 2nd ed. Cambridge University Press, New York.

Trigger, Bruce G., and William R. Swagerty

1996   Entertaining Strangers: North America in the Sixteenth Century. In *The Cambridge History of the Native Peoples of the Americas,* Vol. 1, *North America,* part 1, edited by Bruce G. Trigger and Wilcomb E. Washburn, 325–398. Cambridge University Press, Cambridge, UK.

Trubowitz, Neal L.

1992a   Native American and French on the Central Wabash. In *Calumet and Fleur-de-Lys: Archaeology of Indian and French Contact in the Midcontinent,* edited by John A. Walthall and Thomas E. Emerson, 241–264. Smithsonian Institution Press, Washington, D.C.

1992b   Thanks, but We Prefer to Smoke Our Own: Pipes in the Great Lakes-Riverine Region during the Eighteenth Century. In *Proceedings of the 1989 Smoking Pipe Conference: Selected Papers,* edited by Charles F. Hayes III, Connie Cox Bodner, and Martha L. Sempowski, 97–112. Rochester Museum and Science Center Research Records, no. 22, Rochester, NY.

Turnbaugh, William A.

1977 Elements of Nativistic Pipe Ceremonialism in the Post-Contact Northeast. *Pennsylvania Archaeologist* 47(4):1–7.

1984 *The Material Culture of RI-100, a Mid-17th Century Narragansett Indian Burial Site in North Kingstown, Rhode Island.* University of Rhode Island Press, Kingston.

1993 Assessing the Significance of European Goods in Seventeenth-Century Narragansett Society. In *Ethnohistory and Archaeology: Approaches to Postcontact Change in the Americas*, edited by J. Daniel Rogers and Samuel M. Wilson, 133–160. Plenum Press, New York.

Turner, Frederick Jackson

1891 *The Character and Influence of the Indian Trade in Wisconsin: A Study of the Trading Post as an Institution.* Johns Hopkins University Studies in Historical and Political Science, Baltimore, MD.

Ubelaker, Douglas H., and William M. Bass

1970 Arikara Glassworking Techniques at Leavenworth and Sully Sites. *American Antiquity* 35(4): 467–475.

Van Kirk, Sylvia

1980 *Many Tender Ties: Women in Fur Trade Society, 1670–1870.* University of Oklahoma Press, Norman.

Vaughan, Thomas

1982a Introduction. In *Soft Gold: The Fur Trade and Cultural Exchange on the Northwest Coast of America*, by Thomas Vaughan and Bill Holm, 1–30. Oregon Historical Society, Portland.

1982b The Brilliant Visual Record of the Fur Trade: Annotation. In *Soft Gold: The Fur Trade and Cultural Exchange on the Northwest Coast of America*, by Thomas Vaughan and Bill Holm, 169–278. Oregon Historical Society, Portland.

Veit, Steve

2011 Digging through the Past: Grand Portage, an Archaeological Adventure. *Journal of the Early Americas* 1(5): 26–31.

Vibert, Elizabeth

2010 The Contours of Everyday Life: Food and Identity in the Plateau Fur Trade. In *Gathering Places: Aboriginal and Fur Trade Histories*, edited by Carolyn Podruchny and Laura Peers, 119–148. UBC Press, Vancouver.

Wagner, Mark J.

2003 In All the Solemnity of Profound Smoking: Tobacco Smoking and Pipe Manufacture and Use among the Potawatomi of Illinois. In *Stone Tool Traditions in the Contact Era*, edited by Charles R. Cobb, 109–126. University of Alabama Press, Tuscaloosa.

2011   *The Rhoads Site: A Historic Kickapoo Village on the Illinois Prairie.* Studies in Archaeology, no. 5. Illinois State Archaeological Survey, University of Illinois, Urbana.

Wallace, Anthony F. C.

1999   *Jefferson and the Indians: The Tragic Fate of the First Americans.* Harvard University Press, Cambridge, MA.

Wallerstein, Immanuel

1974   *The Modern World System: Capitalist Agriculture and the Origins of the European World Economy in the Sixteenth Century.* Academic Press, New York.

1979   *The Capitalist World-Economy: Essays.* Cambridge University Press, Cambridge, UK.

Walthall, John A.

1991   French Colonial Fort Massac: Architecture and Ceramic Patterning. In *French Colonial Archaeology: The Illinois Country and the Western Great Lakes,* edited by John A. Walthall, 42–64. University of Illinois Press, Urbana.

Walthall, John A., and Margaret K. Brown

2001   French Colonial Material Culture from an Early Eighteenth-Century Outpost in the Illinois Country. *Illinois Archaeology* 13(1–2): 88–126.

Waselkov, Gregory A.

1978   Evolution of Deer Hunting in the Eastern Woodlands. *Midcontinental Journal of Archaeology* 3: 15–34.

1989   Seventeenth-Century Trade in the Colonial Southeast. *Southeastern Archaeology* 8(2): 117–133.

1997   *The Archaeology of French Colonial North America: English-French Edition.* Guide to Historical Archaeological Literature, no. 5. Society for Historical Archaeology, Uniontown, PA.

1998   The Eighteenth-Century Anglo-Indian Trade in Southeastern North America. In *New Faces of the Fur Trade: Selected Papers of the Seventh North American Fur Trade Conference, Halifax, Nova Scotia, 1995,* edited by Jo-Anne Fiske, Susan Sleeper-Smith, and William Wicken, 193–222. Michigan State University Press, East Lansing.

2009   French Colonial Archaeology. In *International Handbook of Historical Archaeology,* edited by Teresita Majewski and David Gaimster, 613–628. Springer, New York.

Washburn, Wilcomb E., and Bruce G. Trigger

1996   Native Peoples in Euro-American Historiography. In *The Cambridge History of the Native Peoples of the Americas,* Vol. 1, *North America,* part 1, edited by Bruce

G. Trigger and Wilcomb E. Washburn, 61–124. Cambridge University Press, Cambridge, UK.

Way, Royal B.

1919 The U.S. Factory System for Trading with the Indians, 1796–1822. *Mississippi Historical Review* 6(2): 220–235.

Weber, David J.

1971 *The Taos Trappers: The Fur Trade in the Far Southwest, 1540–1846.* University of Oklahoma Press, Norman.

Welters, Linda, Margaret T. Ordoñez, Kathryn Tarleton, and Joyce Smith

1996 European Textiles from Seventeenth-Century New England Indian Cemeteries. In *Historical Archaeology and the Study of American Culture,* edited by Lu Ann De Cunzo and Bernard L. Herman, 193–232. Henry Francis du Pont Winterthur Museum, Winterthur, DE.

Welters, Linda, and Joyce Smith

1985 *Conservation and Analysis of European Textiles from RI-1000: Report to the Rhode Island Historical Preservation Commission.* Rhode Island Historical Preservation Commission, Providence.

Western Michigan University

N.d. Fort St. Joseph Archaeological Project. http://wmich.edu/fortstjoseph/.

Wheeler, Robert C.

1975 The Quetico-Superior Underwater Research Project. In *Voices from the Rapids: An Underwater Search for Fur Trade Artifacts 1960–73,* by Robert C. Wheeler, Walter A. Kenyon, Alan R. Woolworth, and Douglas A. Birk, 7–13. Minnesota Historical Society, St. Paul.

1985 *A Toast to the Fur Trade: A Picture Essay on Its Material Culture.* Wheeler Productions, St. Paul, MN.

Wheeler, Robert C., Walter A. Kenyon, Alan R. Woolworth, and Douglas A. Birk

1975 *Voices from the Rapids: An Underwater Search for Fur Trade Artifacts 1960–73.* Minnesota Historical Society, St. Paul.

Whelan, Mary

1993 Dakota Indian Economics and the Nineteenth-Century Fur Trade. *Ethnohistory* 40(2): 246–276.

White, Bruce M.

1982 Parisian Women's Dogs: A Bibliographic Essay on Cross-Cultural Communication and Trade. In *Where Two Worlds Meet: The Great Lakes Fur Trade,* by Carolyn Gilman, 120–126. Museum Exhibit Series, no. 2. Minnesota Historical Society, St. Paul.

1984 "Give Us a Little Milk": The Social and Cultural Significance of Gift Giving in the Lake Superior Fur Trade. In *Rendezvous: Selected Papers of the Fourth North American Fur Trade Conference, 1981*, edited by Thomas C. Buckley, 185–197. North American Fur Trade Conference, St. Paul, MN.

2004 Grand Portage National Monument Historic Documents Study. Turnstone Historical Research. Report on file at the Grand Portage National Monument, Grand Portage, MN.

White, Carolyn L.

2005 *American Artifacts of Personal Adornment, 1680–1820: A Guide to Identification and Interpretation.* AltaMira Press, Lanham, MD.

White, Richard

2011 *The Middle Ground: Indians, Empires, and Republics in the Great Lakes Region, 1650–1815.* Cambridge University Press, Cambridge, UK.

White, Sophie

2012 *Wild Frenchmen and Frenchified Indians: Material Culture and Race in Colonial Louisiana.* University of Pennsylvania Press, Philadelphia.

Whitner, Robert L.

1984 Makah Commercial Sealing, 1860–1897: A Study in Acculturation and Conflict. In *Rendezvous: Selected Papers of the Fourth North American Fur Trade Conference, 1981*, edited by Thomas C. Buckley, 121–130. North American Fur Trade Conference, St. Paul, MN.

Widder, Keith R.

2013 *Beyond Pontiac's Shadow: Michilimackinac and the Anglo-Indian War of 1763.* Michigan State University Press, East Lansing, and Mackinac State Historic Parks, Mackinac Island, MI.

Wike, Joyce Annabel

1958 Problems in Fur Trade Analysis: The Northwest Coast. *American Anthropologist* 60: 1086–1101.

Wilcox, Michael V.

2009 *The Pueblo Revolt and the Mythology of Conquest: An Indigenous Archaeology of Contact.* University of California Press, Berkeley.

Wilder, Craig Steven

2013 *Ebony and Ivy: Race, Slavery, and the Troubled History of America's Universities.* Bloomsbury Press, New York.

Willoughby, Charles C.

1935 *Antiquities of the New England Indians with Notes on the Ancient Cultures of the Adjacent Territory.* Peabody Museum of Archaeology and Ethnology, Harvard University, Cambridge, MA.

Wilmott, Cory, and Kevin Brownlee

2010 Dressing for the Homeward Journey: Western Anishinaabe Leadership Roles Viewed through Two Nineteenth-Century Burials. In *Gathering Places: Aboriginal and Fur Trade Histories*, edited by Carolyn Podruchny and Laura Peers, 48–89. UBC Press, Vancouver.

Wilson, Douglas C.

2011 Fort Vancouver: History, Archaeology, and the Transformation of the Pacific Northwest. In *Exploring Fort Vancouver*, edited by Douglas C. Wilson and Theresa E. Langford, 1–28. Fort Vancouver National Trust, Vancouver, WA, in association with the University of Washington Press, Seattle.

2014 The Decline and Fall of the Hudson's Bay Company Village at Fort Vancouver. In *Alis Volat Proprisiis: Tales from the Oregon Territory 1848–1859*, edited by Chelsea Rose and Mark Tveskov, 21–42. Occasional Papers no. 9. Association of Oregon Archaeologists, Eugene.

Wilson, Douglas C., Kenneth Ames, Kristine M. Bovy, Virginia Butler, Robert Cromwell, Loren G. Davis, Christopher R. DeCorse, Brian F. Harrison, R. Lee Lyman, Michele L. Punke, Cameron Smith, and Nancy A. Stenholm

2009 *Historical Archaeology at the Middle Village: Station Camp/McGowan Site (45PC106), Station Camp Unit, Lewis and Clark National Park, Pacific County, Washington*. Northwest Cultural Resources Report, no. 1. Washington State Historical Society, Tacoma, and Washington State Department of Transportation, Olympia.

Wilson, Douglas, Robert Cromwell, Douglas Deur, and Roy Watters

2012 Exploring Fort Astoria (AKA Fort George) in Context. Paper presented at the annual Conference on Historical and Underwater Archaeology, Baltimore, MD.

Wilson, Douglas C., and Theresa E. Langford (editors)

2011 *Exploring Fort Vancouver*. Fort Vancouver National Trust, Vancouver, WA, in association with the University of Washington Press, Seattle.

Witthoft, John

1966 Archaeology as a Key to the Colonial Fur Trade. *Minnesota History* 40: 203–209.

Wolf, Eric R.

1959 *Sons of the Shaking Earth*. University of Chicago Press, Chicago.

1982 *Europe and the People without History*. University of California Press, Berkeley.

Wood, W. Raymond

1990 Early Fur Trade on the Northern Plains. In *The Fur Trade in North Dakota*, edited by Virginia L. Heidenreich, 2–16. North Dakota Heritage Center, Bismarck.

Wood, W. Raymond, William J. Hunt Jr., and Randy H. Williams

2011 *Fort Clark and Its Indian Neighbors: A Trading Post on the Upper Missouri*. University of Oklahoma Press, Norman.

Wood, W. Raymond, and Thomas D. Thiessen (editors)

1985 *Early Fur Trade on the Northern Plains: Canadian Traders Among the Mandan and Hidatsa Indians, 1738–1818*. University of Oklahoma Press, Norman.

Woodward, Arthur

1927 Those Green River Knives. *Indian Notes* 4(4): 403–418. Museum of the American Indian, Heye Foundation, New York.

1970 *Denominators of the Fur Trade: An Anthology of Writings on the Material Culture of the Fur Trade*. Socio-Technical Publications, Pasadena, CA.

Woolworth, Alan R.

1982 The Great Carrying Place: Grand Portage. In *Where Two Worlds Meet: The Great Lakes Fur Trade*, by Carolyn Gilman, 110–115. Museum Exhibit Series, no. 2. Minnesota Historical Society, St. Paul.

Woolworth, Alan R., and Douglas A. Birk

1975 Description of the Artifacts Recovered by the Quetico-Superior Underwater Research Project. In *Voices from the Rapids: An Underwater Search for Fur Trade Artifacts 1960–73*, by Robert C. Wheeler, Walter A. Kenyon, Alan R. Woolworth, and Douglas A. Birk, 55–93. Minnesota Historical Society, St. Paul.

Woolworth, Alan, and W. Raymond Wood

1960 *The Archaeology of a Small Trading Post (Kipp's Post, 32MN1) in the Garrison Reservoir, North Dakota*. River Basin Survey Papers, no. 20. Bureau of American Ethnology, Smithsonian Institution Bulletin 176. United States Government Printing Office, Washington, D.C.

Index

Italic letters *b*, *f*, or *t* following a page number indicate a box, figure, or table.

Anthropology as a discipline: evolutionary origin of, 17–21; use of direct historical approach in, 20–21

Archaeology of the fur trade: chronology, 71–72, 81–83, 111, 144; classification by age and function, 72–73, 81, 84–85, 91, 122, 138; collaboration in (*see* Fort St. Joseph Archaeological Project); decades-long examination of traded goods and their transport in, 80, 204–5; forensic approaches to, 98–99; public perception and, 30–31, 194–96, 203–5; site identification, 69–70, 74. *See also* Materiality of the fur trade; Underwater archaeology

Arctic region, 42*t*, 56

Arikaras, 42*f*, 154, 163; attitudes toward Euro-Americans, 155–56; ceramic vessels of, 92–93; fur trade impacts delayed for, 158–59; interaction with Euro-American trade goods by, 82, 157–58

Arrowheads. *See* Projectile points

Artifacts: classification of, 84, 100, 103–4, 122, 136; at Fort St. Joseph, 45*f*, 70; identification of ethnic groups by, 105, 106–7; organic, and their recovery, 74, 79, 80*f*, 83, 126–27, 127*f*

Asian markets, 60; New England and northwest coast in triangular trade with, 63, 64–65, 199; pelts from trapped vs. shot animals for, 94–95; sea mammals for, 62–63, 146, 152, 153, 199

Asian nations, imported goods from, 65, 101, 103, 191

Assimilation: conversion to Christianity and, 49, 165, 168; French vs. English interaction with native peoples, 47–48; native peoples and governmental policies, 26, 65

Astor, John Jacob, 59–60, 61, 66. *See also* Fort Astoria

Autonomy: loss of, and disease epidemics, 158–59; as Native-American power issue, 9, 12, 20, 139, 152, 205; political economy and, 27, 34, 39, 40, 65, 68; retention of, 111, 139

Baidarkas. See under Canoes, kayaks as kind of

Basque fur traders, northeast North America and, 42*t*

Beads, 93*f*, 104, 105, 141; colored, 103, 113, 115;

157; glass, 114, 134, 138; glass, as desirable, 1, 31–32, 91, 103–4, 163, 180; marine shell, 50, 51*f*, 104, 185 (*see also* Wampum); seed, 81, 115, 190; use of, 50–51, 81, 84, 103, 185

Bear, 42*t*, 117, 142, 171, 184; bones of, 144–45, 185; entire, carcasses and butchering evidence, 89, 119

Beaver, 2, 24, 42*t*, 60, 61, 185; as exploited species, 3, 5, 44, 45, 62, 118, 201; felted, hats, 44, 129, 199; pelts supplied by, 48, 86, 120, 153, 155, 168; replaced as mainstay of fur trade, 46, 50, 201

Beaver Club, activities of fur traders in, 8

Bertrand, Joseph, as fur trader, 172

Birch bark canoes, 5*f*, 122, 132; for fur trade transport, 5, 56; northern forest components of, 47, 55, 78; repair of, 169, 170*b*, 184

Bison: bones of, similar to domestic cattle, 184–85; horse trading and hunting, 73, 110, 154; Missouri River Valley and, 153, 154–55, 199, 201; as replacement mainstay of fur trade, 42*t*, 46, 133

Blackfeet, 24, 42*t*

Blacksmithing, firearm repair and gunsmithing as, 94, 116, 150, 169, 181–82, 190

Bodmer, Karl, Mandan life depicted by, 92

Bougainville, Louis-Antoine de, fur production estimates by, 171

Bourgeois House, Fort Union: architectural style of, 160–61; reconstruction of, 159–60

Brandywine Creek 2 site, St. Joseph River Valley, 175

Buffalo. *See* Bison

Building techniques: archaeological identification of, 74–76, 78, 131–32, 138, 195; ethnic differences in, 74, 107, 134–35, 140, 140*f*; at Fort St. Joseph, 178–80, 179*f*, 180*f*

Burial customs, 99; afterlife accompaniments as, 114, 115, 116, 175; body wrappings, 100, 101, 115; commemorative markers, 70, 71*f*

Burnett, William, packs of furs sold by, 172

Buttons, 109, 134; from excavated trading posts, 138, 186; as trade-goods, 63, 103, 124

Cache pits, 135, 138

Cahokia commemoration, revisionist history of, 29

Calumet ceremony: as intercultural mediation, 11, 122, 166, 190–91, 199; stone pipes for, 98, 115, 116f

Canadian territories, 21, 32, 48, 55; colonial trading sites in, 5, 43f; entrepôt in, 5, 128; fur trade in, 10, 25, 34, 58–59; HBC expansion in, 135–40. *See also* French colonialism

Canoes, 127; accidents with, 74, 79, 124–26; kayaks as kind of, 63, 79, 147; large and small, for transport, 5, 5f, 56, 124 (*see also* Birch bark canoes); paddle for, as artifact, 80f, 126; repair materials for, 78, 169, 170b; trade permits (*congés*) for, 45, 107–8, 171

Capitalism: consequences of, 156, 200; fur trade monopolies in, 46, 55, 66; huge profits in trade triangle, 63, 64–65; western, contrasted with Stone Age societies in fur trade, 18, 39; world systems theory and, 23–24, 25–26

Cartier, Jacques, 41, 70

Casa Grande commemoration, revisionist history of, 29

Catchments, as proposed trading spheres, 73

Catlin, George, Mandan life depicted by, 92

Ceramics, 144, 145, 180; archaeological classification of, 122, 138; earthenware, and native presence, 114, 175, 191; native, over time displaced by metals, 24, 92–93; pearlware, recovered from trading posts, 109, 134; recovery of, and pottery design rights loss, 158–59. *See also* Pottery

Chaco Canyon commemoration, revisionist history of, 29

Charlestown, as English colonial trading site, 43f, 143, 144

Cherokees, 42t, 89

Chickasaws, 42t, 146; deerskin production by, 144–46; French war against, 169, 182, 191; gun acquisition by, 144–45; thumbnail scrapers of, 144, 145f

Chimney construction, 76, 135. *See also* Fireplaces

Chipewyans, 25, 42t

Chippewas, transition to wage labor, 24–25. *See also* Ojibwes

Chouart des Groseillers, Médard, inland exploration by, 45

Christianity: assimilation through, 49, 165, 168; introduction of, into St. Joseph River Valley, 166, 173; Jesuits and, 17, 166, 168

Cloth: indicative recoveries of (*see* Lead seals); monetary value of, 52, 118; production of, 186, 187; as remnants in cemeteries, 100, 115

Clothing materials, 116; cotton, 101, 115; wool, 100–101, 115. *See also* Skin clothing

Clothing styles, 129, 162; multiethnic or traditional, of fur tradesmen, 101–2, 122, 190, 192; newly designed, by native women, 111, 115; as trade goods for embellishment, 185–86, 189

Cocumscussoc, as English colonial trading post, Narragansetts and, 50, 114

Coins in trade, 150, 181

Colonialism, 11, 13, 17, 18, 36; comparative studies of, 32–33; postcolonial theory and comparative studies, 33, 34. *See also specific forms of colonialism*

Colonial wars, 195; empire in, 2, 169, 171; fur trade and, 2, 24, 48, 114

Colony Ross. *See under* Fort Ross, as Russian colonial trading site, beginning of

Color pigments, 84, 170b, 190, 191

Columbia River Valley: epidemic spread from Fort Vancouver to, 152–53; expansion of HBC into, 135, 137–40; fur trade rivalries in, 60, 103, 202

Columbus, Christopher, 40; before, and native peoples, 37–39, 69

Competition: French and, 53–56, 54, 82; fur trade and, 2, 5, 56, 58–59, 64, 66, 134; hard bargains and, 11, 91; HBC, 46, 53–56, 103, 135, 202; independent fur traders and, 55–56, 172; market values and, 6, 52

Connecticut River Valley, 89; English colonialism in, 52, 118–19

Cook, Capt. James, exploration by, 63

Copper. *See under* Kettles, copper; Metal trade goods, copper

Cosmology of Native Americans, 39. *See also* Metaphysics of native peoples

Crafts by native peoples, 144; ceramics, 92–93, 114, 175, 191; imported tools and, 96–97, 116f; stone pipes and ritual objects, 96, 115. *See also* Tinkling cones

Credit, 34, 66; land as collateral for, 52, 118; trading posts operating on, 57, 131, 133

Creeks, 42*t*, 144; deerskin production by, 89, 143–44; trade goods and, 141, 146

Crees, 139; as middlemen for Plains Indians, 42*t*, 55

Creolization, 34, 107, 108; as a colonialism process, 11, 147; French colonialism and, 47–48, 107–8

Critical theory: archaeological records and, 13, 192–93, 199; as challenge to dominant ideology bias, 28–29; dominant narrative of manifest destiny, 27, 173, 192

Croghan, George, as Indian agent, 47

Crooks, Ramsay, AFC leadership by, 61

Cumberland House, as HBC post, 55

Currency of the fur trade: coins, 150, 181; deerskins, 169, 170*b*; dentalium shell, 151 (*see also* Wampum); land, 66, 68, 118–19, 202. *See also* Credit

Deer hunting: butchering evidence of entire carcasses from, 89, 119; deerskin trade in southeastern North America, 42*t*, 53, 89, 141–46, 202; harvesting strategies in, 142, 145, 185; hides and skins from, 53, 60, 86, 89, 141–42, 169 (*see also* Hide processing; Skin clothing); subsistence and, 89, 183, 183*t*, 184–85

Dehaître, Antoine. *See* De Lestre, Antoine

Delawares, as Fort Vancouver residents, 139

De Lestre, Antoine: as Fort St. Joseph resident-employee, 169, 170*b*; as gunsmith, 181–82

Dentalium, as currency, 151

Des Groseillers. *See* Chouart des Groseillers, Médard

Detroit, as French-English-AFC colonial trading site, 43*f*, 48, 58, 60, 82, 102–3

De Villiers, Coulon, as agent of The Crown, 170*f*

Diet: changes in, 89, 114–15, 148; ethnic differences in, 87–88, 89, 122; social rank and, 57, 86–87, 108–9, 129; subsistence and (*see* Nutritional resources)

Diplomacy. *See* Intercultural mediation

Diseases in native peoples, 83; diet change and, 89, 114–15; epidemics among, 49, 55, 158–59; social stress and, 147, 152–53

Dogsleds, role in transport, 80

Domestic animals: cattle bones similar to wild bison, 184–85; as meat (*see under* Nutritional resources, meat sources, domestic)

Drake, Sir Francis, exploration of, 64

Duffils, as trucking cloth, 100

Dutch colonialism, 113; fur trade, posts, and routes in, 36, 42*t*, 43*f*, 52

Dutch West India Company, forts established by, 49

Eastman, Seth, native tool use depicted by, 126

Economic approaches to fur trade study, 21–27; complex and simple dynamics in, 21–22; revisionist thinking about, 26–27, 32, 199; world systems theory, 22–26

Effigy forms: pestles in, by native women, 111, 117; smoking pipes in sacred rituals, 115, 116*f*, 118

Eliot, John, Christianity and, 49

Elk, 42*t*, 102, 185, 201

Empowerment, formerly marginalized groups and, 34

Engagés, 57. *See also* Laborers

English colonialism, 32, 42*t*, 43*f*, 48; Connecticut River Valley and, 52, 118–19; deerskin trade for leather industry, 42*t*, 141–42, 143; prohibitions during, 50, 94, 116–17; settlements as priority for, 36, 46, 48–49, 78, 113–14, 123; surveying during, 167, 167*f*, 171

Ethnic relationships, 191; attitudes of Arikaras and Euro-Americans toward each other, 155–56, 158; biases in, and role of native peoples, 13, 16; borrowing cultural traits from others as, 122–23; intermarriage as (*see* Marriage as intercultural union); laborers and, 55, 57, 60, 62, 147; residents of Fort Vancouver and, 139–40; use of goods to express, 105, 106–7

Ethnogenesis and cultural interactions, 34, 108, 193; Arikaras, with Euro-Americans, 82, 157–58; Euro-Americans, with Native Americans, 18–20, 173, 177; European, with indigenous economies, 31–32, 40–41, 82–83

Euro-American populations, 13, 156, 167; interactions with Native Americans and acculturation, 18–20, 173, 177; interdependence of, without natives, 163, 182, 204; trade goods of, and Arikaras, 82, 157–58; unintended consequences faced by, 163, 199–202

European markets: cultural exchanges because of, 2–3, 11, 16; fur trade and, 1, 2–4, 6, 12, 17, 198; interactions with indigenous economies, 31–32, 40–41, 82–83; pelts from trapped vs. shot animals for, 94–95

European nations, 18, 42, 78, 97, 146; colonial pursuits and strategies of, 19, 82, 123, 169; imported goods from, 94, 98, 100–101, 103, 162, 187; power and, 29, 111; raw material for workshops in, 6, 44, 53, 94, 142; Western, and different national perspectives, 17, 33, 96

Face painting, as intercultural mediation, 191

Factor McLoughlin, Chief, agricultural marketing by, 90

Faience ceramics, recovery of, 180

Farm-raised fur-bearers, animal rights and, 197

Fidler, Peter, Nottingham House and, 136

Firearms. See Guns

Fireplaces, 76; at Fort St. Joseph, 178–79, 179f, 180f, 190. See also Chimney construction

Fisher. See Marten

Flintlocks. See Guns

Fond du Lac–Fort St. Louis, as French-NWC-AFC colonial trading area, 43f, 108–9, 130. See also Fort St. Louis de Illinois, as French colonial trading site

Food, symbolism of, 86–87. See also Diet; Nutritional resources

Fort Albany, as HBC colonial trading site, 43f, 85–86

Fort Astoria, as colonial trading site, 43f, 60, 87

Fort Charlotte, underwater archeology near, 126–27, 127f

Fort Clark, as AFC trading site, 43f, 60; architecture to reinforce social hierarchy at, 109, 159, 160f, 161–63; provisions at, 155, 162; steamboat service consequences and, 202-3

Fort Clark State Historic Site, North Dakota, 161–63

Fort de Buade, as French colonial trading site, 48, 165f

Fort de Chartres, as French-English colonial trading site, 43f, 76, 88

Fort Garry, as HBC trading site, 43f, 57

Fort George, as English trading site, 60–61, 139

Fort Hill, as Squakheag village, 118

Fort La Baye, as French colonial trading site, 43f, 165f

Fort La Reine, 46

Fort Massac, as French-English colonial trading site, 43f, 76

Fort McLoughlin, as HBC colonial trading site, 149, 152

Fort Miami, as French colonial trading site, 43f, 70, 165f, 167

Fort Michilimackinac, 94; artifacts and excavation of, in Mackinac City, Michigan, 71, 84, 102, 120; distinct food preferences by ethnicity at, 87–88, 122; establishing chronology for, 71–72; as French-English colonial trading site, 43f, 48, 56, 82, 120, 165f; powder magazine and storeroom in, 76, 108; reconstruction of, 74, 75f, 76, 120–22, 122f; row houses with shared walls at, 121f, 180

Fort Nassau, as Dutch colonial trading site, 49

Fort Orange, as Dutch colonial trading site, 49, 82

Fort Ouiatenon, as French-English colonial trading site, 43f, 72, 78, 88–89, 123, 165f

Fort Pontchartrain, as French colonial trading site, 165f

Fortress of Louisbourg, as French colonial entrepôt, 43f, 74

Fort Ross, as Russian colonial trading site, 43f, 90; archaeological project at, 147–48; beginning of, 109, 147

Forts Folle Avoine Historical Park, Wisconsin, 130–31

Fort St. Joseph (Michigan), 43f, 164–96; archaeology of, 174f, 177–92; artifacts and excavation of, 45f, 70, 74, 89, 90, 174f, 175–76, 180–81, 181f, 188–90, 192; English as operators and traders at, 43f, 171–72, 189; French establishment of, as colonial trading site, 14, 48, 119, 164, 166–71; fur trade legacy at, 192–94; goods supplied to and by inhabitants of, 169–71, 170b, 185–87; lead shot ammunition made locally in, 94, 170b, 190; multiethnic conditions at, 168, 191–92, 192–93; natives

Hamelin, Louis, as Montreal merchant, 169, 170b, 185

HBC. *See* Hudson's Bay Company

Heritage tourism. *See* Tourism

Hidatsas, 42t, 93

Hide processing, 102, 110, 146; beaver, for felted hats, 44, 185; marrow use in, 184–85; scraper technology for, 91–92, 94, 136, 142, 145f, 176; smudge pits in, 95, 142, 176, 177f, 182, 184

Historical archaeology: biases in, and critical theory, 28–29; early investigation of fur trade in, 6–7, 20 (*see also* Fort St. Joseph [Michigan]); ethnocentric biases on role of native peoples in, 13, 16; as fur trade domain, 10, 15; materiality and, 13–14, 16, 31–32, 34, 45f, 50, 68, 198 (*see also* Materiality of the fur trade); understanding American fur trade experience and, 12–13, 69, 204–5. *See also* Interpretive frameworks for fur trade study

Historical resources: archaeologically-based, 6–7, 8–9, 69–73, 205; complementary vs. distinct sources for, 7–8, 13, 14; document-based and oral, 6, 7, 18, 37, 68, 70, 174; racialized distortions and, 8, 173, 195, 203–4; sociopolitical reflections of, 9–10, 13, 15, 16, 31

Historical Society of Michigan, education awards from, 195

Historic preservation: awards for, in Michigan, 195–96; reconstruction and, in Minnesota, 74, 132. *See also* Preservation and reconstruction of fur trading sites

Historic preservation movement, 20

Horses: effect of adopting, on Plains Indians, 110, 154; once feral, in fur trade, 5, 73, 79, 124

Hudson's Bay, 44, 48; trading sphere (catchment) of, 73, 82; watershed of, 55, 62

Hudson's Bay Company (HBC), 32, 79; competition and, 46, 53–56, 103, 135, 202; consolidation of NWC with, 56, 62, 76, 77f, 128; Northern Indians and, 25, 54–55, 64; Orkneymen as workers for, 55, 106; territorial expansion of, and its regional fur trade system, 135–40; trading posts and trade routes of, 43f, 60, 61–62, 78, 87, 153–54; treatment of native peoples by, 57, 140

Human remains, near Fort St. Joseph, 175

Hurons, 42t, 45

Hutchins, Thomas, as English surveyor, 167, 167f, 171

Hybridization, 12; as process of colonialism, 11, 107, 111

Ice chisels, as submerged artifacts, 126

Iconographic rings, archaeological classification of, 122

Illinois River Valley, most common trade goods in, 99–100

Indian Claims Commission, evidence sought by, 9

Indigenous archaeology. *See* Reflexive and indigenous perspectives on fur trade study

Infanticide, as alternative to slavery, 12

Intercultural mediation, 191; calumet ceremony in, 122, 166, 190–91, 199

Intermarriage. *See* Marriage as intercultural union

Interpretive frameworks for fur trade study, 15–35; acculturation theory, 18–20; background for, 15–17; comparative method vs. creolization and glocalization, 32–34; early anthropological contributions to, 17–21; lens adjustment to see a new fur trade, 34–35; postcolonial theory and comparative studies, 33, 34; use of direct historical approach in, 20–21. *See also* Economic approaches to fur trade study; Reflexive and indigenous perspectives on fur trade study

Iroquois, 17, 32, 70; as British allies against the French, 48, 168; trading sphere (catchment) of, 41, 44, 73, 199; traits of, 96, 166. *See also* specific groups

Jay's Treaty, fur trade centers after, 58

John Russell Cutlery Company, skinning knives of, 199

John Sayer's Snake River Post, 76, 77f, 130, 132

Joseph, Saint, New France and, 168

Joseph Ullman and Company, pelt quantity shipments of, 202

Kalm, Peter, available goods noted by, 24, 93

Kashaya Pomos, 42t, 149

Kegs, recovered parts from, 126

Kettles, 93, 93*f*, 170*b*; brass, 1, 22*f*, 175; copper, 79, 92, 93, 96, 138, 150, 180; refashioned, as raw material, 92–93, 116, 188, 191

Kickapoos, 42*t*, 95, 100

King Philip's War, fur trade and, 2, 114

Kinship relations, 116, 200; intermarriage to establish, 40–41, 45, 83; native societies and, 11, 39; racial and political categories transcended by, 192–93

Laborers, 57, 202; canoe, in fur trade transport, 56, 99; ethnicities of, 57, 60, 62; management and morale of, 55, 57–58; physical and symbolic barriers for, 109, 111; provisions for, 56–57, 87, 129, 149, 198; recruitment or termination of, 62, 148; stress markers on skeletal remains of, 98–99

Land otter, 41, 42*t*, 171, 172

Land tenure systems, 18, 50; dispossession and bad debt, 66, 68, 118–19, 202; family hunting territories in, 21, 79; native-controlled, and French outposts, 46–47

Lapidary industry, New England natives and, 96, 115, 116*f*

La Prairie, Joseph, and Forts Folle Avoine, 130–31

La Salle, Sieur René-Robert Cavelier de, 79, 166; commemorative marker for, 70, 71*f*; Fort Miami at St. Joseph River mouth, 167–68

La Vérendrye, Pierre de, western French forts and, 46

Lead mining, 200

Lead seals: archaeological context of, 103, 122, 187; as cloth-related artifact, 104, 114

Lead shot, 94, 124, 138, 162; recovered at Fort St. Joseph, 174*f*, 176, 182, 190

Le Blanc, Francois, residential space of, 108

Lefebre, Jean-Baptist, as tallow provider, 184

Legacy of the fur trade: American psyche and, 3, 13, 84, 165, 192, 194, 197–99; contrasting mythic portrayals of, 203–5; cultural consequences of, 9–10, 195–96, 199–200; ecological consequences of, 200–203; at Fort St. Joseph, 192–94; materiality in, 83–85;

transcultural adoption as Yankee ingenuity, 192, 204

Leisure activities, 8, 123; at Fort St. Joseph, 89, 190–91

Le Prestre de Vauban, Sébastien, fortification principles of, 76, 77*f*, 159

Levake, Henry, intercultural marriage of, 134

Lewis and Clark expedition and tribal trades, 153, 154, 157, 200

Liquor. *See* Alcohol

Little Island Rock Post, American building technique in, 134–35

Log construction, 135, 138

Louisiana: French colonial trading site in, 43*f*, 95, 144; as part of New France, 48, 175

Lyne site, Michigan, 174*f*, 175–76, 176*f*, 177–78, 177*f*

Lynx, 41, 42*t*, 171

Mackenzie, Alexander, as NWC partner, 56

Mackinac, as fur trading center, 58, 133

MacTavish, Simon, as NWC director, 56

Mandans, 154, 156, 199; French fur trade with, 42*t*, 46; geophysical survey of, village, 161–62; impacts of fur trade delayed for, 158–59; traits of, 92, 163

Manifest destiny, 204; dominant narrative of, 156, 173, 192; fur trade role in, 2, 8

Manufacturing, 2, 6, 20

Marine shell, 142, 151; as expression of metaphysics of light, 32, 91; trading of, 37, 73, 137; whelk and clam, in wampum production, 50–51, 51*f*, 185, 186*f*

Maritime trade: American colonialism and, 63–65; consequences of, and American-native relations, 151–52, 152–53; Northwest Coast people's shrewdness in, 67, 151, 156; Northwest Coast regional system for, in furs, 146–53; sea otter and, 42*t*, 63, 146–47, 156, 157; sojourning in, 149, 150

Marriage as intercultural union, 123; as common practice among fur traders, 132, 134, 140; to establish kinship relations, 40–41, 47–48, 168; Euro-native, and its advantages, 107–8; on Northwest Coast, 11–12; offspring of (*see* Creolization; *Métis*)

Marten, 41, 42*t*, 172, 183

Marxian economics, fur trade and, 22, 23, 28

Mashantucket Pequots, 73, 100

Materiality of the fur trade, 69–112; calibrating time in the fur trade era, 81–83; crafts,
96–97, 188, 189*f*; daily activities for utilitarian
purposes, 30, 97–99, 123, 185, 190–91; daily
activities in general, 73, 74, 84, 198; dressing
for the trade, 99–104; fur or food, 85–90;
genesis of fur trade archaeology, 69–73;
identifying people of the trade, 104–11; material legacy of the trade, 83–85, 111–12, 205;
mobility during the fur trade era, 79–80;
navigating the fur trade landscape, 73–79;
technology, 90–96, 102, 116

Maumee River Valley, Fort Miami in, 165*f*

Maximilian, Prince of Wied-Neuwied, Fort
Clark and, 159

McGillivray, William, as fort superintendent, 128

McKenzie, Charles, fur trader attire of, 101–2

Menu pelteries, 42*t*, 44, 120

Mercantilism. *See* Capitalism

Meskwakis, 94, 169, 199

Metal trade goods: brass, 22*f*, 41, 52, 105, 115;
copper, 24, 52, 79, 90, 115, 150, 188; iron, 1, 24,
41, 52, 84, 90, 115, 116, 125, 138, 141; lead, 94,
170*b*; pewter, 176; silver, 72, 141, 175, 176, 176*f*;
steel, 24, 27, 81, 138

Metaphysics of native peoples, 39; afterlife in,
114, 115; communication with the supernatural, 111, 117–18; light and expressions of, 32,
91; values of well-being and ribbonwork in,
96, 111

Métis, 47, 130, 168; as mixed offspring of fur
trade society, 12, 107; as provisioners for
NWC, 55, 57; symbolic meanings of goods
associated with, 91, 111

Miamis, 42*t*, 166–67, 168

Michigan, as part of New France, 48

Michigan government: Governor's Historic
Preservation Award, 195–96; Office of the
State Archaeologist, 175

Michilimackinac, as French trading site, 48, 82.
See also Fort Michilimackinac

Michipicoten, as French-NWC-HBC colonial
trading site, 43*f*

Micmacs, 41, 42*t*, 79

Micmac-style pipe, diplomacy and, 98, 122

Minnesota Historical Society, reconstruction
by, 74, 132

Miscegenation, 12, 204. See also *Métis*

Mississippi River Valley, 11, 42*t*, 88; accident-
prone portage between rivers in, 124–25

Missouri River Valley, 9, 42*t*, 73; agricultural
surplus and intertribal trading in, 156–57;
beaver pelts from, 153, 155, 201; bison robes
from, 153, 154–56; middle region of, 46, 92,
133, 153–54, 156–57, 158–59; palisaded villages
for protection in, 158–59; regional fur trade
system in, 153–63; upper region of, and skinning knives, 2, 199

Mobile, as French colonial trading site, 43*f*, 144

Moccasins, 47, 84; in Great Lakes region, 102–3,
133, 184; leather parts of, recovered, 126–27,
127*f*

Montagnais, 21, 42*t*, 79

Montreal, as French-English colonial trading
site, 82, 169; entrepôt in, 5, 43*f*, 44–45, 95,
119; oversupply of beaver pelts in, 48, 168

Moose bones, 136

Museum collections: historical objects in, and
period chronology, 173. *See also under* Fort
St. Joseph Museum, objects in

Museum of the Fur Trade, Nebraska, activities
of, 9

Muskets. *See* Guns

Muskrat, 61; low numbers of, 133, 136, 183; in *pay
d'en haut*, 42*t*, 89, 125, 133, 172, 201

Nails, 122; as trading post artifacts, 134, 136

Narragansetts, 113–17; cemetery of, 114–15, 117;
disease and, 49, 89; European trade goods
received by, 100, 113–14, 115–17; role in fur
trade, 42*t*, 50–51, 114; wampum production
by, 51, 73

Natchez ceramics, 145

Native American graves, 31; cemeteries of, 100,
114–15, 117; goods distribution in, 70, 100,
114, 116, 175. *See also* Burial customs

Native Americans: acculturation and assimilation of, 12, 18–20, 26, 173; economic interactions of, with Europeans, 31–32, 40–41,

82–83; fur-bearing animals as resource for, 4, 38; as fur producers, 16, 38–39, 141; fur trade and, 1, 2–3, 5, 29, 36–37, 94; inter-tribal trading among, 50, 154, 156–57, 200; portrayals of, 8, 10–11, 57, 203; power issues and autonomy, 9, 12, 20, 40, 139, 152, 205 (*see also* Land tenure systems); power issues and economics, 57–58, 66–67, 82–83, 155–56, 158, 200; power issues and gender (*see* Gender relationships); as refugees, 173, 200, 204; settlement criteria for, 78–79. *See also specific societies*

Native children, 168; adolescents as, 114, 117; diseases and mortality of, 114–15; rearing, as woman's role, 39, 111

Needles, 116; baling, as artifacts, 45*f*, 96, 180, 182, 186; iron, in quill- and beadwork, 96, 186

New Amsterdam, as Dutch-English colonial trading site, 43*f*, 49, 52, 113

New England, 42*t*; fur trade sites and networks in, 13, 73, 113–19; industrial development in, and fur trade, 2, 65, 153; linked to Asian markets, 63, 64–65; native lapidary industry in, 96, 115, 116*f*; native societies in, 32, 40, 94; southern, regional fur trade system before English settlement, 113–19; wampum produced by coastal, natives, 50–51, 73

New France: alliances with native peoples, 168–69, 171, 182; the Crown and, 48, 107–8, 170*b*, 182, 190; re-creation of French culture in North America, 94, 101, 191–91; River of the Miamis in, 166, 168; women of, in public lecture series, 195

New Orleans, as French colonial trading site, 43*f*, 95, 144

New York, fur merchants in, 94

Niles, Michigan, 194; archaeological project partnerships with, 164, 173, 174; commemoration of European settlement in, 173, 196, 204

Nipigon, as French-HBC colonial trading site, 43*f*

North America, 31; colonial trading sites and routes in, 5, 43*f*; encounters of European and native peoples in, 1–2, 10; as fur trade incubator, 3–6; Old Northwest of, 161, 163;

pre-European exchange networks in, 37–38 (*see also under* Regional fur trade systems); summary of fur trade in, 13–14

Northeast groups. *See under* New England, native societies in

Northwest Coast, 152; formline carvings by groups on, 96, 149–50; fur trade networks along, 36, 73, 199 (*see also under* Regional fur trade systems, Pacific Coast and maritime trade); fur traders, their native partners, and fur-bearers in, region, 42*t*, 137; intercultural marriage on, 11–12; negative reciprocity and, groups, 26–27; pre-European trade along, 137, 151, 152; trade goods wanted by, native peoples, 149–51. *See also* Columbia River Valley

North West Company (NWC), 57, 80; founding and later consolidation of, 55–56, 62, 123; French Canadians as workers for, 55, 57, 106–7; palisaded, settlements, 30*f*, 76, 77*f*, 109; regard for native peoples by, 17–18, 129; rivals of, 55, 58, 129, 130–31, 136; status differences within, 108–9, 129; trading posts and trade routes of, 43*f*, 60, 123–29, 130–33, 153–54; water-borne transport between markets by, 79, 119

Nottingham House, as HBC post, 87, 136–37

Nutritional resources: fish, 57, 87–89, 122, 125, 129, 162, 183, 183*t*; meat sources, domestic, 87–88, 90, 122, 129, 183, 183*t*; meat sources, wild, 56, 85, 86–90, 109, 122, 125–26, 129, 162, 183, 183*t*; native diet and, 88, 89, 123, 137, 139, 155, 183, 183*t*; provisions as, 55, 56–57, 78, 87, 89–90, 110, 118, 133, 198; wild and domestic plants, 86, 88, 89, 90, 129, 162. *See also* Diet

NWC. *See* North West Company

Obsidian trade: disruption of, 149

Ocher, as color pigment, 191. *See also* Vermilion

Odawas, 42*t*, 120; as fur-trading middlemen, 49; as trading middlemen, 45

Ojibwes, 11, 42*t*, 49, 94; economic activities of, 19, 130–31, 132–33, 134; food consumption remains of, 85; in Straits of Mackinac area, 120, 166. *See also* Chippewas

Onondagas, 42*t*, 119; crafts of, 92, 96; repurposed trade goods by, 91, 92

Oregon Treaty, 60

Ottawas, 166, 172. *See also* Odawas

Otter. *See* Land otter; Sea otter

Ouiatenon, as French colonial trading site, 48; its successor as French-English fort, 43*f*, 72, 78, 88–89, 123, 165*f*

Pacific Fur Company (PFC), Astoria as focal point of, 61

Pacific Northwest region. *See* Northwest Coast

Palisades, 160; forts with, 30, 109, 130–31, 160, 168; NWC settlements with, 76, 77*f*, 109; villages with, 158–59

Panton, Leslie, & Company, deerskins exported by, 89

Pays d'en haut. See Great Lakes region, western (*pays d'en haut*)

Peague. *See* Wampum

Pedlars, as independent traders, 55–56

Pemmican, 155; production of, 47, 56, 110; sale or trade of, 55, 57, 133

Personal adornment. *See* Adornments

PFC (Pacific Fur Company), 61

Phoenix buttons, 103

Pipes, 72, 84; clay, 97, 111, 114, 117, 134, 138, 162, 190; red pipestone, 50, 119, 162; stone, 96, 97–98, 106, 115, 116*f*, 117–18, 122; stone, at Fort St. Joseph, 174*f*, 175, 190–91

Plains Indians, 42*t*, 55, 81; bison and, 155, 201; gender relations among, 23, 110

Politics, 22, 31, 98; alliances in, and racial perspectives, 192–93; autonomy in, 27, 34, 39, 40, 65, 68; colonialism and, 29–30; sociopolitical reflections in data, 9–10, 13, 15, 16, 33

Pontiac's War: fur trade and, 2, 24; native rebellion against English, 171–72

Pony beads, 81

Postcolonial theory, 136, 193; comparative studies and, 33, 34

Potawatomis: gaming pieces of, 89, 190; settlement of, near Fort St. Joseph, 78–79, 167, 167*f*, 175; tribal movements of, 166, 173; used fur-trading Seneca middlemen, 42*t*, 49

Potlatch ceremony, 149

Pottery, 24; loss of rights to, designs, 158–59; shell-tempered, at Fort St. Joseph, 174*f*, 175

Preservation and reconstruction of fur trading sites: building styles and construction, 74–76, 78; facsimile re-creation, 74, 128, 132, 159–60; fortification principles, 76, 77*f*; obstacles to reconstruction, 173–74; special purpose buildings, 76–78

Projectile points, 175; arrowheads as, 182, 190

Pynchon, William, trading activity of, 52

Quebec, as French-English colonial trading site, 43*f*, 95, 199

Quetico-Superior Underwater Research Project, archaeology in, 125–26

Rabbit, 42*t*

RAC. *See* Russian-American Company

Raccoon, 61, 65; western Great Lakes region and, 42*t*, 60, 172, 183, 185, 201

Racial perspectives, 12, 13, 140; class solidarity and, in fur trade, 24, 139–40; creation of stereotypes from, 17, 38; dominance as moral success in, 8, 9; hierarchies in, 87, 156; political alliances and, transcended by kinship relations, 192–93

Radisson, Pierre, exploration by, 45

Red River carts, 62; for transport between markets, 57, 58*f*, 80, 133

Reflexive and indigenous perspectives on fur trade study, 27–32; colonialism vs. native interpretation and public perception, 29–30; critical analysis of material culture, 31–32; critical theory used by native peoples, 28; nonsustainable returns vs. some degree of autonomy, 27; power of European nations in, 29; revisionist history of commemorative native sites, 29

Regional fur trade systems, 113–63, 198; Missouri River Valley for pelts and robes, 153–63; Old Northwest in microcosm, 163; Pacific Coast and maritime trade, 146–53; southeastern North America and deerskin trade, 141–46; southern New England prelude to English settlement, 113–19; territorial expansion of HBC, 135–40; western Great Lakes region, 119–35

Religious missions: Jesuit, in North America, 17, 166, 168; materials of, and archaeology, 122, 191

Rhoads site, Illinois, 95, 96, 176

RI-1000, Rhode Island, 114–18. *See also* Narragansetts

Rituals: in mediation, 122, 166, 190–91, 199; sacred, and effigy pipes, 115, 116*f*; at trading posts in, 97–98

Rock Island, Lake Michigan, 166

Rocky Mountain fur trade, competition in, 5

Ross Colony. *See under* Fort Ross, as Russian colonial trading site, beginning of

Rupert's Land, 55, 62

Russian-American Company (RAC), 55; compared to other fur companies, 32, 64, 149; established Fort Ross for agricultural supplies, 90, 147; territories of, 62–63, 64

Russian colonialism, 36, 41, 65, 147; California and, 32, 33, 63, 148; settlements of, 148, 149; trading regions, posts and routes in, 42*t*, 43*f*

St. Joseph, as French colonial trading site. *See* Fort St. Joseph (Michigan)

St. Joseph River Valley, 165*f*; archaeological investigation of fur trade in, 172–74, 174*f* (*see also under* Fort St. Joseph [Michigan], archaeology of); French regime in, 14, 166; Native American sites in, 175–77

St. Lawrence River Valley, 73; beaver in, 24, 201; fur trade expansion west and north of, 21, 36, 119–20; Montreal as exchange center, 44, 199

St. Louis, trading sphere (catchment) of, 59, 73, 154

St. Louis River, accident-prone portage and, 124–25

Salvage archaeology, Missouri River Valley and, 9

Savannah, as English colonial port, 143

Savannah Portage, as notorious connector, 124–25

Sayer, John, as proprietor, 76, 77*f*, 130, 131–33

Sayer's Fort, as colonial trading site, 43*f*, 77*f*, 109, 130, 131–33

Sea otter: Asian markets for, 62–63; decline of, 63, 64, 149, 201–2; maritime trade and, 42*t*, 146–47, 152, 199

Secwepemcs, 139; excavation of postcolonial village and, 138–39

Seed beads, users of, 81, 115, 190

Senecas, 110; fur-bearing species and, 86, 120; as middlemen for western Indians, 42*t*, 49–50

Seven Year's War: fur trade and, 2, 48, 171; myth replacement as result of, 203–4

Sexual union. *See* Marriage as intercultural union

Shaganappi, universal repair of Red River carts with, 80

Shamanism, 111, 117–18

Shawnees, 42*t*; plea by its prophet to, 66–67, 158

Sitka, Russian settlement at, 149

Skin clothing, 115; contrasted to wool, 100, 101; leather industry and, 141–42; material preparation for (*see* Hide processing); as superior to unacceptable English cloth, 64, 101

Skinning knives, fur trade regions and, 2, 143, 199

Slavery, 109; African and Native American, connection to fur trade, 1–2, 204; as base of cotton industry and demise of deerskin trade, 144, 146; native peoples and, 12, 137

Smoking (tobacco): casual use of, 124, 191; ceremonial use of, 11, 115, 116*f*, 118; effects of, on skeletal remains, 98–99; as gender privilege or cultural taboo, 111, 117–18; pipes for, 97–98, 106, 122. *See also* Pipes; Tobacco

Smoking (deerskins and hides), as part of tanning process, 94, 102. *See also* Smudge pits

Smudge pits, 205; as corn holes at Fort St. Joseph, 174*f*, 176, 177*f*, 182; in hide processing, 95, 142, 176, 177*f*, 182, 184; processing of deerskins in, 94, 142

Snake River trading site. *See* Sayer's Fort

Snowshoes, role in transport, 47, 79

Society for Historical Archaeology, 70

Southeastern region, 42*t*; contributing factors in collapse of deerskin trade in, 144, 146; deerskin in fur trade system of, 53, 141–46

Southwest region. *See* Greater Southwest region

Spanish colonialism, 42t, 149, 154; Fort St. Joseph and, 172, 173; horse trading in, 5, 73, 154

Squakheags, 42t; evidence of tension among, 89, 118

State Historical Society of North Dakota, 161

State Historical Society of Wisconsin, 131

Status relationships, evidence of: diet and clothing, 57, 86–87, 97, 101–2, 103, 108–9, 129, 162; divisions of labor, 110–11, 137; privileges, 12, 109, 137; residential size, style, and placement, 30, 74, 78, 107, 108, 109, 140, 140f, 156, 159; use of goods to express, 105, 109, 127, 149

Storage practices, 76, 132; cache pits, 135, 138, 181; gunsmith's cache, 181, 181f

Straits of Mackinac, 87, 166; French penetration through, 119, 120

Stress: occupational, markers, 98–99; overhunting and, 83, 89, 201–2; social environment and, 41, 89, 147, 152–53, 200

Subarctic region, fur traders, their native partners, and fur-bearers in, 42t

Subsistence. See Diet; Nutritional resources; see also under Animal bones, marrow from;

Sumptuary laws, renegotiation of, 103

Support the Fort, Inc., collaborative archaeology and, 174, 194

Tallow, 170b, 184; multiple uses of, 169, 191

Tanning, 102, 136. See also Hide processing

Technology and materiality of the fur trade: ceramics, 92–93 (see also Ceramics); guns, 93–95, 116–17 (see also under Blacksmithing, firearm repair and gunsmithing as); hide processing and clothing production in, 91–92, 96–97, 102–4 (see also Hide processing; Skin clothing); imported tools, 96–97, 115, 116f; metallurgies, 90–91, 92, 93f 96, 116–17; pipes for smoking, 96, 97–99, 116f, 117 (see also Pipes; Smoking [tobacco]); traditional technologies abandoned, 24, 91, 92

Tenskwatawa, traditional culture and, 66–67, 158

Thimbles, 109; brass, repurposed for ornaments, 105, 105f; as syncretic symbols, 106, 111; as trade goods, 103, 186–87

Thompson's River Post: in HBC's Caledonia

department, 137–39; native settlement excavation nearby, 138–39

Thread, as traded goods, 81

Tinkling cones: buckles associated with, 189–90; production at Fort St. Joseph of, 105–6, 105f, 187–89, 189f; reuse of trade goods for, 84, 186–87, 188, 191

Tlingits, 137; as middlemen for interior coast trade, 42t, 64; as selective trade goods consumers, 64, 149, 150, 151

Tobacco, 11, 97, 106; access to, at trading posts, 129, 133, 156; domestic vs. imported species of, 98, 111, 156; as exchanged goods in fur trade, 58, 64, 65, 84, 138. See also Smoking (tobacco)

Toboggans, role in transport, 5, 47, 79–80

Totemic significance, symbols in adornments, 116f, 117. See also Effigy forms

Tourism: fur trade destinations and, 9, 16; public education and, 9, 14, 30–31; reconstructions in, 30, 30f

Trading posts, 4f, 133, 205; archaeological interest in, 8–9; as compounds, 76–78, 77f; establishment of, 49, 50, 114, 167–68; evidence of rituals at, 97–98; military function of, 74, 76, 168; native proximity to, and dependency, 21, 78–79, 123; site selection and settlement criteria for, 50, 78–79, 114; as U.S. government factories, 65–66, 67t. See also specific trading posts

Transportation modes: animal-borne, 5, 79–80, 124; interactive native networks of, 37, 56, 73; overland technologies, 5, 47, 57, 58f, 79–80, 124, 133; packaging bundles for, 45f, 95–96; water-borne, 3, 5, 5f, 44, 46, 78, 79, 95, 119, 124, 202–3

Treaty of Ghent, boundary changes after, 60, 133

Treaty of Paris, changes after, 55, 59, 128, 130

Treaty of Utrecht, French competition after, 54, 82

Tribute (iasak), furs as form of, 41, 147

U.S. government, 130; alliances with native peoples, 60, 65, 98; control of Fort St. Joseph

MICHAEL S. NASSANEY is Professor of Anthropology at Western Michigan University. His research interests include colonialism, material analysis, historical archaeology, public archaeology, and the archaeology and ethnohistory of eastern North America. He is the editor of the book series The American Experience in Archaeological Perspective, in which this volume appears, and has published extensively on the archaeology of the eastern United States, including the recent co-edited volume *Archaeology and Community Service Learning*.

The American Experience in Archaeological Perspective

EDITED BY MICHAEL S. NASSANEY

The books in this series explore an event, process, setting, or institution that was significant in the formative experience of contemporary America. Each volume frames the topic beyond an individual site and attempts to give the reader a flavor of the theoretical, methodological, and substantive issues that researchers face in their examination of that topic or theme. These books are comprehensive overviews that provide serious students and scholars with an understanding of contemporary and past inquiries on a broad theme in American history and culture.

CPSIA information can be obtained
at www.ICGtesting.com
Printed in the USA
LVOW11*0747310117

522710LV00003B/12/P